Love in America

Love in America

Gender and self-development

FRANCESCA M. CANCIAN

University of California, Irvine

The right of the
University of Cambridge
to print and sell
all manner of books
was granted by
Henry VIII in 1534.
The University has printed
and published continuously
since 1584.

CAMBRIDGE UNIVERSITY PRESS

Cambridge

New York   Port Chester   Melbourne   Sydney

Published by the Press Syndicate of the University of Cambridge
The Pitt Building, Trumpington Street, Cambridge CB2 1RP
40 West 20th Street, New York, NY 10011, USA
10 Stamford Road, Oakleigh, Melbourne 3166, Australia

First published 1987
Reprinted 1987
First paperback edition 1990

Printed in the United States of America

British Library cataloguing in publication data
Cancian, Francesca M.
Love in America: gender and self-development.
1. Love
1. Title.
152.4 BF575.L.8

Library of Congress cataloging in publication data
Cancian, Francesca M.
Love in America.
Bibliography.
Includes index.
1. Sex role – United States.
2. Androgyny (Psychology).
3. Love 1. Title.
HQ1075.5.U6C36 1987   305.3'0973   87-10277
C.2   67513
ISBN 0-521-34202-3 hardback
ISBN 0-521-39691-3 paperback

To Maria and Steve
and to Jean

Contents

Figures

Tables

Acknowledgments

Many colleagues and friends contributed to this project. The case studies are the work of several very gifted interviewers: Eileen Pinkerton, Nancy Broomfield, Kitty Rowley, and Kim Thompson. Several research assistants helped in the data analysis, especially Michael Tracy, Clynta Jackson, and Paul Raper who did most of the content analysis of magazines. Barbara Metzger's intelligent editing improved my prose and Cheryl Larsson typed the manuscript with skill and good humor. A grant from the National Endowment for the Humanities supported the beginning stages of the work.

Steve Gordon, Arlie Hochschild, Lillian Rubin, and Ann Swidler helped me to start on this project by sharing their knowledge and their hunches. Conversations with Gary Thom, Graham Little, Scott Swain, and Wendy Lozano clarified my ideas. I benefited immensely from the reaction of colleagues and friends who read drafts of the book. Steven Gordon, Gerald Handel, Mark Poster, Francisco Ramirez, Rose Wendel, and Beatrice Whiting gave me thoughtful comments on an early draft, and the detailed criticisms and suggestions of Carol Browner, Rachel Kahn-Hut, Peggy Thoits, and Barbara Risman were especially helpful. Richard Almond, Albert Bergesen, and Norbert Wiley commented on several chapters, and my husband, Frank Cancian, helped me on every draft with careful, incisive criticisms and useful suggestions. Finally, I want to thank my husband and my friends Alyn Bartick, Ellie and Henry Fagin, Sally Hufbauer, and Judy Krieger, who read numerous drafts, endured my elation, obsession, and despair, and sustained me through this project.

Introduction

1
Love vs. self-development

Since the 1950s Americans have gained considerable freedom in their personal lives. Choices that used to be condemned, such as living together without being married, or remaining single or childless, have become acceptable options. Family and gender roles are much more flexible and being free to develop oneself is becoming a goal for both women and men.

The price of greater freedom, according to most scholars, is a weakening of close relationships. Now that many women are leaving their traditional role of caring for others, we seem to be moving towards a "culture of narcissism" in which no one is responsible for love and nurturance. Many observers believe that family relations have been strained to the breaking point by the self-centeredness of recent decades. To strengthen close relationships, they argue, we must stop pursuing self-development and reassert the importance of enduring commitments and obligations.[1]

These observers compare two images of private life: (1) the traditional family, based on restricting individual freedom, especially for women, and (2) the contemporary pattern of limited commitments between independent individuals, each focused on his or her own self-development. They conclude that there is a fundamental conflict between family bonds and self-development, and that we must choose between them.

There is a third alternative that most scholars ignore. A new image of love that combines enduring love with self-development has emerged in popular culture. Many Americans believe that to develop their individual potential, they need a supportive, intimate relationship with their spouse or lover. They see self-development and love as mutually reinforcing, not conflicting, and their view is supported by social and psychoanalytic theories of self-development. In this popular image, love and self-development both grow from the mutual interdependence of two people, not from extreme independence, nor from the one-way dependency of a woman on a man encouraged by traditional marriage.

My purpose is to examine these three images of heterosexual love: traditional marriage, independence, and interdependence. I will describe how they developed historically, and examine how they are shaping contemporary close relationships. Middle-class marriage is my major focus, but I also consider couples who are living together and working-class marriage.

FEMININE LOVE AND MASCULINE SELF-DEVELOPMENT

The apparent conflict between love and self-development is linked to the polarization of gender roles. Since the nineteenth century the feminine sphere of love and the family has been split off from the masculine sphere of self-assertion and work, as numerous historians have documented.[2] Women were expected to provide affection and care at home and forego autonomous achievement, while men provided money for the family and sought individual success, foregoing close attachments with their children or friends. Through marriage, people could become whole, vicariously realizing in their spouses the qualities that they denied in themselves. The distinction between the emotionally expressive wife and the competent, instrumental husband provided a blueprint for marital love and family behavior. But it implied that if women as well as men pursued self-development, the family would collapse.

Contemporary gender role stereotypes still show this split between feminine love and masculine self-assertion. According to several studies, most Americans distinguish feminine and masculine as follows:[3]

Feminine qualities	*Masculine qualities*
1 Dependent	1 Independent
2 Submissive	2 Dominant
3 Not self-confident	3 Very self-confident
4 Illogical and passive	4 Logical and active
5 Expresses tender feelings	5 Hides emotions
6 Aware of others' feelings	6 Not aware of others' feelings
7 Gentle	7 Aggressive

Gender roles portray women as dependent, loving and incapable of practical action, while men are portrayed as independent and competent, needing no help from others, and incapable of giving emotional support. These beliefs effect our behavior, as well as our expectations of ourselves and others; for example, research indicates that most boys try to hide their tender feelings and are rewarded for doing so.[4] In particular, gender stereotypes reinforce the power of men over women by describing men as naturally dominant, and implying that women need heterosexual love much more than men do.

Gender roles describe men and women in terms of opposed, mutually exclusive qualities. Insofar as love is identified with the feminine role, and self-development with the masculine role, love and self-development are also seen as opposed.

The dominant definition of love in our culture is feminized. Love is identified with women and with qualities seen as feminine, such as tenderness and expressing feelings. We tend to ignore the practical, material aspects of love such as giving help or sharing activities – qualities associated with masculinity and strength. Identifying love with expressing feelings is biased towards the way women prefer to behave in a love relationship. Women are more skilled and more interested than men in talking about feelings, while men are more interested in giving practical help, as I will show in Chapter 5.

The feminization of love encourages women to focus their lives on love and family, and implies that strong family bonds depend on maintaining traditional gender roles. Since men have difficulty in expressing tender emotions, women must devote themselves to love, otherwise there will be little love for anyone. Researchers have ignored this process, although they have documented the other social forces that lead women and not men to specialize in love, such as encouraging girls to play with dolls and work as babysitters, expecting mothers to be the primary parent, and paying men higher wages than women.[5]

While love has been feminized, our conception of self-development has been masculinized. Becoming a healthy personality typically means developing from a dependent child to an autonomous, independent adult, in psychological theories of personality development. Thus, for Erik Erikson, the individual ideally passes from an initial crisis of "trust versus mistrust" to "autonomy," "initiative," "industry," and "identity." Only with full adulthood does the issue become "intimacy versus isolation." As Carol Gilligan comments, "development itself comes to be identified with separation, and attachments appear to be developmental impediments."[6] Women emphasize attachment in their personal development, Gilligan found. But women are judged by a masculine standard and their close ties to others are interpreted as a sign of being developmentally retarded, overly "field-dependent," or insufficiently individuated. This masculine conception of self-development is one of the social forces that encourages men, and not women, to assert themselves and develop their capacity for independent achievement.

The split between feminine love and masculine self-development persists despite the trend to more flexible gender roles. It is part of our language and our culture. David Bakan, in *The Duality of Human Existence*, points to a basic contrast in Western society between masculine "agency" and feminine "communion":

Agency manifests itself in self-protection, self-assertion, and self-expansion; communion manifests itself in the sense of being at one with other organisms. Agency manifests itself in the formation of separations, communion in the lack of separations. Agency manifests itself in isolation, alienation, and aloneness; communion in contact, openness, and union.[7]

Modern thought from our everyday discussions to academic analyses is pervaded by a series of related dualisms: mind vs. body, doing vs. being, reason vs. passion, abstract vs. concrete. Underlying these dualisms is the opposition of masculine freedom to develop oneself vs. feminine attachment to others.[8]

GENDER IN A CONTEMPORARY MARRIAGE

The pervasive effects of split gender roles on marriage can be seen in the experience of Lyn and Tommy Gilmore, a couple in their middle thirties who were intensively interviewed for this book.[9] Lyn Gilmore was a housewife until recently, and her husband is a successful engineer in an aerospace company near their home in a southern California suburb. They have been married for fourteen years and have three daughters, aged 5, 8, and 11.

A few months before the interview, Lyn returned to college, and the year before she took a psychology course on communication and self-assertion, and had several months of psychotherapy. "Right now," says her husband Tommy, "she's expanding and she's trying to move out into a self-sufficient, stand-by-herself type person." He has adapted to these changes by supporting Lyn's return to school and taking on some of the child care and housework.

Despite these changes, they conform to traditional gender roles in many ways. Tommy focuses on individual achievement and independence in all aspects of his life except his marriage. "I enjoy my job very much . . . I enjoy the challenge of it. It's high stress, very demanding, very technical, and it requires a lot of, it demands a lot of me." He seems very involved in his marriage, and the only change he would like in his relation to Lyn, he said, was "I would change it so we have more time together." But this independent man has few other attachments. "I'm a loner, not making many friends, acquaintances, life in the fast lane, that kind of thing. As soon as something is almost done, I lose interest in it and am ready to move on to the next." Lyn, in contrast, has several close friends.

Both Lyn and Tommy define their personalities in sex-stereotyped ways. When Tommy is asked to describe Lyn in one word, he says: "Feeling. She's the most feeling person I ever knew. Sometimes she feels too much for people." Later he adds: "When things don't work, she gets very emotional . . . she can't see or she can't listen to comments from outside the thing she's looking at." Lyn describes Tommy as "someone who sees solutions better than I do . . . he sees the overview." But she also believes that his intellectual superiority is a facade covering his sensitive ego, something she has to work around. For example, when the solution to a problem "doesn't come from his mind, and it comes from me," she mentions her idea and then drops it until he brings up the idea as his own.

Gender also determines the division of labor in the family. Tommy provides all the income, while Lyn is responsible for the cooking, child care, and housework. Although Tommy does a lot of the work at home, it is defined as "babysitting" or "helping Lyn," and she is careful to thank him for his efforts.

The division of personality traits and activities by gender is creating conflicts in the family. Lyn complains about Tommy's aggressive treatment of the children: "He's always been one of these people who say 'do what I say or I'm going to slug you' which he never does, but it's always that verbal I'm-going-to-clobber-you stuff. They don't really react to that very well." She also longs for sensitive, emphatic communication with her husband. "I'm working on changing our intimacy level," she comments, but the change is progressing very, very slowly. For Lyn, like many women, intimacy focuses on talking, while for Tommy it focuses on sex.

For the Gilmores love is feminized. It is primarily Lyn's responsibility and her conception of love dominates. The split between the loving, dependent woman and the achieving, independent man structures their marriage. But their relationship is also influenced by a different, more androgynous image of marriage – a marriage that is the joint responsibility of both partners and helps both of them develop themselves.[10]

ANDROGYNOUS LOVE AND SELF: TRENDS AND DEBATES

The trend to more androgynous images of love and self has been visible since the end of the nineteenth century. The separation of the home and the workplace had contradictory effects. At first it polarized gender roles, but in later decades it encouraged a growing interest in self-development that is undermining these roles. During the twentieth century, the glorification of independence and individualism for the masculine role and the public sphere spread to women and the private sphere. Wives increasingly joined the paid labor force, which made them less economically dependent on their husbands, and strengthened their aspirations for self-development.

By the seventies, self-development was a primary value for both men and women, and more androgynous images of love and self were developing. National surveys reported a shift towards more flexible, androgynous gender roles, and more concern with private life and expressing feelings. Americans increasingly described a good marriage or love relationships in terms of both partners communicating openly, developing an autonomous self, and working on the relationship.[11] This new ideal of love is more androgynous because the man and woman are equally responsible for the relationship; and they are both openly dependent on the other, and committed to self-development. However, love is still feminized in that emotional and verbal expression are emphasized.

Conceptions of the ideal self are also becoming more androgynous, and portray a developed person as someone who combines feminine intimacy and emotional expression with masculine independence and competence. This expanded, androgynous self is replacing the older ideal of a restricted masculine self – the ideal of a self-made man who is independent, emotionally controlled, and economically successful.

Love and self-development are mutually reinforcing, not opposed, in the new ideals, in part because gender roles are not polarized. The combined emphasis on intimacy and self-development also reflects the influence of popular psychology and the new therapies of the human potential movement, leading some scholars to label new ideals as "therapeutic" images of love.[12]

Is the trend to androgyny and self-development beneficial or harmful for close relationships? This question is the focus of much of the current debate about the family. Most scholars, including Robert Bellah *et al.*, Ralph Turner, and Christopher Lasch, argue that the therapeutic perspective has had predominantly negative effects on personal life, and is undermining committed relationships and real self-development. The human potential movement encourages an "empty" or "impulsive" self, in their view, a self focused on expressing individual needs and desires that are ungrounded in social ties or shared culture. Personal life, they charge, is becoming a marketplace where individuals negotiate temporary relations that best meet their needs, while therapy instructs them in skilled negotiation and provides a model of brief relationships of limited commitment.[13]

These critics have an inaccurate, overly negative view of recent trends. In particular, they do not understand how self-development and enduring love can be mutually reinforcing.

Their misinterpretation stems from a failure to distinguish between two different images of love and self-development in popular culture, which I label "Independence" and "Interdependence." The Independence image undermines committed relationships, as the critics charge, but the image of Interdependence strengthens commitment.

In the Independent image of love a person first develops an independent self and then love follows. Developing one's self consists mainly in expressing one's needs and feelings. This perspective easily leads to the "me first," "I do my thing, you do yours" orientation that has received so much attention from the mass media. In the Interdependent image, self-development and committed love occur together, and mutual support is emphasized. For example, M. Scott Peck's 1985 bestseller on self-development and spiritual growth, *The Road Less Traveled*, counsels that the journey to individual growth is "the ultimate goal of life," but "significant journeys cannot be accomplished without the nurture provided by a successful marriage . . ."[14]

While the critics consider only the Independence image, I focus on Interdependence, and emphasize the positive effects of the search for self-development. The Interdependence blueprint suggests a realistic way of integrating self-development and enduring love, in my view, and is a better model for relationships than traditional family and gender roles. Moreover, people in androgynous, Interdependent relationships tend to be healthier and happier. The ideal of Interdependent love has several problems. It overemphasizes expressing emotions and ignores material interdependence, and the focus on emotions and the self may encourage people to withdraw from public life, as the critics charge. But, as I will try to demonstrate, it is a better model for close relationships than the alternatives.

Both the Independence and Interdependence images have an important influence on the close relationships of many Americans. For example, in the Gilmore's marriage, Lyn's search for self-development has involved greater interdependence – more cooperation and sharing in raising the children, more gratifying sexual intimacy, and the opportunity to expand beyond the limits of rigid gender roles, all without any apparent weakening of their mutual love and commitment. On the other hand, Tommy sometimes complains that Lyn is becoming too self-centered and independent. She "becomes so self-sufficient that sometimes she steps on other people's toes. And she loses track of the sight that other people have the same rights or the same needs to be just as independent."

Why have most scholars been blind to the more positive, interdependent side of self-development? There is plenty of evidence that the interest in personal growth during the seventies was linked to close relationships; intimacy, not isolation, was a sign of a developed self.[15] But observers usually dismissed this preoccupation with intimacy as a symptom of weakening close relationships, or as a survival of traditional family values that persisted in spite of the new concern with self.[16]

Theoretical assumptions about social life explain part of this negative reaction. Critics like Bellah, believing that a good society requires strong communities and a shared moral code, are alarmed by the increasing tolerance and declining respect for authority that has accompanied the

trend to self-development. They assume that valuing individual fulfillment and accepting a diversity of changing life styles will lead to anomie
and the breakdown of social bonds.

Social scientists and intellectuals also resist seeing the link between adult
self-development and intimacy. They devalue the "feminine" realm of
attachments, as Carol Gilligan has pointed out, and follow the masculine
pattern of identifying the self with abstract moral principles, the general
community, or the distant intimacies of childhood, not with current close
relationships. Theories in psychoanalysis and social psychology showing
how the self develops in committed relationships are generally ignored,
and the importance of intimacy in therapy is usually misunderstood.
Scholars fail to see that the warm relationship between therapist and
patient is an important part of what makes the patient better – more
self-developed and more capable of love.

Some scholars see the positive side of self-development. Peter Clecak
argues that it is part of a larger, progressive development in American
culture since the fifties: a quest for "personal fulfillment within small
communities of significant others," that includes the political activists of
the sixties and the human potential movement.[17] These movements have
improved the quality of life for many Americans, Clecak argues, and they
usually integrate self-development with intimacy and family ties. But
close relationships are not a major focus for Clecak, nor for most others
with a positive perspective on recent cultural change.[18] That topic is the
agenda for this book.

PLAN OF THE BOOK: ARGUMENTS AND EVIDENCE

The book has three parts. Part I presents the historical development of
feminine and androgynous love. I trace the split between feminine love
and masculine self-development in the nineteenth century, and then I
describe the twentieth-century trend from role to self – the shift away
from rigid family and gender roles, towards self-fulfillment, flexible
roles, and androgynous love. A positive evaluation of the trend from role
to self is supported by Marxist and feminist theoretical assumptions. The
negative evaluation of most scholars, I argue, rests on theories that
exaggerate the benefits of constraining rules and fixed family and gender
roles.

Part II examines feminized love in contemporary close relationships. A
feminine image of love continues to be influential in popular culture and
academic studies; love is identified with emotional expression, not
practical help, and women are expected to be responsible for close
relationships. The feminization of love encourages women to be dependent and preoccupied with relationships, and men to be independent and

preoccupied with work. This overspecialization results in illness and premature death for both sexes, and it produces intense conflicts in marriage between women who want more closeness and men who withdraw, as a case study of a marriage illustrates.

In Part III I focus on the new, more androgynous images of love that combine love and self-development, and give both partners responsibility for the relationship. A psychoanalytic perspective on the self shows how love and self-development can reinforce each other, and clarifies the limits of therapy as a model for love. The kind of love relationship that best fosters self-development, from this perspective, is secure and flexible, and includes both emotional and material interdependence. Case studies of several couples show how interdependent, androgynous relationships can foster both self-development and enduring love. Examples of androgynous love among friends illustrate the possibilities of committed love without pre-set roles, while loving relationships among relatives show the benefits of material and emotional interdependence among a group of people.

In the future, I conclude, the trend from role to self will continue, and androgynous love will be more important. This trend may lead us to more interdependent relationships or more independence and isolation. The outcome partly depends on economic and political changes in the wider society.

The evidence to support these arguments was generated by many methods of research, partly because I am integrating sociological, historical, and psychological perspectives, and partly because I believe that a statement is more likely to be true if it is supported by evidence from diverse sources.

Changes in images of love are documented by examining popular magazines between 1900 to 1979. I analyzed the content of 124 randomly selected articles on how to have a happy marriage, and the results give strong support for a trend from role to self. Historical and sociological studies by other researchers confirm this trend.

Evidence on contemporary close relationships was obtained from a series of surveys and intensive interviews in southern California, conducted by my students between 1980 and 1983. A survey of 133 adults showed that the ideal of Interdependence is more widely accepted than Independence. Structured interviews with 46 heterosexual couples showed that polarized gender roles and feminized love frequently produce conflicts over intimacy. Finally, intensive, open-ended interviews about close relationships were conducted with 32 individuals, and their relatives and friends. These interviews provide the case studies, such as the description of the Gilmores, that show how general social factors operate within concrete relationships. (The interviews are the source of all quotations that are not attributed to other researchers.) The respondents in these studies came from diverse backgrounds, but were not randomly selected; they were primarily acquaintances of the interviewers. Appendix I describes the samples and the research methods in detail.

Studies by other researchers – including national surveys, community studies and interviews – supplement my evidence on contemporary close relationships. This evidence strongly supports the argument that women and men tend to have different styles of love, and also indicates that polarized gender roles have negative effects on health. The positive effects of androgynous love and Interdependence have not been clearly established, but several studies show that Interdependence is becoming an increasingly influential blueprint of love. In sum, images of love in America clearly have shifted towards flexible roles and self-development, and this change is probably an improvement over the past.

I
The history of love

2

The feminization of love in the nineteenth century

The split between feminine love and masculine self-development emerged in the nineteenth century, with the transformation from an agrarian to a capitalist economy. Economic production moved out of the household, changing family life and people's conceptions of love and gender. In the short run, this transformation created the ideals of feminine love and a masculine self. In the long run, it led to androgynous ideals of love and self. By tracing their historical development, we can see how our ideas of love were formed by the new division of labor, by changing relations of dependency between women and men, and by the ideology of separate spheres.[1]

Before the nineteenth century, the dominant image of family life was that women and men were both responsible for love, and family members were dependent on each other both materially and emotionally. The ideal of the independent individual was still weak; gender roles were not polarized, and the private sphere of family life was closely integrated with the public community.

In the colonial communities of New England, the household was the arena for affection, economic production, education, and social welfare. The typical family was, in the words of the historian John Demos, "a little commonwealth," a miniature community governed by the same rules as the wider community.[2]

The integration of activities in the family produced a certain integration of instrumental and expressive traits in the personalities of men and women.[3] Husbands and wives were involved in similar economic activities, and shared the task of caring for household members. The patriarch was expected to guide and nurture all the dependents in his household, which often included apprentices and servants, and both sexes were instructed by their ministers to be loving and affectionate within the family.[4] Benjamin Wadsworth's book, *The Well-Ordered Family*, published in 1712, advised that "the duty of love is mutual, it should be performed by each to each of them." Husbands were instructed to temper their authority with love: "Though he governs her, he must not treat her as a servant but as his own flesh, he must love her as himself." And love included sexuality. Men were told, in the words of the Bible, to "rejoice with the wife of thy youth. Let her breasts satisfy thee at all times. And be always ravished with her love."[5]

Men owned almost all the property and monopolized positions of power in the community, while women were responsible for the care of infants and of the sick and disabled, but the activities and personality traits associated with love were not highly differentiated by gender. As the historian Mary Ryan summarizes the evidence:

> when early Americans spoke of love they were not withdrawing into a female byway of human experience. Domestic affection, like sex and economics, was not segregated into male and female spheres ... The reciprocal ideal of conjugal love ... grew out of the day-to-day cooperation, sharing, and closeness of the diversified home economy.[6]

THE SEPARATION OF MEN'S AND WOMEN'S ACTIVITIES IN A CASH ECONOMY

By the end of the eighteenth century, a great transformation was occurring. The family and personal relationships were being separated from economic production, and there was a parallel separation of human personality traits by gender. Love and family attachments were being defined as women's sphere while economic production and individual achievement were in men's sphere. The feminization of love and the masculinization of work intensified the divergence between men's and women's activities and personalities, and produced ways of loving that were more congenial to women than to men. Mary Ryan describes how this transformation took place in upstate New York. A similar transformation has occurred in much of the world during the last two centuries.[7]

At the beginning of the nineteenth century, Oneida County was a sparsely populated frontier, where most families lived on subsistence farms. Households were headed by the patriarch and produced their own food and clothing, bartering some of their produce for spices, liquor, and other luxury goods in one of the few local stores.[8] The household also conducted family worship, educated its children, and took care of the sick and the indigent. The church and town watched over the household and tried to ensure that it carried out these duties.[9]

Personal relationships within the household were relatively formal and hierarchical. Obedience of the wife and apprentices to the household head and of children to their parents was a primary virtue, and all adults were expected to be hardworking and religious. Children were viewed as miniature adults, and stern discipline was used to break a child's will and turn the child from individual desire to obedience to parents and church. The emotional bonds between husband and wife were not emphasized, and there was little physical privacy in the house for the couple. Marital intimacy, in the modern sense of emotional expression and verbal disclosure of personal experience, was probably rare. Instead, husband and wife were likely to share a more formal and wordless kind of love, based on duty, working together, mutual help, and sex.

The activities of both men and women focused on productive work near the home and on caring for household members. Women had a major role in economic production, usually taking charge of planting the family vegetable garden, caring for poultry and cattle, and making thread, cloth, and clothing, and other products. Men as well as women were responsible for the well-being of household members, and for their religious education, although men were doubtless expected to be more severe and demanding. Men worked near their homes, often assisted by family members, and were home during the day for meals and other family activities. Moreover, there was no sharp distinction between "private" and "public". The household was a hierarchical work group supervised by church and town, and intimate attachments or individual self-expression were not cultivated; thus people behaved much the same at home and in the community.

The patriarchal household began to disintegrate between 1815 and 1840. As land became scarce, shops and crafts began to replace agriculture as the major economic activity. Cash replaced barter as a mode of exchange, and merchants in the 1830s lured farmers with advertisements such as "cash for wool."[10] The new economic opportunities to work as artisans, shopkeepers, or commercial farmers were mostly open to men, but the cotton mills offered employment to young unmarried women. At first, the factories were small; families worked together under the father's leadership and were often paid in kind rather than cash. Thus an advertisement in the Utica *Patriot* in 1813 announced, "A few sober and industrious families of at least five children each, over the age of eight years, are wanted at the Cotton Factory."[11] But by 1840, the factories were larger; workers were all recruited individually, not as families, and they were paid in cash. Husbands in the towns typically worked as craftsmen or shopkeepers in establishments that were attached to the homes, but the most prosperous merchants worked away from home. Wives stayed at home and did not work for money.

As the workplace became more separate from home and family, relationships at work became impersonal. The distinction between the warm, personal, private sphere and the cold public sphere was emerging. Paul Johnson describes the changes in the shoe factories and among building crews of Rochester, New York, a community that became the fastest growing city in the nation in the 1820s as agriculture became commercialized and the Erie Canal was completed. In 1820, merchants and master craftsmen "lived above, behind, or very near their places of business, and employees boarded in their homes." The master was responsible for the moral behavior of his workmen; they were defined as dependents in his household. "Work, leisure and domestic life were acted out in the same place and by the same people . . ."[12]

In the following decade, the size of workshops grew larger, and workmen increasingly lived apart from their employer. For example, while in 1827 one in four shoemakers lived with his employer, only one in twenty was doing so by 1834.[13] Masters were becoming businessmen, spending most of their time away from the workshops buying labor and raw materials and selling finished goods. At the same time, they were demanding new standards of discipline at work. "Masters increased the pace, scale, and regularity of production, and they hired young strangers with whom they shared no more than contractual obligations."[14]

By the 1840s, the split between men's sphere at work and women's sphere at home was well under way. The male world of business and public life had become an unpredictable arena of competition among individuals. People moved from farm to town and from one town to another in search of work, competing with the growing number of foreign workers and fearful of the recurrent business slumps. Men's daily work increasingly became divorced from personal relationships and cooperation, and men also became separated from religion, as they stopped attending church and leading family prayers. Historians detect a mood of expansiveness and unlimited opportunity in American public life in the early nineteenth century. At the same time, there was an under-current of fear, a sense of slipping away into a chaos of "individual men devouring each other in the struggle for success."[15]

As public life became more impersonal, immoral, and uncertain, the female world of the family was becoming more intensely personal, pure, and circumscribed. Households became smaller as the birth rate declined and fewer households had apprentices and boarders. The ties between household, church, and town diminished, as husbands withdrew from the family and from the church, and town governments became more impersonal. The family less often acted as an efficient work team. Economic production, education and health care moved out of the home into factories, offices, schools, and hospitals. Women continued to work hard at home, producing clothing, preparing food, and caring for family members, but the focus of their lives was to care for their children and their husbands.

Women's task of childrearing expanded as children were defined as vulnerable innocents in great need of care. Moreover, the proper raising of children became increasingly important to the middle class as the class position of sons and daughters came to depend more on character and education than on inheritance of land. Childrearing, according to Paul Johnson, "fell more and more to mothers. They were warned not to beat their children . . . , but to mix discipline with love, and to develop moral sensibilities that would make them useful citizens of a Christian republic."[16] The relationship between mother and child became emotionally intense and oriented to the individual development of the child (but not the mother). In Ryan's words, the center of the household shifted "from patriarchal authority to maternal affection."[17]

Between the worlds of work and home, a new arena of missionary societies, lodges, and clubs was developing. Young men joined lodges to have a place to stay when they left home and went to clubs for fellowship. Women joined religious and moral reform societies as a way of having an impact on the wider society and a context for carrying on close friendships with women. These sex-segregated voluntary organizations bridged the growing gap between the public and private spheres.

THE IDEOLOGY OF SEPARATE SPHERES

As the daily activities of men and women grew further apart, a new world view emerged. It exaggerated the differences between "the home" and "the world" and polarized the ideal personalities of women and men. It was an ideology that was adopted by affluent Americans as well as the working class and is still influential today.[18]

The ideology of separate spheres is clearly evident in the magazines, church newsletters, and sermons of the nineteenth century, and has been well described by several historians.[19] In brief, this ideology portrayed the home as an "oasis in the desert," a spiritual "sanctuary." A New England minister proclaimed in 1827 that

> it is at home, where man . . . seeks a refuge from the vexations and embarrassments of business, an enchanting repose from exertion, a relaxation from care by the interchange of affection: where some of his finest sympathies, tastes, and moral and religious feelings are formed and nourished: – where is the treasury of pure disinterested love, such as is seldom found in the busy walks of a selfish and calculating world.[20]

Home is good and pure in this image and also somewhat immaterial and unreal – home centers on feeling and ideals, not productive physical activities like preparing meals or caring for infants.

In contrast, in the tough, material outside world "we see the general good, sacrificed to the advancement of personal interest," according to the *Ladies' Magazine* in 1830. "We behold every principle of justice and honor, and even the dictates of common honesty disregarded, and the delicacy of our moral sense is wounded."[21]

These two different worlds were dominated by two different personalities – the feminine and the masculine. The ideal woman was pious, pure, domestic, and submissive, in the words of historian Barbara Welter; a pious, emotional giver of care who depended on her husband to provide money and to deal with the threatening outside world. The ideal was described in a sermon on women:

> How interesting and important are the duties devolved on females as WIVES . . . the counsellor and friend of the husband; who makes it her daily study to lighten his cares, to soothe his sorrows, and to augment his joys; who like a guardian angel, watches over his interests [and] . . . constantly endeavors to render him more virtuous . . .[22]

A letter from General William Pender to his wife during the Civil War illustrates how husbands expected their wives to be moral arbiters:

> Honey, whenever I try to reflect upon the future and to resolve to do better, I think of you first and your image rises up . . . so that I have almost come to feel that you are a part of my religion. Whenever I find my mind wandering upon bad and sinful thoughts I try to think of my good and pure wife and they leave me at once. My dear wife you have no idea of the excellent opinion I have of your goodness and sweetness. You are truly my good Angel.[23]

Motherhood was the key to being a real woman. The virtues of motherhood were extolled in *The Ladies' Companion* in 1838. Fathers could not inculcate morality in children because the father,

> weary with the heat and burden of life's summer day or trampling with unwilling foot the decaying leaves of life's autumn, has forgotten the sympathies of life's joyous springtime . . . The acquisition of wealth, the advancement of his children in worldly honor – these are his self-imposed tasks.

It was his wife's duty to develop the child's character, to form "the infant mind as yet untainted by contact with evil . . . like wax beneath the plastic hand of the mother."[24] An ideal woman centered her life on love of husband and children, a love expressed mostly through emotions and piety, not practical action.

The ideal woman could also be powerful, both as the ruler of her domestic domain and as a moral reformer working with other women to help the weak and punish the wicked. Thus popular magazines between the middle of the eighteenth and the middle of the nineteenth century portrayed women as increasingly powerful, especially in childrearing, morality, and courtship.[25] But if she were to avoid censure, her power had to be based on her special feminine qualities – her superior ability to love, to be good, and to serve others – and not on masculine qualities such as self-interest, anger, or a desire for control.[26] According to an 1839 article on matrimony, "the man bears rule over his wife's person and conduct. She bears rule over his inclinations: he governs by law; she by persuasion ... The empire of the woman is an empire of softness ... her commands are caresses, her menaces are tears."[27]

The masculine ideal, tailored to fit the emerging capitalist economy, was to be an independent, self-made man. Key male virtues included self-control, economic success, courage, and upright character. *A Voice to the Married*, published in 1841, advised young men that "a good character must be formed, it must be made – it must be built by our individual exertions." Nineteenth-century writers called on men to be disciplined and courageous and to concentrate their energies, in order to prosper in the world outside the home, which was "a vast wilderness' where they were "naked and alone surrounded by savages" in "a rage of competitive battle."[28] Thus Demos identifies the central masculine virtues as strength, cunning and endurance. Men's strength depended on controlling and restraining their emotions and their sexuality. A medical text counseled men that "reserve is the grand secret of power everywhere." "Be noble, generous, just, self-sacrificing, continent, manly in all things – and no woman worthy of you can help loving you in the best sense of the word."[29] An abundant medical literature described the dire consequences of masturbation and excessive sexual intercourse. One text warns that with masturbation "all the intellectual faculties are weakened. The man becomes a coward; sighs and weeps like a hysterical woman. He loses all decision and dignity of character."[30] With the polarization of gender roles, male vices are female virtues, as Charles Rosenberg has commented.

The masculine conception of self-development that is still influential today is rooted in this nineteenth-century male ideal. Independence, self-control, and achievement are the major values of this ideal self while intimacy, emotional expression, and other feminine qualities are devalued.

An ideal man was not perfectly suited for family life. Trained for competitive battles and self-reliance, he might well suffocate in a cozy Victorian home. This conflict was reflected in the existence of two contradictory male ideals: the family man and the independent adventurer. From the point of view of most mothers, ministers, and prospective brides, the ideal man was probably a dependable family man, a good provider, and devout Christian. Nineteenth-century marriage manuals defined the ideal husband as a home-loving Christian and a man of good character who avoided "idleness, intemperate use of intoxicating drinks ... licentiousness in every form, gambling, swearing and the keeping [of] late hours at night."[31]

But many of the nineteenth-century heroes – the mountainmen, ship's captains, and cowboys – were undomesticated adventurers. They had abandoned the civilized world of women and the family for a life of danger and comradeship among men. According to Leslie Fielder's analysis of novels, the central myth of American culture is the tale of a boy or man who escapes from society to an island or wilderness where mother can't come and where he can enjoy innocent, violent adventures with a special male companion.[32] In this myth, marriage represents captivity and emasculation by sexless, virtuous women. The ideal is heroic action with men, not passionate love with women, as it usually is in European novels. Heroes from Tom Sawyer and Captain Ahab to the contemporary private eye all fit this pattern, which is an extreme version of the myth of male independence from women and families.

In sum, the ideology of separate spheres reinforced the new division of labor, and portrayed a world of independent, self-made men and dependent, loving women. The ideal family was portrayed as a harmonious, stable, nuclear household with an economically successful father and an angelic mother.

The reality of family life in the nineteenth century was of course much more diverse and turbulent than this ideology, even among the white middle class. Death disrupted many families. Marriages were just as likely to be broken in 1850 as 1950, if we combine the effects of death and divorce, because in 1850 so many people died young. Not until the 1960s was there a substantial rise in broken marriages, because of a sharp increase in divorce. Many households included other people besides the nuclear family. Affluent families usually had servants, while poorer families took in boarders.[33] Husbands sometimes rebelled against the provider role and deserted their wives, and wives were often less docile and more interested in sex than the Victorian image of "the angel in the house" suggests. Many women retreated into illness or rebelled against their confinement at home by joining religious or reform organizations or by remaining single.[34]

For the working class, immigrant groups, and black slaves, reality was probably farther from the ideal, although the evidence for these groups is scanty. Working-class men and their families often moved from city to city in search of work. For example, only 40% of the unskilled laborers who had lived in Newburyport, Massachusetts, in 1850 were still there in 1860.[35] When work was available, the husband's wages often could not support his family so his children and wife had to work. Less than 36% of the men working in Massachusetts factories in 1897 earned enough to support their families.[36] Immigrant groups often maintained the family patterns of their homelands, and slave families also had special traditions as well as a unique burden of oppression. Despite this diversity, however, these families too were strongly influenced by Victorian ideals, according to historian Carl Degler:

> The majority of Afro-American children in the 19th and 20th centuries lived in a nuclear family with both parents present, in which the father was not only the recognized head of the household but the primary breadwinner as well ... Among the immigrants, as among the Black and native families, the wife and mother was the heart of the home; it was she who managed the home and reared the children. Upon her fell the responsibility for seeing that the home was a proper place for the children and an attractive place for the husband.[37]

THE FEMINIZATION OF LOVE

With the split between home and work, and the polarization of gender roles, love became a feminine quality. A Unitarian minister described the female as "accustomed to feel, oftener than to reason." An Episcopalian praised women for possessing "all the milder virtues of humanity," and "a more exquisite sensibility than men ... The God of heaven has more exquisitivily [sic] attuned their souls to love, to sympathy and compassion."[38] Women's superior ability to love was seen as enabling them to comfort and care for their children and husbands.

As women gained control of love, the cultural images of love shifted towards emphasizing tenderness, expression of emotion, and weakness. When mothers replaced fathers as the parent with day-to-day authority, the methods of childrearing shifted from the stern will-breaking methods of agrarian times to socialization through giving and withholding love. Conceptions of God's love also shifted towards sweetness and tenderness. God was seen as an "indulgent parent," a "submissive, meek and forgiving" Christ.[39] In religious revivals, and in women's friendships, there was a new emphasis on recognizing private feelings and communicating them in an intimate relationship in which one could unfold one's whole heart.[40] Conceptions of marital love also shifted towards greater emphasis on affectionate feelings.

In *The Feminization of American Culture*, Ann Douglas argues that religion and popular literature were dominated by middle-class women and Protestant ministers in the nineteenth century. Women's status was declining as the household lost many of its functions, and ministers were becoming less powerful as the church lost its control over daily life and society became secularized. Excluded from effective public action, they took over activities devalued in industrializing America, and created an ineffectual, sentimental mass culture reflecting their own powerlessness. The literature and the religion they produced emphasized subjective feelings and suffering, and opposed virile action, rebellion, and objective analysis. As this simplified outline of her argument may show, Douglas is more admiring than I am of "masculine" assertion and independence, more critical of "feminine" emotion, and less interested in integrating the two spheres. But her analysis suggests how love was changed and distorted by being identified with women.

Feminized love was defined as what women did in the home; it had nothing to do with how men related to each other at work. Love became a private feeling, disassociated from public life, economic production, and practical action to help others. Many middle-class women challenged this private conception of love in the latter part of the nineteenth century. They expanded domestic love to include being "social housekeepers" and "mothers of the world." In the name of feminine love, hundreds of thousands of women organized to stamp out the vice of liquor, and smaller numbers worked to help the poor or abolish child labor.[41] But by the 1920s women's love was private once again.

Equating women's activities with love and men's activities with work produced a distorted perception of activities of both sexes. Men's attachments and dependency were obscured, and women's productive labor was labeled love. A great deal of work remained to be done at home, especially for the majority of women who lacked servants. But women's domestic labor was less visible and less respected than it had been in the agrarian economy.[42] Women were not paid for housework, while outside the home people usually worked for wages. The labor involved in women's expanding new task of shopping, spending money for goods, was especially obscured by identifying work with getting money. There was also an increasing divergence in the quality of work experience. Women's work at home "retained the irregularity, the responsiveness to immediate and natural demands, and the intermixture with social occasion common to preindustrial occupations."[43] Outside the home, work was regulated by clock time and the demands of machines. Gradually the concept of work excluded women's labor in the home and emphasized the masculine ideals of individualism, achievement, discipline, and competition.

Another effect of the feminization of love was to encourage a florescence of intimate friendships between women in the late eighteenth and the nineteenth century. The historian Nancy Cott points out that "the identification of women with the heart . . . implied that they would find truly reciprocal interpersonal relationships only with other women."[44] Moreover, the equality between women compared favorably to women's subordination to men. Friendship among women was also encouraged by the sociability among women in all-female schools and charitable and religious societies.

Frontier women bitterly complained about the absence of female friends, and the correspondence of educated women often reveals a passionate, enduring commitment to a life-long woman friend. Luella Case, a married woman from Massachusetts, wrote to her old friend Sarah in the 1830s after discovering a poem that Sarah had written to her: "words seem inadequate to express the sense I feel of your – what shall I say, *friendship*? No, I will rather call if affection, for you know I confessed as one of my weaknesses, an inordinate desire *to be loved*." And as a visit from Sarah ended, she felt "most lonely" having "no gentle voice to talk with, or read to me, no sweet beaming countenance to echo the feelings expressed, none of that gentlest of all sympathies, that of a pure, and truehearted female . . ."[45] Intense love between women friends, more accepted in the nineteenth century than now, was expressed in fondling, endearments, and love letters, concludes historian Lillian Faderman, but rarely included genital sex.[46] Victorian women thus turned to other women and to their children for love, more than to men.

LOVE, DEPENDENCY, AND POWER

Power relations in the family and the economy were also affected by the new beliefs in feminine love and masculine independence. These beliefs strengthened men's power advantage at home. They also covered up the material dependency and exploitation that were the major causes of power differences in the family and the workplace.

Women in the nineteenth century became extremely economically dependent on their husbands, probably more so than before or after the Victorian era. In the colonial period, women were actively involved in the domestic economy; after the Victorian era, increasing numbers of women entered the workforce. But in the nineteenth century it was shameful for a wife to work, even if she was a widow. An advice book for married women pointed out that "the average woman recognizes the value of money," but her desire to make money "battles perpetually with her desire to do nothing which is strong-minded and unladylike."[47] Married women who had worked as teachers usually would not be rehired after they married, and offices and stores often would not employ older married women.[48] Three-fourths of the female industrial workers in large cities in the 1880s were younger than twenty-five and 96% of them were single.[49]

Other family relationships became less dependent with the transition to capitalism. Economic survival was no longer based on working in the family farm or shop; individual wage labor was an alternative. Sons and daughters no longer depended on inheriting land from their father, and family members increasingly turned to outside government and private organizations rather than each other for education and health care. But wives became more dependent on husbands.

For example, Emma Goldman reports matter-of-factly that despite the poverty of her family, she quit her factory job in 1887 when she married the young man who worked next to her in the shop. After describing her reactions to her husband's impotence, she continues:

> My own passion had subsided. The material anxiety of making ends meet excluded everything else. I had stopped work: it was considered disgraceful for a married woman to go to the shop. Jacob was earning fifteen dollars a week . . . Life became insupportable.[50]

Increasing economic dependency was the basis for what many social historians see as a decline in the power of wives during the Victorian era,[51] but the connection was obscured by the ideology of innate differences between the sexes. In this world view, women were powerless because they were naturally affectionate and docile, as an article by the antislavery writer Lydia Maria Child illustrates:

> The comparison between women and the colored race is striking. Both are characterized by affection more than by intellect; both have a strong development of the religious sentiment; both are exceedingly adhesive in their attachments; both, comparatively speaking, have a tendency to submission, and hence, both have been kept in subjection by physical force, and considered rather in the light of property, than as individuals.[52]

This perspective denies the material basis of women's dependency, and emphasizes women's need for affection and their natural morality and submissiveness. Part of the feminization of love was the belief that women had an enormous need for love and tenderness while men were naturally independent and had much less need for enduring, non-sexual love. This imbalance in emotional dependency bolstered the power of men over women.

In the workplace, too, relations of material dependency were obscured by polarized gender roles. Men were defined as naturally independent, amoral, and isolated, the other side of defining women as naturally dependent, moral, and affectionate. This ideology of the isolated (male) individual accompanied and justified the rise of capitalism, as Marxist scholars have pointed out.[53] Workers were encouraged to see themselves as independent, competitive, and self-made. If they were rich or poor, it was the result of their own individual merit, not relations of dependency with other people. And if they were real men, they would thrive on the impersonal, competitive relationships that prevailed at work. Personal, caring relationships were restricted to women and the home; they should not be expected in the public sphere. The ideology of independent individuals and "free" workers replaced the old patriarchal model of dependent workers who were subordinate members of their master's household. Johnson describes how new ideals of independence and self-control emerged in Rochester in the 1820s and thirties, fueled by a religious revival that emphasized the "moral free agency" of each individual to reject evil and choose Christ.[54] This ideology implied that employers had no responsibility to their workers beyond paying them a minimal wage;

> the belief that every man was spiritually free and self-governing enabled masters to present a relationship that denied human interdependence as the realization of Christian ideals ... workmen who continued to drink and carouse and stay away from church were no longer considered errant children; they were free moral agents who had chosen to oppose the Coming Kingdom. They could be hired when they were needed, fired without a qualm when they were not.[55]

Thus the new division of labor in the family and the workplace intensified the material dependency of wives and of workmen, but these relations of unequal resources and power were covered over by an ideology that focused on the characteristics of individuals. The economic dependency of women was masked by the belief that women were inherently loving. The economic dependency of workers was masked by the belief that men were independent and self-made and free to determine their own social position.

The ideals of love and self-development that emerged in the nineteenth century justified inequality, especially at the workplace, by denying the material dependency among people. Our ideals of love and self continue to ignore material interdependence, as I will show later, perhaps because recognizing this interdependence would threaten the legitimacy of our economic system.

ANDROGYNY AND INTIMACY

As we have seen, the transition from agrarian to capitalist society polarized gender roles, feminized love and led to a masculinized ideal self. But in the long term, the transition led to more androgynous conceptions of gender, love, and self, and more intimacy between husband and wife. The new androgynous ideal combined masculine autonomy and feminine affection. Emotional expression became more valued for both sexes and intimate relationships in the private sphere became the main arena for developing one's unique self. In contrast, the masculine ideal self that accompanied the rise of capitalism emphasized independence, emotional control, and success in the public sphere. Conceptions of love also became more androgynous, as feminized love was superceded by new ideals of husband–wife companionship and open communication. Ideals of intimacy and androgyny did not become powerful in American culture until the twentieth century, in my view, although these ideals were visible much earlier, during the transition to capitalism.

In contrast to my interpretation, that of Lawrence Stone, a historian of the English family, does not distinguish between the long-term and short-term effects of capitalism. He argues that the rise of capitalism was accompanied by new values of "affective individualism" that emphasized self-development and intimate bonds with others. Stone describes how "human relationships were increasingly seen in economic terms, governed by the rules of the free market" because of the growth of a market economy and wage labor, together with other trends such as urbanization and geographical mobility. In the old world view, "the purpose in life was to assure the continuity of the family, the clan, the village or the state, not to maximize the well-being of the individual."[56] The new world view emphasized

> firstly, a growing introspection and interest in the individual personality; and secondly, a demand for personal autonomy and a corresponding respect for the individual's right to privacy, to self-expression, and to the free exercise of his will within limits set by the need for social cohesion...

Combining individualism with a focus on personal experience and feelings, the new world view was manifest in warmer, more affectionate family relationships and in "a wholly new scale and intensity of interest in the self."[57]

However, affective individualism probably did not predominate until much later than Stone asserts. The evidence that he cites primarily shows that love became feminized, not androgynous, with the rise of capitalism. For example, he notes the enormous popularity of romantic novels (read mostly by women) and the greater intimacy of the mother–child relationship.

Other scholars have noted signs of affective individualism during the rise of capitalism in nineteenth-century America. William Goode argues that with industrialization the American family became more affectionate and equalitarian, increasingly emphasizing the need for all its members to develop their unique selves. Eli Zaretsky discusses the emergence of a new sphere of personal life in nineteenth-century America as work became less satisfying and people turned to personal relationships and internal experiences for gratification.[58] And Robert Bellah *et al.* describe the "expressive individualism" that began to develop in the middle of the nineteenth century. In this new perspective, "the expansive and deeply feeling self" was the mark of a successful life, along with rich experience and the freedom to express oneself. In contrast, the older " utilitarian individualism" advocated "a life devoted to the calculating pursuit of one's own material interest."[59]

Some historians argue that this trend to affection produced more intimate and equal marriages in the nineteenth century, and they cite letters and diaries exhibiting a high degree of mutual love and dependency in marriages.[60] However, my reading of the evidence is that intimacy between wife and husband remained rare as long as their activities were so different and their power was so unequal. Thus Nancy Cott points out that "exaggerated sex-role distinctions may have succeeded in making women uncomfortable with men (and vice versa) as often as rendering the two sexes complementary."[61] She also argues that marital love was weakened by the subservience of women to men in a period in which traditional dependency relations were dissolving and peer relationships were increasingly valued.

Evidence of the lack of intimacy between husband and wife comes from nineteenth-century marriage manuals, which rarely mention affection or companionship. According to these manuals, a sound marriage is based on being religious, industrious, and healthy, and sex is for the purpose of procreation only. Women are advised to seek a husband who values home life and has good morals and then to obey him and be hardworking and good tempered. The quality of the relationship between husband and wife is relatively unimportant.[62] Other signs of marital estrangement include the complaints of married people in their letters and diaries, the disapproval of sexuality, the enormous rise in prostitution, and the decrease in the marriage rate toward the end of the nineteenth century.[63]

In the twentieth century, women and men became more similar and more equal. Wives joined their husbands in working for wages and both sexes came to place a high value on intimacy and self-development. But in the nineteenth century, the separation of the home and the workplace primarily created inequality and estrangement between the sexes, and a split between feminine love and masculine self-development.

3

From role to self: the emergence of androgynous love in the twentieth century

In the long run, the social changes that began in the nineteenth century destroyed Victorian family patterns. The ideal of masculine independence spread to women and the private sphere, undermining people's willingness to be restricted by narrow family and gender roles. Wives became less subordinate and absorbed by mothering, as they had fewer children and increasingly joined the labor force, and many husbands became less consumed by their work as leisure time expanded and jobs became bureaucratized. Through most of the twentieth century, there has been a trend towards more fluid, androgynous family roles and more involvement in self-development and personal life. Americans have become more concerned with individual happiness and pleasure, more tolerant of alternative life styles, more committed to equality for women and men, and more prone to divorce.

The trend to androgynous love has been discontinuous. In eras that emphasized personal liberation like the twenties and the late sixties the trend accelerated, while in the fifties the long-range trend reversed as gender roles became more rigid and tolerance declined. These discontinuities can be used to identify different periods in the social organization of marriage, each dominated by a different family blueprint, or a different mix of blueprints.[1] Each blueprint combines a cultural image of the ideal marriage with expectations for daily life that guide behavior.

Figure 1 presents the major blueprints of marriage since the nineteenth century. First is the Victorian blueprint of Family Duty in which love is the woman's responsibility. Then come the three blueprints that dominate contemporary marriage: the more traditional Companionship blueprint that first evolved in the twenties, and the newer blueprints of Independence and Interdependence in which the woman and the man share the obligation to work on their relationship, and the goal of self-development replaces conformity to roles. This chapter gives a general description of these changes in blueprints of marriage, and then presents quantitative data on the major trends.

	Who is responsible for love?	What is love?
Feminized love		
Family Duty (nineteenth century)	woman	fulfill duty to family
Companionship (1920–)	woman	intimacy in marriage
Androgynous love		
Independence (1970–)	woman and man	individual self-development and intimacy
Interdependence (1970–)	woman and man	mutual self-development, intimacy, and support

Figure 1   Blueprints of love

THE DECLINE OF THE FAMILY DUTY BLUEPRINT

The Family Duty blueprint was the first solution to the problem of maintaining family bonds in an increasingly individualistic society. According to this image of family life, as we have seen, the ideal family was a nuclear household consisting of a father who left home every day to make the money to support the family, a loving mother who was the center of family life, and the children. Marriage was forever, and a man had considerable authority over his wife and children. The relation between husband and wife began with falling in love and might develop into companionship, although intimacy and sexual relations between spouses were not central and both spouses had important ties with relatives and friends of their own sex. The key relation was an intense, emotional tie between mothers and children, and raising moral, respectable, and healthy children was a woman's major task.

This ideal dominated in the United States from about 1840 to 1880 and then began to show signs of decline.[2] The divorce rate was increasing at the end of the century, and it doubled between 1900 and 1920. The proportion of women remaining single was rising, and so many affluent women were childless that some social critics raised the spectre of "race suicide" and "race sterility." Others criticized the family as an oppressive institution that deprived Americans of freedom and equality. Feminists attacked the tyranny of husbands over wives; plays like Ibsen's *A Doll's House* attached the childlike position of women; advocates of free love protested against sexual repression; and sociologists viewed the difficulty of divorce as an unnecessary impediment to self-development.

By the turn of the century there was widespread debate in government, churches, and the mass media on the future of the family, the decline of sexual morality, and especially divorce. Opponents of divorce believed that it would destroy the family, which they saw as the basis of civilization. Divorce was attributed to "dangerous individualism," especially individualism in women, and women were charged with being spoiled, romantic, "jealous of men and usurpers of the male's time-honored functions." But by 1910, the opposition was overwhelmed and divorce was accepted.[3]

The 1920s witnessed the dissolution of Victorian family patterns. Social commentators believed that a "revolution in manners and morals" was sweeping the country, and, according to William Chafe, "almost all agreed that the age was one of unprecedented personal liberation."[4] The historian of the family, Arthur Calhoun, writing in 1917, believed he was witnessing the passing of patriarchy and devotion to the family, as people became more and more individualistic.

In the Roaring Twenties, college students and other young people cast aside Victorian clothes and pursued sexual liberation and exciting personal experiences.[5] The institution of dating developed – the pattern of young men and women seeing each other without chaperones, and without any intention of marriage, to "have a good time." High school students in Muncie, Indiana, in 1924 went to necking and petting parties and only with difficulty could be persuaded to be home for dinner three nights a week. On college campuses, dedication to social reform gave way to social activities organized by sororities and fraternities.[6] Women from respectable families smoked in public, wore short skirts and cosmetics, worked as secretaries before they married, and modeled the new image of a woman with an expensive wardrobe and sex appeal. The response of many older, more conservative Americans to all this was horror at the decline of morality and the sexual orgies (real and imagined) of the young.[7]

The causes of the decline of the Family Duty blueprint include changes in the sexual division of labor and an increasing value placed on self-fulfillment. Women's daily activities shifted away from motherhood and towards more participation in the public sphere. The ideal of the free, self-made man was spreading, and women were beginning to be seen as similar and equal to men, as persons who should develop themselves. The declining birth rate reduced the burdens of motherhood, although many housewives were busier than ever as standards for a clean and attractive home rose. Employment opportunities for women expanded through the growth of respectable jobs such as being a secretary or a saleswoman. "Nowadays," said suffragist Frances Willard in 1897, "a girl may be anything from a college president down to a seamstress or a cash girl. It depends only upon the girl what rank she shall take in her chosen calling."[8] In fact, most working women were segregated in a few low-paying jobs, and it remained shameful for married women to work, but being a single career woman was becoming a respected way of life.[9]

The Victorian ideal that woman's place was in the home was also challenged by women's participation in the Temperance Movement and in other social reform movements of the early twentieth century. The movement for women's suffrage, which obtained the vote for women in 1920 and involved an estimated two million women, most directly undermined the Family Duty blueprint.[10] The suffragists used the rhetoric of separate spheres and argued that women needed the vote because they were more moral and altruistic than men, but women's suffrage removed a major barrier to women's participation in public life.[11]

Men's lives also changed as routine white-collar jobs expanded with the growth of large corporations, and the forty-hour work week became more common. Men's work became more sedentary and regimented, and less heroic. According to several social historians, as many men found less validation for their masculinity in work, their personal identification with their jobs diminished and they became more involved with their personal lives, their families, and leisure activities.[12] Work probably continued to be the center of life for men pursuing challenging and prestigious careers, but personal life became increasingly important for men as the twentieth century advanced.[13]

The increasing focus on personal life and self-development and decreasing commitment to traditional roles was fueled by several changes. Security – experiencing the world as safe and abundant – seems to promote a concern with self-development, and the average person's sense of security probably rose in the early twentieth century because of gradual improvements in the standard of living and the widespread economic boom during the early twenties.[14] The growth of consumerism and advertising also encouraged people to develop new personal needs and try to fulfill them. "The American citizen's first importance to his country," editorialized the Muncie newspaper in the 1920s, is "that of consumer."[15] Valuing self-development and independence over conformity to roles was also encouraged by public education, which expanded enormously for both sexes.[16] In 1924, high-school diplomas were awarded to 213,000 men and 281,000 women, an increase since 1900 of about 500 percent for both sexes, while the population had only increased by 50 percent.[17] Finally, the social reform movements of the Progressive Era challenged traditional roles and political institutions, and the unpopularity of World War I further undermined established authority, leading people to seek direction and meaning in their own personal lives.[18]

THE COMPANIONSHIP BLUEPRINT

As the Victorian blueprint of duty to family roles was disintegrating, a new ideal was being articulated in academia and the mass media: the Companionship family. This blueprint identified the family with marriage, not parenthood, and emphasized emotional and sexual intimacy between husband and wife.

Sociologists proposed a new family ideal focused on affection and supporting each other's personalities, now that families had lost their traditional economic and social functions. The modern family was "a unity of interacting personalities" in the famous phrase of sociologist Ernest Burgess, and had evolved "from institution to companionship."[19] The first principles of family life, according to Burgess, are "that the highest personal happiness comes from marriage based on romantic love" and "that love and marriage are essentially personal and private and are, perhaps, even more than other aspects of life to be controlled by the individual himself."[20] Marriage, in this view, is a private arena of self-fulfillment, not duty. With the spread of the Companionship blueprint, affective individualism and a more androgynous self became part of mainstream American culture.

For the first time, popular advice books suggested that having children might weaken a family, and in 1931, for the first time, there were more advertisements for cosmetics than for food in the *Ladies' Home Journal*. Being an attractive companion was becoming more important than being a competent homemaker. Dorothy Dix, in her syndicated newspaper column for women, advised: "The old idea used to be that the way for a woman to help her husband was by being thrifty and industrious . . . but a domestic drudge is not a help to her husband, she is a hindrance . . . The woman who cultivates a circle of worth-while people, who belongs to clubs, who makes herself interesting and agreeable . . . is a help to her husband."[21]

The Companionship family blueprint emphasized the similarity of husband and wife much more than the Family Duty blueprint. Both partners were expected to need and to give affection and understanding, and increasingly, both were expected to enjoy sexual intimacy. But love was still feminized, and wives were still expected to be economically dependent and submissive to their husbands. Marriage was to be all of a woman's life but only part of a man's. There was no column by Dorothy Dix instructing a man on how to be a help to his wife, and the magazines of the period consistently told women that it was their responsibility to create successful marriages.[22] Despite some changes towards androgyny, gender roles remained fairly polarized in the Companionship blueprint.

The reality of family life in the twenties, according to Robert and Helen

Lynd's study of Muncie, is more similar to the Family Duty blueprint than to the world of Companionship marriage and libertine flappers. In the business class (the top 30 percent of the families), wives did not work, and the social status of the family was a primary concern to both husband and wife. Most couples did not place a very high value on companionship in marriage, and frankness between spouses was not encouraged. Husbands described wives as purer, morally better, and more emotional and impractical than men, and their wives agreed. The motto of one of the women's clubs was "Men are God's trees; Women are his flowers."[23] Social life was organized primarily around couples, although men and women were also active in sex-segregated clubs and friendships were important to the women. Wives were very child-centered, while husbands had little contact with their children beyond meals and family auto trips. Husbands were, however, beginning to share in the housework. In the working class, a substantial minority of the wives worked, but marital relations were even farther from the Companionship ideal. Husbands and wives rarely talked, and in the absence of other methods of birth control wives kept away from their husbands sexually. Only the beginnings of the Companionship family were observable in Muncie; an intimate emotional and sexual bond between two developing personalities was seldom achieved or even strongly desired. Contrary to what many historians have suggested, marital intimacy was rare, as late as the twenties.

The Great Depression from 1929 to 1941 was probably the major force in reversing the trend towards individual freedom of the twenties. As the economy collapsed, people faced an insecure, hostile environment, and adopted a rigid version of the Companionship ideal that emphasized traditional family and gender roles more than personal development. Although domestic politics became more radical in the thirties, with the growing power of labor unions and the social programs of the New Deal, family life became more conservative.

College students in the early thirties expressed less approval of divorce and extramarital sex than in the twenties and there was a rise in the proportion of students who intended to marry and have children.[24] Opposition to women's entering the labor force reappeared as more and more men lost their jobs, and employers increasingly denied married women the right to work. A survey of 1,500 school systems in 1930 reported that 77% refused to hire wives and 63% fired women teachers if they married. When the Gallup Poll asked Americans in 1936 whether wives should work if their husbands were employed, 82% said "no."[25] Women's magazines "urged their readers to return to femininity and constructed an elaborate ideology in support of the home and marriage to facilitate the process," according to historian William Chafe.[26] *The Ladies'*

Home Journal told its readers that "the creation and fulfillment of a successful home is a bit of craftsmanship that compares favorably with building a beautiful cathedral," while *McCall's* observed that only as a wife and mother could the American woman "arrive at her true eminence."[27]

The effects of economic insecurity on commitment to traditional family roles is documented by Glen Elder's study of people who grew up during the Depression. Compared with people whose families had not suffered economically, men and women from families that had suffered substantial economic losses in the Depression placed a greater value on family life as opposed to work and leisure, and were more interested in raising children and less interested in husband–wife companionship. The deprived men actually had a larger number of children, on the average, than men from non-deprived backgrounds. Another finding that supports the link between economic deprivation and traditionalism is that working-class people have more traditional attitudes about family and gender than middle-class people.[28]

World War II ended the Depression and interrupted normal life for many families as men went off to war and women to work. Between 1940 and 1944, the proportion of married women in the labor force rose from 17% to 26%.[29] Although there was an effort to push women workers back into the home after the war, married women continued to enter the work force in growing numbers, radically changing the division of labor between husbands and wives that had persisted since the nineteenth century.

The postwar decades were a period of extreme commitment to the family and to split gender roles. People married earlier, had more children, and avoided childlessness, causing the famous baby boom. The divorce rate stayed unusually steady,[30] and new suburban tracts provided a setting for a family-centered way of life. There was a resurgence of antifeminism and a revival of the nineteenth-century theme of separate spheres. Thus the head of one women's college advocated that preparing women for "the task of creating a good home and raising good children" be made the primary purposes of women's colleges.[31] Women's magazines described the joys of femininity and togetherness, and public opinion, which had supported wives working during the war, once again opposed their working if their husbands could support them. Most people also supported a traditional division of labor in which men determined where a family lived and how it spent its money.[32] Yet all the while, more and more wives were working.

The blueprint for family life was a revised version of the Companionship family of the twenties and thirties.[33] The Companionship ideal of the fifties was based on intimate affection between husband and wife. Although the relation between mother and children was vitally important, a woman was warned not to let motherhood weaken her relation with her husband or to smother her children with too much attention. The couple was expected to lead an active social life but not to have close ties outside the nuclear family. The Victorian ideology of separate spheres was still partly intact; it was the husband's job to support the family, while the wife was the center of home life. But the authority of the husband had declined – he was to be more of a pal to his children and more of a companion to his wife. The concept of family togetherness – of Mom, Dad, and the kids barbecuing dinner together in the backyard – softened the separation of men's and women's spheres. Marriage began with falling in love and developed into companionship; but if love died, divorce might be the best solution.

This family ideal was endorsed by most intellectuals and social scientists in the postwar era. Talcott Parsons provided a theoretical justification with his argument that a well-functioning family required an instrumental father and an expressive mother. Other sociologists obscured the gender differentiation in the Companionship model by emphasizing its equality and flexibility in comparison with the patriarchal Victorian family or the marriages of conservative Americans. Few observers noted that as long as marriage was defined as the wife's responsibility and love was feminized, emphasizing companionship increased her dependency on her husband.[34] The Victorian wife at least had her separate sphere of children and women friends. For the wife in a Companionship marriage, her husband was her sphere, and her life was focused on getting the right emotional response from him. The price of Companionship marriage was high, especially for the educated, middle-class women who valued their independence the most.[35]

The strong commitment to traditional family roles throughout the fifties and early sixties is somewhat puzzling since many social conditions encouraged androgyny and self-development. A growing number of wives had jobs and became less economically dependent on their husbands. By 1965, 45% of married women with school-age children worked, compared with 26% in 1948. There was an unprecedented economic prosperity in the postwar era, and a very large expansion of public higher education. One would expect these conditions to accelerate the trend from role to self, but this did not happen until the late sixties, when a wave of protest movements and the Vietnam War produced a counter-culture that rejected traditional roles and beliefs, including the Companionship family blueprint.[36]

THE DECLINE OF THE COMPANIONSHIP BLUEPRINT

Another period of personal liberation began in the sixties. This time many observers felt that a major boundary of social organization had been crossed – that we had passed from an era in which people's private lives were regulated by the obligations of family roles into a new era of the self.[37] There was a rapid reversal of the familism of the fifties. Divorces accelerated sharply and fertility declined to an all time low. The rate of couples living together without being married doubled between 1970 and 1979, and there was a large increase in the number of persons living alone. Premarital sexual experience, which had been increasing since the twenties, became much more frequent; for example, the percentage of single seventeen-year-old girls who had experienced sex rose from 27 to 41% between 1971 and 1976.[38]

The trend towards wives working for money was probably the underlying cause of the decline of the Companionship family. But the immediate cause was the anti-establishment social movements of the sixties and seventies. The sixties began a period of "revolution in manners and morals" similar to the twenties, literally a "counterculture."[39] The civil rights movement, the antiwar movement, and the women's movement involved a large minority of Americans in demonstrations, drug trips, petition campaigns and consciousness-raising groups, all of which undermined the patriotism and devotion to family of the postwar era.

The women's movement, in particular, attacked the Companionship family blueprint. Conservative feminists endorsed the "two-career family," in which both husband and wife were equally committed to glamorous careers and to childrearing and homemaking. Radical feminists rejected the family as the preferred living arrangement and developed images of homosexual households or socialist collectives. By the early seventies ideas about gender equality diffused throughout the nation as the women's movement received a great deal of media coverage and achieved a rapid series of legislative victories supporting expanded opportunities for women in the labor force and in education.[40]

Once again, a strong women's movement had undermined traditional family roles. As long as family blueprints emphasized self-sacrifice and polarized gender roles, women's freedom conflicted with family bonds. Thus Carl Degler concludes his history of women and the family in America by observing that "the great values for which the family stands are at odds . . . with those of the women's movement."[41]

Companionship family roles were also attacked by the human potential movement. Popular psychology books like Gail Sheehy's *Passages* rejected the role of successful provider and cheerful housewife as hypocritical and deadening. They urged people to free themselves from restrictive obligations, get in touch with their feelings, and experience their full potential. New therapies and growth centers sprung up – encounter groups, Esalen, Primal Scream, EST – all of them encouraging adult men and women to develop themselves and reject traditional roles. In contrast to the orthodox therapies of previous decades that had urged patients to adjust to traditional family and gender roles, the new therapies preached androgyny, and urged men and women to reject the expectations of others and develop their own true selves.[42]

The decline of the Companionship blueprint was welcomed by some groups and opposed by others. Not surprisingly, women supported the new flexibility in gender roles more than men, especially highly educated professional women.[43] These women valued independence the most and could benefit the most from improved career opportunities. Thus, in the political struggle over abortion, the "pro-choice" activists were mostly well-educated, career-oriented women who placed a high value on individual freedom and self-development. The "pro-life" women were primarily less educated housewives with a deep commitment to religion and to the traditional roles of the loving housewife and the strong husband who provides for her.[44] For these women and for many other Americans, the Companionship family continued to be their ideal.

THE NEW BLUEPRINTS: INDEPENDENCE AND INTERDEPENDENCE

By the middle of the seventies, new androgynous images of close relationships were beginning to crystallize. A prolonged economic recession dampened people's aspirations for freedom, and academics and the mass media began to criticize the human potential movement as selfish and narcissistic.[45] The need for intimacy began to seem more pressing than the need to combat oppressive family and gender roles.

The new blueprints emphasize three sets of qualities that I label "self-fulfillment," "flexible roles," and "intimacy and open communication." First, in the new images of love, both partners are expected to develop a fulfilled and independent self, instead of sacrificing themselves for the other person. Second, family and gender roles are flexible and are continually renegotiated. Third, the relationship centers on intimate communication of needs and feelings, and on openly confronting problems. Self-development and love are integrated in these blueprints, and love is the responsibility of the man as well as the woman. The Independence and the Interdependence blueprints both emphasize these qualities; they differ on the issue of self-sufficiency and independence vs. mutual support and commitment.

The new blueprints of relationships began to emerge in the middle of the sixties, according to a study of women's magazines. Women were advised that they must develop an independent self in order to be loving, and they were told to build a vital, spontaneous relationship without fixed rules, by communicating openly about feelings and working through conflicts. In contrast, in the fifties, "putting aside of self was defined as loving behavior," and women were advised to sacrifice themselves for their families, follow traditional sex roles, and strive for harmony and togetherness.[46]

When Ann Swidler interviewed sixty residents of an affluent California suburb around 1980, she found that most of them emphasized self-fulfillment and accepted the "therepautic ideal" of love promoted by psychologists and the human potential movement. They believed that love is partly expressed by sharing oneself and one's feelings; therefore, a person must develop a somewhat independent self in order to be loving. For example, a young wife explained that she had had problems with her husband, Thomas, because "I was doing things just for him and ignoring things for myself. Now, since her therapy, she feels more independent and self-confident. "The better I feel about myself, I feel I have a whole lot that I can contribute to Thomas."[47]

"Good communiction" is crucial in the new blueprints, both to express one's self, and to negotiate a unique, flexible relationship in the absence of definite family and gender roles. Verbal communication is also part of being intimate and "working on" the relationship. As a college man commented, "You have to work at your marriage, it's like a job." A poll conducted for *Playboy* magazine in 1976 indicates the importance of communication to contemporary American men. "Someone to be totally open and honest with" was the most frequently mentioned quality for an ideal lover.[48]

The new blueprints are radically androgynous and anti-institutional. The themes of self-fulfillment and intimate communication resemble the Companionship blueprint, and its concern with personality development and marital interaction. But unlike the Companionship ideal, the new blueprints do not legitimate predetermined roles or a sexual division of labor; they are blueprints for "relationships," not marriages. Both partners are expected to work on the relationship, communicate openly and develop themselves. Wives are advised to cultivate independent interests and goals, while husbands are encouraged to express their feelings. Love is no longer part of women's special sphere.

The Independence blueprint adds to these themes a strong emphasis on being self-sufficient and avoiding obligations. Developing an independent self and expressing one's needs and feelings is seen as a precondition to love. In contrast, couples who follow the Interdependence blueprint believe that they owe each other mutual support and affection, and that love is a precondition to full self-development.

Sociologists disagree about the relative importance of these two blueprints. Robert Bellah and his associates conclude that Independence is becoming the dominant image of love in America. People are increasingly avoiding commitments, they argue and support their interpretation by quoting from Swidler's interviews. For example a counselor commented: "I guess, if there is anyone who needs to owe anybody anything, it is honesty in letting each other know how they feel about each other, and that if feelings change, to be open and receptive, to accept those changes, knowing that people in a relationship are not cement."[49]

In contrast, my study of 133 adults in 1980 indicates that Interdependence, not Independence, is the dominant blueprint of love. The respondents, who came from diverse social backrounds, were asked about the "qualities that are most important for a good marriage or love relationship" (see Appendix I for details of the study). Contrary to the argument of Bellah *et al.*, the second most frequently mentioned quality was "support and caring." "Good, open communication" was most frequently mentioned, while "tolerance, flexibility and understanding" was third, "honesty" was fourth, and "commitment" was fifth.[50] Individuals who emphasized "support and caring" usually talked about the obligation to be nurturant and attentive, and many of them connected support and caring with self-development. For example, when a thirty-year-old minister in San Diego was asked what he most valued in his wife, he replied:

> I trust her to react in a reaffirming way to me when I share with her ... I know that she will respond to me in a positive way. She will share the pain or frustration or triumph of the day with me, and I feel like what I have to say about me is very important, because it's me in a sense.

Although there is disagreement about the importance of mutual support and commitment in contemporary relationships, researchers agree on the growing importance of self-fulfillment, flexible roles, and intimate, open communication. With the decline of the Companionship blueprint, the trend from role to self accelerated, producing new, more androgynous images of love.

It is possible that another shift back to traditional roles has begun, partly as a result of the continued economic difficulties of the seventies and eighties. The slight drop in the divorce rate and the reversal of feminist gains in affirmative action and abortion rights may be signs of such a shift. But the evidence that would document this change is not yet available.

EVIDENCE FROM POPULAR MAGAZINES

The changes in family blueprints that I have just described are clearly reflected in magazine articles that give advice on how to have a happy marriage. I analyzed a sample of articles from 1900 to 1979 and measured the proportion of articles in each decade that endorsed the traditional

Family Duty and Companionship blueprints vs. the modern themes of self-fulfillment, flexible roles, and intimacy. The results confirm the long-range trend from role to self during the twentieth century, and also show that the twenties and sixties were unusually modern while the fifties were unusually traditional. Studies by other researchers show this same pattern of change.

I examined 128 articles on marriage from high circulation magazines like the *Ladies' Home Journal*, *McCalls*, and *The Reader's Digest*. The articles are addressed primarily to women, and advise them on how to produce a happy, loving marriage and how to overcome feelings of disappointment and loneliness. For each five-year period, I randomly selected eight articles listed in the *Readers' Guide to Periodicals* under the topic "Marriage." The content of each article was coded according to the dominant message that the article seemed to communicate to readers.[51]

The categories used to analyze the articles focused on self-fulfillment, flexible roles, and intimacy and open communication. One category that measured self-fulfillment was "self-sacrifice vs. self-fulfillment." An example of endorsing self-sacrifice is a 1909 editorial in *Harper's Bazaar* that advised: "Marriage means self-discipline. Marriage is *not* for the individual, but for the race ... Marriage is the slow growth of two persons into one – one person with one pursuit, one mind, one heart, one interest ... one ideal."[52] In contrast, a *Ladies' Home Journal* article in 1978, illustrating the self-fulfillment theme, warned that it was a myth to believe that marriage should "meet all the emotional needs of both spouses," that it "is an all-encompassing blend of two personalities fused into one. A marriage like this leaves no breathing space for two individuals to retain their own personalities."[53]

A category for measuring flexible roles was "rigid vs. flexible female gender role." The traditional side of this category is illustrated by a 1940s article which comments that, compared to men, "women have much less time for action, being absorbed, consciously or unconsciously, by their preoccupation with love and maternity."[54] Intimate communication was measured by the category "avoid conflict, and keep up a front vs. communicate openly and confront problems." Illustrating the modern view of communication, an article in the *Reader's Digest* in 1974 asserted that "if spouses are thoughtful toward each other on *all* occasions, they probably have a sick marriage."[55]

Table 1 shows the number of articles in each decade that support traditional vs. modern themes in these three categories. The percent of modern themes – combining the three categories – gradually rises, as shown at the bottom of the table. There are also discontinuities; for instance, there are more articles endorsing flexible gender roles in the 1920s than in the next three decades. Thus a 1925 article in *The Ladies'*

Table 1 *Trends in magazine articles on marriage, 1900–1979: number of articles supporting traditional vs. modern themes*

Traditional [T]		Modern [M]	1900–1909		1910–1919		1920–1929		1930–1939		1940–1949		1950–1959		1960–1969		1970–1979	
			T	M	T	M	T	M	T	M	T	M	T	M	T	M	T	M
1 self-sacrifice compromise	vs.	self-fulfillment individuality	7	1	4	3	5	1	7	2	10	0	11	0	7	7	5	2
2 rigid female role	vs.	flexible female role	10	7	14	4	8	10	11	7	8	9	13	5	8	10	6	13
3 avoid conflict, keep up a front	vs.	communicate openly confront problems	1	2	2	0	3	2	5	3	4	0	4	6	4	8	3	10
Percent of modern themes			36%		26%		45%		34%		29%		28%		57%		64%	

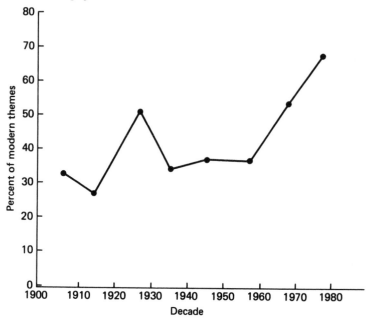

Figure 2 Modern themes in magazine articles on marriage, 1900–1979: percent of themes supporting self-fulfillment, flexible roles, and intimacy

Home Journal proclaimed: "The woman of today acknowledges no master." Women now regard marriage as "a social partnership, an adventure, an experiment even, but it must always be on a fifty-fifty basis."[56] And in every decade, there is considerable variation in what the magazines are saying, and a substantial number of both traditional and modern themes.

The trend from role to self and the discontinuities in this trend are more clearly displayed in the graph in Figure 2. The graph shows the percent of themes in each decade that support self-fulfillment, flexible roles, and intimate communication, combining eight categories that include the three already discussed. For example, "flexible roles" is measured by the previously discussed category about the female role, as well as categories about the male role and the acceptability of divorce (see Appendix II for details).

The graph shows a trend to modern themes over the twentieth century. In the first two decades of the century, about 30% of the themes are modern, compared to about 70 percent in the 1970s. There is also a clear up-and-down pattern of change, with modern themes predominating in the twenties and again in the sixties and seventies.

The causes of the trend from role to self, as I have discussed, probably include economic prosperity, increasing leisure and education, and the tendency of women as well as men to work for individual wages. The discontinuities can partly be explained by the same factors; in particular, economic hard times apparently reversed the trend in the thirties. Other researchers have emphasized demographic shifts in explaining disconti- nuities in American family life, and unpopular wars may also be impor- tant.[57]

The intriguing association between the women's movement and images of marriage suggests other explanations of the discontinuities – explanations that point to the great importance of gender roles in understanding the American family. A strong women's movement accompanied or preceded the extreme emphasis on personal freedom and self-fulfillment in the twenties and again in the late sixties. The women's movement, as measured by the amount of coverage of women in *The New York Times* and popular magazines, was strongest between 1905 and 1920. It reached its low point between 1950 and the early sixties, and then rose again in the late sixties (see Appendix III). The rise and fall of the women's movement thus parallels the rise and fall of modern images of marriage, as shown in Figure 2, except that the highpoint of the movement around 1910 preceded the change in marital images by about a decade.

This relationship between the women's movement and the trend from role to self is not surprising, and has been noted by social historians. The women's movement usually has urged women to avoid self-sacrifice and traditional gender roles, and participating in the movement probably made women more powerful and independent of their families as they acquired new skills and friends, and new ideas about women's proper place.

The conflict between traditional family roles and women's rights may also produce a self-generating cycle of change. When there is a strong commitment to a traditional family blueprint (i.e., the Family Duty or Companionship blueprint), individual freedom and self-development are suppressed, especially for women. But freedom and self-development are highly valued in America, leading to a conflict that eventually undermines the blueprint and produces a period of personal liberation like the 1920s. Greater freedom to develop oneself, especially for women, then threatens people's needs for attachments, creating a readiness to accept a new family blueprint. This cyclic tendency, if it exists, will be weakened by the diffusion of the Interdependence blueprint, which combines stable attach- ments and self-development.

Whatever the causes of the changing images of marriage, two patterns of change emerge clearly from my analysis of magazine articles. There has been a gradual trend towards self-fulfillment, flexible roles, and intimate communication, as well as some major discontinuities.

MORE EVIDENCE ON THE TREND FROM ROLE TO SELF

Studies by other researchers strongly support my findings on the trend in popular images of marriage. I examined all quantitative studies of changing beliefs about marriage and gender in the twentieth century, and found that the trend to self-fulfillment, flexible roles, and intimate communication was documented by many independent researchers. There are virtually no findings that contradict my results, and the evidence of a major change from role to self since the late sixties is especially strong.[58] There is less evidence on the discontinuities, partly because few studies consider a long enough time span to detect reversals of trends.

Two large surveys of a random sample of Americans show that the trend from role to self applies across social strata and geographical regions. Joseph Veroff, Elizabeth Douvan, and Richard Kulka compared the results of national surveys done in 1957 and 1976. They found a change towards "(1) diminution of role standards as the basis for defining adjustment; (2) increased focus on self-expressiveness and self-direction in social life; (3) a shift in concern from social organizational integration to personal intimacy."[59] For example, Americans in 1976 gave more emphasis to personality traits when they described themselves, and less to moral qualities. They talked to others more about their personal problems, expressed more concern with achieving intimacy in marriage, and were also more tolerant of people who remained single.

Daniel Yankelovich's surveys of young adults in the seventies reported similar findings. Americans are rejecting "the old credo that if they work hard, stay out of trouble, and put their family and others ahead of their own personal satisfaction, then they will be rewarded with a good living," he concluded. College students rejected traditional beliefs more than non-college youths, following the usual pattern of the upper classes being more modern; but for both groups, expressing yourself, love, and friendship were the top-rated values, and their main goal was "finding just the right life style for expressing their psychological potential."[60] By the early eighties, Yankelovich estimated that 80% of Americans were involved in some way in the quest for self-fulfillment – in self-help groups, women's liberation, holistic health, and other activities – while almost 20% were strongly committed. Several studies of fiction and non-fiction articles in popular magazines also detected a growing emphasis on self-fulfillment, flexible roles, and intimacy since the fifties. Another sign of the concern with self was the growing popularity of seeing a therapist – the American Association of Marriage and Family Therapy expanded from 237 members in 1960 to 11,941 in 1985.[61]

Changes in women's roles are part of the shift from self-sacrifice to self-fulfillment. For example, the proportion of women supporting the statement "A man can make long-range plans for his life, but a woman has to take things as they come" declined from about 45% to about 11% between 1964 and 1970. And national surveys show a pervasive and substantial shift toward egalitarianism in sex-role attitudes since 1962. There is also evidence that motherhood is becoming less important; since 1960, the birth rate has declined, women and men have wanted fewer children and have rated children as less important to a good marriage.[62]

More flexible family and gender roles – the second component of the trend from role to self – is part of a general trend towards tolerance. Increasing tolerance of diversity and change, and declining rigidity of rules and moral standards, has been one of the major changes in American values over the past two centuries,[63] despite occasional reversals, as in the 1950s when there was little tolerance for diversity in either family life or politics. Children's readers since 1800 have included fewer and fewer moral teachings.[64] Surveys of college students reveal a gradual decline in the number of acts judged "wrong" or "bad" between 1919 and the sixties, with especially sharp declines in the twenties. Students have gradually shifted away from a strict and detailed moral code that condemned sexual misbehavior, lying, extravagance, selfishness, and idleness. These codes have been replaced by "more reflective and internalized moral orientations" that condemned violations of the sanctity of the individual and acts that directly harmed others.[65] "Other-directedness" or wanting to please others has declined sharply since the early fifties.[66] Commitment to orthodox religion has also declined. For example, the percentage of high-school students in Muncie agreeing that "Christianity is the one true religion and all people should be converted to it" dropped from 94% in 1924 to 38% in 1977. This study of Muncie also documented a trend towards more flexible gender roles. Parents defined fewer chores as "girls' work" or "boys' work" in the seventies than in 1924, and high-school students' ideals for mothers and fathers were much more similar to each other.[67]

Changes in behavior, such as the rising divorce rate, attest to the growing flexibility, diversity, and impermanence of close relationships. About 10% of the marriages begun in 1900 ended in divorce, compared with an estimated 50% of those begun in the seventies.[68] By the eighties, colleges were housing men and women in the same dormitories, homosexuals were organizing political demonstrations and electing candidates to protect their interests, and a growing number of respectable couples were openly living together without being married.[69] These actions were difficult even to imagine in the fifties.

The long-term trend to intimate communication is less well documented, since there are few studies on this topic. However, recent surveys showing that good communication is valued above all other qualities, like the previously mentioned *Playboy* survey, suggest that there has been a major rise in valuing good communication since the sixties. Another sign of the increasing value of intimacy is the growing importance of sexual pleasure in marriage. The idea that sex for enjoyment rather than procreation is central to a good marriage began to spread at the turn of the century and seems to have been widely accepted by the thirties. Michael Gordon concludes from his study of American marriage manuals from 1830 to 1940 that sex was redefined as fun between 1920 and 1940.[70]

The average American's beliefs about marriage clearly have shifted towards emphasizing self-fulfillment, flexible roles and intimacy. Although the Companionship blueprint remains important, especially for the less affluent, many people are accepting the new blueprints of androgynous love.

The family and gender roles of the nineteenth century created a conflict between self-development and love, especially for women. In the twentieth century, the trend from role to self undermined these roles, and by the seventies the new Independence and Interdependence blueprints were advising women and men to integrate self-development and love.

Most observers are pessimistic about these changes. In their view, the new blueprints emphasize separation and individual needs too much to be a workable alternative. They believe that the Companionship blueprint is the only reliable guide to committed relationships, and that traditional family and gender roles are necessary to preserve family attachments. This gloomy evaluation of the trend from role to self is wrong, I believe. An examination of the theoretical ideas of these critics will clarify why they are too positive about the past and too negative about current trends.

4

The history of love: theories and debates

The debate on the family focuses on how far we have moved from role to self and on whether the change is good or bad. Underlying the debate are different theoretical ideas about the causes of family change, and the nature of a good society. Scholars generally agree on the directions of change: the split between the feminine home and the masculine workplace in the nineteenth century, and the shift towards self-development in the twentieth century. But is the family being undermined by the trend to androgyny and self-development? Do we need traditional roles in order to maintain committed relationships? On these questions there is considerable disagreement.

Observers such as Christopher Lasch and Robert Bellah believe that contemporary blueprints of love are destroying enduring relationships and real self-development. Mutual commitment and a shared moral code are necessary, they argue, to sustain an intimate relationship and develop coherent selves. But the human potential movement encourages people to reject these commitments, and to manage their private lives according to the selfish individualism of the marketplace. For other critics, the women's movement and the trend to androgyny are the main danger, because they threaten us with a society where women as well as men care mostly about their individual success.

In contrast to this pessimistic outlook, I am optimistic about the shift from role to self. I argue that the Interdependence blueprint is a workable guide to intimacy and personal growth, a blueprint that has many advantages over the major alternative – Companionship marriage and feminized love.

CAUSES OF CHANGE

Critics of the trend to self-development typically imply that the family is on the verge of collapse. They underestimate the persistence of traditional family and gender roles because they ignore the stability of two social

49

factors that maintain these roles: the division of labor, and relations of dependency between women and men.[1]

The new division of labor accompanying capitalism or industrialism was the most important cause of modern family and gender roles, according to both functionalist theorists like Talcott Parsons, and Marxists like Eli Zaretsky. This division of labor differentiated the public and private sphere by: (1) separating economic production from the household, and (2) organizing the economy around impersonal, competitive relations and the family around personal, loving relations. It also polarized gender roles by: (3) specializing activities, so wives were responsible for family relations and husbands were responsible for earning money, and (4) basing gender identity on these specialized activities, so that femininity focused on love and masculinity on work. This division of labor was the foundation of the Family Duty and Companionship blueprints. It polarized gender roles, feminized love, and led Americans to look to the family and private life as their haven in a heartless world.

The separation of public and private spheres has not changed appreciably since the nineteenth century. Gender roles have changed, with a dramatic increase in wives working and a shift towards more androgynous conceptions of masculinity and feminity. But most Americans continue to expect the husband to be the main breadwinner; women continue to do most of the childrearing, and the stereotypes of the loving woman and the competent man persist.

Continuity in the division of labor has produced considerable continuity in family and gender roles, as the evidence reviewed in Chapter 11 demonstrates. The problems of oppressive roles are still with us – isolated men obsessed with work and submissive women obsessed with intimacy. The weakening of family ties is not our only problem.

Obviously family life and images of love have shifted a great deal towards emphasizing self-fulfillment and more flexible roles, but the critics of self-development exaggerate the degree of change. As long as the division of labor remains stable, something like the Companionship family will persist as one important blueprint for close relationships.

Relations of economic and emotional dependency between women and men, which are related to the division of labor, have also persisted, maintaining the roles of dominant, independent husbands and submissive, dependent wives. Mutual dependency is the root of power relations, as sociological exchange theory makes clear.[2] Power, in this perspective, comes from owning or controlling a valued resource and supplying it to someone who needs it. Thus the balance of power between a man and a woman depends on the balance of resources that the other overtly needs; covert or repressed needs do not affect power. The resource may be love, money, or assistance – anything a person believes he needs from another and cannot get from an alternative source, although money is especially important in our culture.[3] Most researchers seem to agree on the link between dependency and power, but except for feminists and Marxists, they often neglect to use it in interpreting family relationships.

The division of labor established in the nineteenth century increased the power of husbands over wives by making women more economically dependent on men. As more wives earned money, this dependency lessened, but it will persist as long as women's wages continue to be substantially lower than men's wages. Women also became more emotionally dependent on men, as intimate relations with men became the focus of their daily lives. Beliefs about gender that emphasized women's need for heterosexual love and minimized men's need for love further amplified the imbalance in dependency and power between the sexes. The imbalance is lessening, as men place more value on their close relationships and women focus more on friends and work, but according to recent surveys, love is still more important to women than to men.[4] As long as the imbalance in material and emotional dependency persists, so will many aspects of traditional family and gender roles.

EVALUATING THE TREND FROM ROLE TO SELF: CLASSIC ISSUES

However far we have traveled on the road to androgynous love, is this change mostly beneficial or harmful for our private lives? The answer is partly an empirical issue, and hinges on which blueprint of love is dominant – Independence or Interdependence. But classic theoretical issues are also involved. First, there is the issue of constraint versus freedom: do people need stronger social values and roles to provide security and structure, or do they need more freedom and power to direct their own lives and develop their potential? Gender is the second issue: is it more natural and socially useful if women focus on love and men on work, or if they are both androgynous? These have been central questions in social theory since the nineteenth century. The answers proposed by classic theorists – especially Emile Durkheim and Karl Marx – provide a framework for evaluating the trend from role to self and for understanding the current debate about the family.

The need for constraint

Durkheim and Marx offer opposing views on whether constraint or freedom is the basic problem of modern society. Steven Lukes observed that "Durkheim saw human nature as essentially in need of limits and discipline," while Marx assumed that the full realization of human powers requires

> a world in which man is free to apply himself to whatever activity he chooses and where his activities and his way of seeing himself and other men are not dictated by a system within which he and they play specific roles ... Social constraint is for Marx a denial and for Durkheim a condition of human freedom and self-realization.[5]

Durkheim argued that people need rules to limit their desires and define a meaningful way of life that binds them together in a secure moral community.[6] They need to believe in values and obligations that they experience as external and constraining and that are enforced by the authority of the group. Shared beliefs and values not only can restrain disruptive emotions and promote mutual commitment and support; they are also essential for developing a separate, coherent self capable of meaningful choices. Our actions have meaning only in the context of a world view or belief system, and commitment to a world view depends on being part of a group that supports our beliefs. Being with the group intensifies our personal vitality, our sense that we are real and worthwhile because our way of life is good and makes sense. Without this social integration, we become excessively self-centered and despairing, and may even turn to suicide. Thus, committed relationships and self-development require restrictive rules and a potentially repressive moral community. Anomie, or the collapse of traditional values and community ties, is the root of our troubles. From Durkheim's perspective, the change from strong family roles to tolerance of diversity is a change for the worse.

There is an anti-democratic, pro-authority bias in Durkheim's position. He exaggerates the dangers of pluralism and uncertainty, and minimizes the dangers of a uniform moral code – the intolerance, sexism, and justification of inequality that typify periods of moral consensus like the fifties. But he is probably correct in pointing to the need for some constraining beliefs in order to achieve a secure relationship and a meaningful sense of self. Security seems to encourage self-development. The positive psychological effects of economic security are shown by studies of unemployment and economic depressions; and security in close relationships also seems to be important – the confidence that one's partner will not leave and will be supportive and behave in expected ways.[7] A world view that structures and justifies one's self and one's relationships is also likely to encourage self-development, as Durkheim argued. Enduring relationships and self-development thus depend on constraining beliefs and expectations that are shared with others. These "others," however, can be limited to one's partner and a network of friends and acquaintances. Beliefs that are part of a unified national culture, such as marital roles, usually are overly restrictive and are part of an oppressive hierarchy of power. Contrary to Durkheim, I am arguing that values and rules do not need to be experienced as external and as embodied in superior authorities. They can be developed and changed by the participants themselves, as the cases I describe later illustrate. Such a decentralized and democratized culture can provide the benefits of shared beliefs with a minimum of restriction and domination.[8]

Contemporary critics of self-development who praise moral codes, following Durkheim, also tend to glorify the traditional rural community, following decline-of-community theorists. Decline-of-community theorists celebrate rural village life in which family ties were strong and people knew each other and were united by bonds of cooperation and shared religion.[9] They see these warm communities as having been destroyed by modernization, especially the development of an impersonal market place, urbanization, mobility, and the decay of traditional beliefs. The modern concern with freedom, self-development, and individualism is for them a sign of the decay of community. If we want secure attachments, they argue, we will have to return to the more restricted way of life of the past; love and self-development cannot be integrated.

The father of the decline-of-community perspective is Ferdinand Tönnies. He distinguished between warm, familial "community" relationships (*Gemeinschaft*), and cold, efficient "society" relationships (*Gesellschaft*). According to Tönnies, the nuclear family is the prototype of *Gemeinschaft* and combines emotional bonds and instrumental exchange. Relations are based on blood and kinship and are strengthened by living together for a long time, helping each other, and sharing possessions and experiences. Less intense forms of *Gemeinschaft* relations are extended kinship, neighborhood, and friendship. In all these relations, people do not treat each other as means to an end; the relationship is an end in itself. *Gesellschaft* relations are also based on exchanging goods and services, but relations are "transitory and superficial," limited to the specific things to be exchanged. Each individual "is by himself and isolated," relating to others as a means to increase his private goods.[10]

Tönnies's emphasis on material interdependence in all relationships is useful. He does not restrict love to women and the private sphere – *Gemeinschaft* includes the relationships between fathers and children and among friends, neighbors, and co-workers. But his major theme, counter to my position, is that warm human relationships are incompatible with self-development. For Tönnies, as for Bellah and other contemporary critics, modern individualism rests on independence and isolation, not interdependence.

The decline-of-community position implies that we have become a society of isolated individuals without strong family bonds or other dependable human ties, but this exaggerates the degree of change and romanticizes the past. There is strong demographic evidence that the past was not much warmer or more secure than the present. The proportion of marriages broken by death *and* divorce did not rise significantly in the twentieth century because the rise in divorce was offset by a decline in mortality until around 1970.[11] Geographical mobility was very high in the working class in the nineteenth century, and also has not increased greatly for the average American in the past hundred years. Although there probably was more contact and interdependence among extended kin in the past, for centuries most people in Europe and North America have lived in nuclear households.[12]

Durkheimian and decline-of-community theorists also ignore the rich social life that is possible in modern society. Many studies have documented the vitality of friendship networks, specialized subcultures, voluntary associations, and urban neighborhoods. The decline of community ties, for most Americans, has not been very large, and the decreasing authority of the national culture has been partly offset by the increasing authority of subcultures.[13]

For Durkheim and Tönnies, the underlying problem of modern life is that we are cut off from family and community ties and confused by a jumble of conflicting beliefs and life styles. What we lack is security, connection, and constraining beliefs that define our goals and limit our desires.

The need for freedom

For Marx, in contrast, our major problem stems from the exploitation and domination of the many by the few. What people need is more freedom to develop their potential, more power in controlling their society and determining how they will live.

Marx argues that individuals must be free or self-directed at work in order to develop their potential. The economy and the state must be organized in such a way that people collectively control what they produce and determine how it will be distributed. But – to greatly simplify his theory – modern society creates alienation, not freedom, because of private property and the class structure. Some people control economic production and take more than their share of the goods, while others are forced to work for the ruling groups in order to support themselves and their families. The rigid division of labor also blocks self-development by denying people the variety, creativity, and conscious choice they need to develop their potential. The solution, for Marxists, is to abolish private property and create a society of free individuals who collectively control the economy and are unfettered by repressive roles.

But Marx is not clear on what will bind people together and ensure stable attachments in this ideal society. He sees social laws and rules as repressive and ignores their positive contribution. Thus, Marxists tend to fall back on a "natural love" argument: if people were not corrupted and oppressed by class differences and ideology, their natural loving tendencies would create a harmonious society in which everyone could find both love and freedom.[14]

Two Marxist ideas are especially useful in interpreting the trend from role to self. Firstly, Marx emphasizes the value of being free to develop one's full potential. Secondly, he identifies social conditions that promote self-development: democratizing economic and political relations so that people would be more powerful or self-directed, and changing the division of labor so that people would engage in a broader variety of activities.[15]

However, most Marxists are pessimistic about the recent trend to self-development because it has not been accompanied by change in property and the control of economic production. Real self-development, in their view, cannot be restricted to the private sphere and the expression of feelings.

The pessimism of most Marxists is exaggerated, in my view. They typically discount gradual reform and see all developments in capitalist society as destructive and oppressive. This unrelieved negativism is contradicted by evidence that the quality of life has improved substantially for the average American in the past fifty years; for example, economic security, education, and leisure time have increased and mental and physical health have improved.[16] Capitalism does block self-development in many ways, as the Marxists charge: inequality deprives poorer Americans of economic security, lowers their self-esteem, and severly restricts their freedom; and most Americans remain relatively powerless in the public sphere. None the less, there have been significant reforms and improvements, including, I argue, the change from Companionship marriage to Interdependent relationships.

In sum, emphasizing the need for constraint leads to a negative evaluation of the trend to self-development. Emphasizing the need for freedom leads to a positive evaluation unless, like many Marxists, one assumes that positive trends in capitalist America are very unlikely.

SPLIT GENDER ROLES VERSUS ANDROGYNY

The desirability of polarized gender roles is the second theoretical issue shaping people's evaluation of the trend from role to self. A closely related issue is the impact of separating the public and private spheres. Those who value androgyny and the integration of public and private life will be more likely to welcome the trend from role to self. Those who believe that women's place is in the home, and that women are naturally more loving than men, will disapprove of the trend to self-development, and will support the separation of public and private life.

Some scholars argue that biological sex differences make it preferable to follow traditional family and gender roles. However, historical and cross-cultural variation in gender shows that the American split between the expressive wife and the instrumental husband is not built into the human organism (see Appendix IV). Others use theories about the functional requirements of society to justify polarized gender roles, and a sharp division between the private and public spheres.

According to Talcott Parsons, the most influential functionalist in recent decades, the split between the feminine, expressive family and the masculine, instrumental workplace is a social arrangement that fulfills the needs of individuals and of society. The modern family and the economy specialize in different functions and need to emphasize different kinds of social relations. Family relations need to be emotionally expressive, accepting, and concerned with the whole person in order to carry out the functions of raising children and maintaining the personality of adults. Relations at work need to emphasize rationality, performance, and impersonal standards to fulfill the function of efficient production. The division of labor between family and economy is necessarily linked to polarized gender roles. Because women bear children, they focus on the expressive home while men's lives focus on the instrumental workplace. These gender roles are beneficial and will persist, according to Parsons, although he also describes the strains in the feminine role.[17]

Other theorists legitimate polarized gender roles by using gender-linked conceptions of self-development and love. They emphasize the masculine aspects of self-development – being instrumental, independent, and rational – and portray the ideal adult as an independent person with a successful career, unrestricted by obligations to care for others. Directions of development where women are likely to excel such as attachment to others, are ignored.[18] This view implies that some people – presumably women – must forego self-development and specialize in caring for others, since a society without care and nurturance is difficult to imagine. Polarized gender roles are also supported by feminine conceptions of love that emphasize verbal self-disclosure and expressing tender feelings. Such conceptions ignore masculine styles of love like providing protection and practical help, and imply that only women really know how to love.

On the other hand, the benefits of androgyny are also a persistent theme in social theory and research. Most feminists have advocated moving towards androgyny, and integrating public and private life. Marxists too have criticized traditional gender roles as a form of oppression, and have forecast a more androgynous future in which women and men would be loving, productive, and creative. For Marxists, given their focus on power and material exchange, it is obvious that the marriage of an instrumental man who controls the money and property and an expressive woman who controls "love" will result in the woman being powerless and exploited.[19]

The benefits of androgyny are also supported by research, although the findings are not conclusive. Illness and early death are more likely to occur among men who are preoccupied with work and women who are preoccupied with relationships, as I will discuss later, and children seem to develop better if both parents are emotionally expressive and there is no sharp differentiation between an expressive mother and an instrumental father. Androgynous individuals tend to be more flexible and have higher self-esteem, according to psychological studies, but some researchers find the highest levels of adjustment among individuals who rate high on masculinity. Finally, marriages in which partners want a high degree of companionship are happier if both husband and wife can be expressive. In general, androgynous individuals seem to have better close relationships.[20]

Criticism of the trend from role to self is rooted in two ideas about what is good for individuals and society. Firstly, people need constraining rules and strong community ties. Secondly, love and work are accomplished better if women specialize in love and men specialize in work. Since there is good reason to doubt both propositions, much criticism of self-development and androgyny rests on shaky foundations. A positive evaluation of self-development is rooted in the opposing ideas that people need to be free of domination and oppressive roles, and that the split between masculine and feminine, public and private, is destructive.

THE CURRENT DEBATE: IN PRAISE OF CONSTRAINT AND AUTHORITY

The growing interest in self-development has been condemned by most contemporary scholars, who follow Durkheim and the decline-of-community theorists. *The Triumph of the Therapeutic*, written by Philip Rieff in the sixties, presented the major issues. Culture, according to Rieff, is based on faith and on obedience to the authorities that embody moral demands. By submitting to cultural controls, we are saved from chaos and emptiness, and gain a commitment to larger "communal purposes in which alone the self can be realized and satisfied."[21] The emerging therapeutic world view is an anti-culture, substituting individual feelings and well-being for faith in collective morality. Therapy undermines faith and authority by teaching a tolerant, skeptical attitude towards all moral codes. It advocates "limiting the power of the super-ego and therewith, of culture."[22]

In *Habits of the Heart*, Robert Bellah *et al.* make a similar critique of the "therapeutic ethic," although they are more cautious and balanced than Rieff. "The meaning of one's life for most Americans," they assert, "is to become one's own person," a process that is largely negative, and involves "breaking free from family, community, and inherited ideas." In the pursuit of freedom "we have jettisoned too much," and need to revitalize our biblical and republican moral traditions.[23]

As our culture becomes increasingly voluntaristic, individual preferences and experience have become our only moral guide, Bellah observes, and we lack "any objectifiable criteria of right and wrong." Instead of real communities that integrate private and public life, and bring together a variety of people, modern Americans belong to "lifestyle enclaves" of their choice – a network of similar people that focus on some segment of private life. Instead of a language for talking about relationships that justifies commitments to others, people are adopting a therapeutic language that "denies all forms of obligations and commitment in relationships, replacing them only with the ideal of full, open, honest communication among self-actualized individuals . . . [24]

Without the guidance of a moral code, Bellah argues, our search for self-development and intimacy will fail. A coherent self requires a shared vision that links individual lives to the wider society. Enduring close relationships depend on moral traditions that legitimate mutual commitments and obligations. The search for self-fulfillment undermines commitment because it legitimates only self-interest and the expression and sharing of feelings. When these individual needs are no longer met, the relationship must end.

This evaluation of the trend from role to self has a strong negative bias and elitist, anti-democratic implications, even though that is not the authors' intention. Bellah *et al.* underestimate the costs of moral communities – how they justify exploitation and inequality, and oppress women and other "deviants." They point to these problems in passing, but their main argument is that Americans suffer from an "individualism grown cancerous" and need less freedom and more commitment to a shared moral code.[25] Their criticism of "lifestyle enclaves" is also elitist, implying that cultural standards cannot be diverse and decentralized. Research findings, however, suggest that subcultures and networks of similar people can successfully anchor a person's identity and provide guidelines for action.[26] Finally, they underestimate the positive features of the popular search for self-development. They miss the importance of interdependence and mutual support in contemporary relationships, both in people's behavior and in the language they use in talking about relationships. And they misrepresent therapy as a cool relationship that teaches people to be distanced and manipulative. Thus, the couples who turn to therapy to improve their relationships are victims of "ideological confusion," in their view.[27] In fact, the warm relationship that is gradually established in successful intensive therapy often does teach people to be more intimate, as I will show later.

A more legitimate criticism by Bellah *et al.* is that the average American is more narrowly focused on his or her private life than in the past, producing an increasing separation of the self from the public sphere. However, others conclude that the plethora of self-help groups, local activists, and single-issue groups indicate a rising level of community involvement.[28]

One would expect contemporary Marxists to be less elitist and more sympathetic to self-development than the Durkheimians, but most of them are not. A prime example is Christopher Lasch, who rejects Marx's stress on the freedom to develop one's potential, emphasizing instead the usefulness of social constraint, and using some of the same arguments as Rieff and Bellah. Lasch mourns the decay of traditional authority and moral commitments and implies that life was better in the fifties, when clear family and gender roles ordered our lives.[29] The elements of Marxism that Lasch retains are a concern with political and economic factors, a criticism of all developments in capitalist society, and occasional references to the need for a socialist revolution.

For Lasch, the growing concern with intimacy and self-development is a symptom of the destruction of family bonds and all human relationships by capitalism. Preoccupation with the self is part of the ideology of independence and competition fostered by capitalism. We are becoming a society of isolated individuals, increasingly oppressed by the ruling class, corporate managers, experts, and the government. Even when individuals manage to obtain what they want, they are not free, because their wants have been manipulated by the mass media and the cultural apparatus of our consumer society.

Real self-development requires becoming aware of the conflicts within oneself and within society and working for social change, argue Lasch and other Marxist social critics.[30] But self-development has been co-opted by the establishment. People now remain unaware of their internal conflicts, accept the status quo, and seek instant self-development by paying for a weekend workshop on personal growth. Similarly, real intimacy requires long-term interdependence and commitments, and an expressive, non-market orientation. But capitalist culture lures people to seek intimacy through acquiring the right cars, clothes, and social skills and attracting someone who will immediately make them feel good. The new therapies contribute to the breakdown of personal relations by instructing people to avoid investing themselves in relationships. Private life has become as stressful and warlike as work, and "the family – the last refuge of love and decency," which "has been slowly coming apart for more than a hundred years," is decaying.[31]

Part of the decay of the nuclear family, Lasch argues, is that parents, especially fathers, have lost their power. Psychologists, social workers, and other experts have invaded the family, destroying the confidence of parents and making them confused and anxious, so they offer their children neither an intense emotional relationship nor clear standards for behavior. Their children develop an ethic of immediate gratification instead of internalizing a coherent set of values that would lead them to sacrifice for others, and help them achieve real self-development and intimacy.[32]

Many of Lasch's criticisms of contemporary culture are partly valid – they reveal the weaknesses of the Independence blueprint and the need for commitment to other people and to moral standards. But his analysis displays the usual problems of a Durkheimian, decline-of-community approach: he exaggerates the collapse of social ties, romanticizes the past, and underestimates the costs of patriarchal authority. The elitist tendencies of *Habits of the Heart* are magnified in Lasch's work, and he discounts the popular search for intimacy and self-development as a futile, self-defeating enterprise. However, most people are not as deluded and victimized by the system as Lasch asserts, according to numerous studies of contemporary Americans. Most seekers for self-development seem to be following the Interdependence blueprint, and they are making small but substantial steps to a better private life.[33]

THE CURRENT DEBATE: POSSIBILITIES OF FREEDOM

Marxist scholars who are positive about the trend to self-development have more respect for the desires and opinions of "common" people. They retain Marx's idea that the goal of progressive change is to give individuals freedom to develop their potential, and observe an expansion of this freedom for the average American in recent decades.

Eli Zaretsky, one of the few Marxist social critics who is positive about the human potential movement, shares some of my optimism about the trend from role to self. He sees the development of personal life and the concern with self-fulfillment as a product of capitalism that has contradictory effects on individual freedom. In nineteenth-century America, "proletarianization split off the outer world of alienated labor from an inner world of personal feeling," Zaretsky argues, in a historical analysis that I have incorporated in the previous chapters.[34] This development of a separate sphere of personal life, together with the shortening of the work week, created new needs for intimate relationships and self-gratification among the masses of people, needs that were strengthened by advertising.

The growing interest in self-development reflects an expansion of freedom and power, a "profound democratization" of "the ethic of personal fulfillment," compared to previous eras when personal fulfillment was restricted to the elite.[35] But there are also new sources of alienation and powerlessness. The needs for intimacy generated by capitalism tend to be all-engulfing and mystifying, Zaretsky argues, because they are experienced as completely subjective – split off from the outside world of community, work, and politics. People experience their love life as mysterious – one day they fall in love and then for some inexplicable reason love fades and they are alone again. In a socialist society, he believes, people would better understand the material and social bases of love, and their personal needs would be fulfilled in the workplace and the community as well as at home.

Other observers are more positive about recent trends. The most enthusiastic, who are popular writers, embrace even the worst features of the trend from role to self – the overemphasis on independence and the alienation from public life.[36] A more balanced optimistic view is presented by Peter Clecak. The quest for self-fulfillment, he argues, has produced a "democratization of personhood" and a greater involvement in the public sphere for most Americans, although it also has had negative consequences such as encouraging selfishness. This quest includes the human potential movement, the political activists of the sixties, contemporary feminists, and the Christian revival. They are united by "their accent on personal experience; their wish for a community of affective, touching selves; and their comparatively light regard for authority, doctrine, and received institutions."[37] These movements have successfully challenged the political and cultural domination of the male W.A.S.P. elite, Clecak concludes, creating a more decentralized, pluralistic society that provides greater self-fulfillment for the average American.

Where Bellah and Lasch see misguided individualists or deluded victims of capitalism, seeking self-fulfillment and intimacy, but achieving empty isolation, Clecak sees successful creators of new social forms that provide more love and self-development. Studies of contemporary Americans tend to support Clecak's more optimistic assessment.[38]

THE CURRENT DEBATE: SPLIT GENDER ROLES VS. ANDROGYNY

The nature of gender is the second dimension underlying current debates on the trend from role to self. One would expect feminists to support the quest for self-development, because it is linked to androgyny, and anti-feminists on the radical right to oppose it. But there is more opposition in both groups than support.

For the radical right, the Parsonian ideal of an instrumental husband

and an expressive wife is the natural and right kind of family. For example, Marabel Morgan's national best seller, *The Total Woman*, proclaims that "God ordained man to be the head of the family, its president," while his wife is ordained to be "the executive vice-president," charged with maintaining an affectionate, sexually exciting marriage, raising the children, and imparting religion.[39]

Love and marriage are a woman's life, says Morgan, in language reminiscent of the Victorian celebration of woman's special sphere: "It is only when a woman surrenders her life to her husband, reveres and worships him, and is willing to serve him, that she becomes really beautiful to him. She becomes a priceless jewel, the glory of feminity, his queen." A wife has absolute power in the sphere of domestic affection. It is possible for almost any wife "to have her husband absolutely adore her in just a few weeks' time." But to be a powerful queen at home, a woman must sacrifice any claims to independent achievement outside the home. "Only after you have met your spiritual needs, the needs of your husband and your children, should you think of your profession or the public."[40] The same message comes from Phyllis Schlafly, the organizer of a powerful anti-E.R.A. (Equal Rights Amentment) organization, who is scornfully quoted in a feminist pamphlet as asserting that "self-fulfillment is not compatible with a happy marriage, with family life or with motherhood ... Motherhood has to be self-sacrificing: this is what marriage and motherhood is all about."[41]

But the radical right also tries to incorporate some contemporary themes into its call for a return to the past. Thus on the first page of her book, Marabel Morgan confides that when she was first married, she and her husband "had marvelous communication, so things looked very promising." But they gradually stopped talking and had a "communication breakdown." Then she developed her Total Woman program and applied it to her marriage "with stunning results." Her husband Charlie "began to talk to me in his old way. At times he could hardly get his words out fast enough ... He began to share his dreams and activities eyeball to eyeball again ... With communication reopened, romance was not far behind."[42] Thus the main reward that Morgan promised her many women readers was the modern goal of intimate communication with their husbands.

The radical right ignores the disadvantages of polarized gender roles, and the contradiction between expecting intimacy in marriage and advising spouses to be unequal in power and dissimilar in their activities and attitudes. They present an idealized image of the happy traditional family that conveys a sexist and conservative political message: the world will be a happy place again if women just go back home and put the family in order – economic and political problems are not the issue.[43]

The strength of the radical right position is that it voices many people's concerns about their families and their own emotional security and offers a clear solution – revitalize the Companionship family – even though the solution is unrealistic given the high rates of divorce and female employment. The radical right acknowledges the superior power and financial resources of men and the demands of childrearing, and implicitly or explicitly advises women to make the most of their dependent position.

Feminists, as one would expect, oppose the radical right on all these issues and reject the Companionship family roles that subjugate women. Moderate feminists like Betty Friedan welcome the trend from role to self and envision a new form of the family where women and men share equally in childrearing and providing money. But most feminist scholars seem to reject the possibility of androgynous marriage in our time. Given the persistent inequality in men's and women's power, income, and childrearing responsibilities, they argue, heterosexual relationships will oppress women and should be avoided.[44]

Marxist or socialist feminists attack the trend towards self-development as another pernicious outgrowth of capitalism, just as Lasch does, although they do not share Lasch's nostalgia for the past. Thus Bárbara Ehrenreich and Dierdre English charge that the ideas of the human potential movement lead to a "ruthless self-centeredness" and an extension of the capitalist market mentality into close relationships.

> The primary assumption is that each person in a relationship has a set of emotional, sexual, or other 'needs' which he or she wants met. If they are no longer being satisfied by a friend or sexual partner, then that bond may be broken just as reasonably as a buyer would take his business away from a seller if he found a better price. The *needs* have an inherent legitimacy – the *people* are replaceable.[45]

As individual needs become all-important, women are abandoning their traditional nurturant roles, and are adopting the instrumental attitudes of men. And men, encouraged by the human potential movement and attacks on the traditional male role, are choosing a life of self-centered consumerism and personal growth instead of providing for their wives and children, Ehrenreich argues in a more recent book.[46]

The split gender roles of the past "denied women any future other than service to the family," according to Ehrenreich and English, but "the new psychology seemed to deny human bonds altogether – for women or for men." They conclude on a pessimistic note. "The alternative to the suffocation of domesticity turns out to be the old rational nightmare: a world dominated by the Market, socially atomized, bereft of 'human' values."[47] Like Lasch, Ehrenreich and English focus on the

Independence blueprint and on the evils of capitalism, and can see nothing positive in the trend from role to self.

The hostility of most feminist and Marxist scholars towards the new images of love is surprising, since they advocate androgyny and self-development as general goals. One explanation may be their negativism – their skepticism about all developments in a capitalist or sexist society.[48] Another factor may be the difficulty of breaking away from gender-linked conceptions of love and self. Love traditionally means something women do in traditional families, even for feminists and Marxists. Thus the only way to protect enduring love is to forfeit women's rights to develop themselves, something that Lasch seems willing to recommend, but feminists reject, leaving them no positive alternative. Self-development means a ruthless pursuit of individual needs – an extension of the ideology of the self-made man – not developing new capacities within an interdependent, mutually supportive relationship. Thus, scholars with socialist sympathies often reject the trend to self-development.

There are some signs that Marxists and feminists are becoming more positive about the human potential movement, perhaps because it is becoming clearer that interdependence and mutual support is part of self-development for many Americans. For example, Barbara Ehrenriech, in a recent book, praises the human potential movement for freeing men and women from oppressive roles, and for increasing "the possibility of honest communication between the sexes . . . "[49] Feminist and Marxist scholars should nourish and guide the progressive aspects of the human potential movement, in addition to criticizing its faults, given their assumptions about human nature and a good society. Hopefully, more of them will follow the example of people like Eli Zaretsky, and provide this intellectual leadership.

In sum, classic issues of social theory shape our understanding of the history of love and the family. If we attend to the social foundations of heterosexual love – the division of labor and the balance of dependence – we conclude that gender inequality and traditional family forms will persist for some time. We are not on the verge of becoming a society of equal and isolated individuals pursuing our selfish interests. Companionship marriage and the roles of expressive wife and instrumental husband will be part of American society for many decades, but only as one acceptable life style among others, not as the only right way to love.

Our evaluation of changes in the family depends on our ideas about freedom and gender, and about the possibility of gradual progress in American society. These basic questions about human nature and society can be clarified by evidence, but probably not resolved. Those who emphasize the fundamental differences between the sexes and the need for authority and a constraining moral code, will condemn the trend to self-development and androgyny, and will support a revitalization of traditional family and gender roles. Those who emphasize the similarity between men and women and need for greater freedom to develop one's self, are more likely to see the benefits of current trends and the costs of feminized love.

II
Feminized love and its costs

5
Feminine and masculine love

Most Americans have an incomplete, feminine conception of love. We identify love with emotional expression and talking about feelings, aspects of love that women prefer and in which women tend to be more skilled than men. We often ignore the instrumental and physical aspects of love that men prefer, such as providing help, sharing activities, and sex. Those that follow the Companionship blueprint feminize love further by giving women the primary responsibility for maintaining a loving relationship.

Our feminine conception of love exaggerates the difference between men's and women's ability to love, and their need for love. It reinforces men's power advantage, and encourages women to overspecialize in relationships, while men overspecialize in work. The following chapters demonstrate how this inequality and overspecialization has strong negative effects on the health of women and men, and on intimate relationships between the sexes.

DEFINITIONS OF LOVE

"Love is active, doing something for your good even if it bothers me" says a fundamentalist Christian. "Love is sharing, the real sharing of feelings" says a divorced secretary who is in love again. In Ancient Greece, the ideal love was the adoration of a man for a beautiful young boy who was his lover. In the thirteenth century, the exemplar of love was the chaste devotion of a knight for another man's wife. In Puritan New England, love between husband and wife was the ideal, and in Victorian times, the asexual devotion of a mother for her child seemed the essence of love.[1]

What is a useful definition of enduring love in the contemporary United States? On what grounds can I reject the feminine definition of love in favor of a broader, androgynous definition that includes the masculine style of love? One guideline for a definition comes from the prototypes of enduring love – the relations between committed lovers, husband and wife, parent and child. These relationships combine practical assistance with physical and emotional closeness. Studies of attachment between infants and their mothers emphasize the importance of being protected and fed as well as being touched and held. In marriage, according to most family sociologists, both practical help and affection are part of enduring love, or "the affection we feel for those with whom our lives are deeply intertwined."[2] Our own informal observations often point in the same direction: if we consider the relationships that are the prototypes of enduring love, it seems that love is a combination of instrumental and expressive qualities.

Historical studies provide a second guideline for defining love. In pre-capitalist America, as we have seen, love was a complex whole that included feelings and working together. Then love was split into feminine and masculine fragments by the separation of the home and the work-place. This historical analysis suggests that affection, material help, and routine cooperation are all part of love.

Consistent with these guidelines, my working definition of enduring love between adults is: a relationship where a small number of people both (1) express affection, acceptance, and other positive feelings to each other, and (2) provide each other with care and practical assistance. Love also includes (3) commitment – an intention to maintain the affection and the assistance for a long time, despite difficulties; and (4) specialness – giving the loved person priority over others. The concept of love in all contemporary adult relationships – with a spouse, friend, relative, or lover – seems to emphasize these four qualitites. Enduring sexual love for people who live together also includes sexual intimacy and physical affection, as well as cooperation in the routine tasks of daily life. Finally, the new images of love add the qualities of promoting each other's self-development, and communicating and understanding each other's personal feelings and experiences. My focus is on enduring sexual love between men and women. I will for the sake of simplicity refer to it as "love," and use the terms "attachments" and "close relationships" more broadly, to include relations with friends, relatives, and lovers.

In contrast to this broad definition of love, a narrower, feminized definition dominates both contemporary scholarship and public opinion. Most scholars who study love or close friendship focus on qualities that are stereotypically feminine, especially talking about feelings.[3] For example, Abraham Maslow defines love as "a feeling of tenderness and affection with great enjoyment, happiness, satisfaction, elation and even ecstasy." Among healthy individuals, "there is a growing intimacy and honesty and self-expression."[4] Studies of friendship usually distinguish close friends from acquaintances on the basis of how much personal information is disclosed, and research on married couples and lovers emphasizes communication and self-disclosure. Thus, a study of older couples identifies love as a "basic need" in marriage, along with personality fulfillment, respect, communication, finding meaning, and integrating past experience. Love is measured by four questions about feelings: for example, whether one's spouse expresses "a feeling of being emotionally close to me." Providing practical help, money, or sex are not considered to be among the basic needs satisfied by marriage.[5] A recent book on marital love by Lillian Rubin also emphasizes emotional expression. She focuses on intimacy, which she defines as "reciprocal expression of feeling and thought, not out of fear or dependent need, but out of a wish to know another's inner life and be able to share one's own."[6] Intimacy is distinct from nurturance or caretaking, she argues, and men are usually unable to be intimate.

Among the general public also, love is defined primarily as expressing feelings and verbal disclosure, not as instrumental help, especially among the more affluent.[7] Recent surveys show that most people identify "open, honest communications" as the most important quality of love relationship,[8] while a contemporary dictionary defines love as "strong affection for another arising out of kinship or personal ties" and as attraction based on sexual desire, affection, and tenderness.[9]

These contemporary definitions of love clearly emphasize qualities that are seen as feminine in our culture. A study of gender roles in 1968 found that warmth, expressiveness, and talkativeness were seen as appropriate for females, and not males. In 1978 the core features of gender stereotypes were unchanged although fewer qualities were seen as appropriate for only one sex. Expressing tender feelings, being gentle and very aware of the feelings of others were still ideal qualities for women and not men. The desirable qualities for men and not women included being very independent, unemotional, and interested in sex.[10] Thus sexuality is the only "masculine" component in popular definitions of love. Both scholars and the general public continue to use a feminized definition of love.

FEMINISTS ON LOVE AND GENDER

In the nineteenth century, the feminization of love was part of the ideology of separate spheres that polarized gender roles. In the fifties, sociologists, like Talcott Parsons, defending gender differentiation in the nuclear family, emphasized the "natural" division between expressive wives and instrumental husbands. Today it is feminist scholars like Nancy Chodorow and Carol Gilligan who are among the most influential defenders of feminine love. Although their purpose is to attack our system of gender roles, their theories partly reinforce this system by arguing that women are loving and connected to others while men are separate.

Nancy Chodorow's psychoanalytic theory has been especially influential. Her argument – in greatly simplified form – is that as infants, both boys and girls have a strong identification and intimate attachment with their mothers. Since boys grow up to be men, they must repress this early identification and in the process they repress their capacity for intimacy. Girls retain their early identification since they will grow up to be women like their mothers, and throughout their lives females see themselves as connected to others. As a result of this process, Chodorow argues, "girls come to define and experience themselves as continuous with others; ... boys come to define themselves as more separate and distinct."[11] This theory implies that love is feminine – women are more open to love than men and this gender difference will remain as long as women are the primary caretakers of infants.

Several scholars have used Chodorow's theory to develop the idea that love and attachment are fundamental aspects of women's personality, but not men's. Carol Gilligan's influential book on female personality development asserts that women define their identity "by a standard of responsibility and care." The predominant female image is "a network of connection, a web of relationships that is sustained by a process of communication." In contrast, males favor a "hierarchical ordering, with its imagery of winning and losing and the potential for violence which it contains." "Although the world of the self that men describe at times includes 'people' and 'deep attachments,' no particular person or relationship is mentioned ... Thus the male 'I' is defined in separation ... "[12] Lillian Rubin's recent books make a similar argument. These works imply that women will be loving and men will be separate as long as infants are raised by women.[13]

On the other hand, feminist historians and psychologists like Mary Ryan and Jean Baker Miller have developed an incisive criticism of the feminized perspective on love. They argue that the type of love in which women specialize is distorted and partial, because it is split off from productivity and power – qualities associated with the masculine role and the public sphere. Mary Ryan's work shows how love became women's responsibility in the nineteenth century, and the conception of love shifted towards emphasizing tenderness, powerlessness, and the expression of emotion.[14] Jean Baker Miller argues that women's ways of loving – their need to be attached to a man and to serve others – result from women's powerlessness. A better way of loving would integrate power with women's style of love.[15] Ryan and Miller emphasize the flexibility of gender roles and the inadequacy of a concept of love that includes only the feminine half of human qualities. In contrast, Chodorow emphasizes the rigidity of gender differences after childhood, and defines love in terms of feminine qualities. The two theoretical approaches are not as inconsistent as my simplified sketches suggest, and many scholars combine them. However, they have different empirical implications. Chodorow's approach, but not Ryan's, implies that women are much more loving than men.[16]

EVIDENCE ON WOMEN'S ''SUPERIORITY'' IN LOVE

A large number of studies show that women are more interested and more skilled in love than men. However, most of these studies are biased measures based on feminine styles of loving, such as verbal self-disclosure, emotional expression, and willingness to report that one has close relationships. When less biased measures are used, such as how often people see their friends and relatives, the differences between women and men are often small.

Women have a greater number of close relationships than men. At all stages of the life cycle, women see their relatives more often. Men and women report closer relations with their mothers than their fathers, and are generally closer to female kin. Thus an average Yale man in the seventies talked about himself more with his mother than his father, and was more satisfied with his relation with his mother. His most frequent grievance with his father was that he gave too little of himself and was cold and uninvolved; his grievance with his mother was that she gave too much of herself and was alternately overprotective and punitive. A recent national survey concludes that ''men in our society appear to find close interpersonal relations with their children problematic.''[17]

Throughout their lives, women are more likely to have a confidant – a person to whom they disclose personal experiences and feelings. Girls prefer to be with one friend or a small group, while boys usually play competitive games in large groups. Men usually get together with friends for sports or other activities, while women explicitly meet to talk and be together.[18]

Many men are very isolated, given their weak ties with their family and kin. Among blue-collar couples interviewed in 1950, 64% of the husbands had no confidants besides their spouses, compared with 24% of the wives.[19] The predominantly upper-middle-class men interviewed by Daniel Levinson in the seventies were no less isolated. He concluded that ''close friendship with a man or a woman is rarely experienced by American men.''[20] Most men apparently have no loving relationships besides their wives or lovers, and given the estrangement that often occurs in marriage, many men must have no loving relationships at all.

Several psychologists have suggested that there is a natural reversal of these specialized roles in middle age, as men become more concerned with relationships and women turn towards independence and achievement; but there is little evidence, as far as I know, showing that men's relationships become more numerous or more intimate after middle age, and some evidence to the contrary.[21]

Women are also more skilled than men in talking about relationships. Women disclose more about personal experiences than men and are expected to disclose more. Men who deviate and talk a lot about their personal experience are defined as too feminine and poorly adjusted.[22] Women value talking about feelings and relationships, whether they are working class or middle class. Working-class wives prefer to talk about themselves, their close relationships with family and friends, and their homes, while their husbands prefer to talk about cars, sports, work and politics. The same gender-specific preferences are expressed by college students.[23]

Men do talk more about one area of personal experience – their victories and achievements; but talking about success is associated with being powerful, not intimate. Women say more about their fears and disappointments, and it is sharing one's weaknesses that usually is interpreted as a sign of intimacy.[24] Women are also more accepting of the expression of intense feelings, including love, sadness, and fear, and more skilled in interpreting other people's emotions.[25]

Finally, in their leisure time women are drawn to love and human entanglements, while men are drawn to competititon with other men. Women prefer watching the emotional struggles on daytime soap operas or, if they are more educated, the highbrow soap operas on educational channels. Most men like to watch competitive and often aggressive sports. Reading tastes show the same pattern. Women read novels about love, while men's magazines feature stories about adventure and encounters with death by groups of men.[26]

However, this evidence on women's greater involvement and skill in love is not as strong as it appears. Part of the reason that men seem so much less loving than women is that men's behavior is measured with a feminine ruler. Most research considers only the kinds of loving behavior that are associated with the feminine role, such as talking about personal troubles, and rarely compares women and men on masculine qualities such as giving practical help or being interested in sexual intercourse.

When less biased measures are used, the behavior of men and women is often quite similar. For example, in a careful study of kinship relations among young adults in a southern city, Bert Adams found that women were much more likely than men to say that their parents and relatives were very important in their lives (58% of women and 37% of men). In actual contact with relatives there were much smaller differences (88% of women and 81% of men whose parents lived in the city saw them weekly). He concludes that "differences between males and females in relations with parents are discernible primarily in the subjective sphere; contact frequencies are quite similar."[27]

The differences between the sexes are often small even when biased measures are used. For example, Marjorie Lowenthal and Clayton Haven reported the widely quoted finding that elderly women were more likely than men to have a friend with whom they could talk about their personal troubles – clearly a measure of a traditionally feminine behavior. The figures revealed that 81% of the married women and 74% of the married men had a confidant – not a sizable difference.[28] On the other hand, whatever the measure, virtually all studies find that women are more involved in close relationships than men, even if the difference is small.

In sum, women are moderately superior to men in love – they have more close relationships and care more about them, and they also seem to be more skilled at love, especially those aspects of love that involve expressing feelings and being vulnerable. But this does not mean that men are separate and unconcerned with close relationships. When national surveys ask people what is most important in their lives, women tend to put family bonds first while men put family bonds first or second, along with work.[29] For both sexes, love is very important.

EVIDENCE ON THE MASCULINE STYLE OF LOVE

Men tend to have a distinctive style of love that focuses on practical help, shared physical activities, spending time together, and sex. The major elements of the masculine style of love emerge in Margaret Reedy's study of 102 upper-middle-class couples in the late seventies. She showed individuals statements describing aspects of love and asked them to rate how well the statements described their marriages. On the whole, husband and wife had similar views of their marriage, but several sex differences emerged. Giving practical help and spending time together were more important to men. They were more likely to give high ratings to statements like: "When she needs help I help her" and "She would rather spend her time with me than with anyone else." Men also described themselves as more sexually attracted, and endorsed such statements as: "I get physically excited and aroused just thinking about her." In addition, emotional security was less important to men than women, and men were less likely to describe the relationship as secure, safe, and comforting.[30] Several hundred young, highly educated couples studied in the late seventies showed a similar pattern. The husbands gave greater emphasis to feeling responsible for their partner's well-being and putting their spouse's needs first, as well as to spending time together. The wives gave greater importance to emotional involvement and verbal self-disclosure, but also were more concerned than the men about maintaining their separate activities and their independence.[31]

The different significance of practical help to men and women was demonstrated by seven couples who recorded their own interactions for several days. They noted how pleasant their relations were and also counted how often their spouse did a helpful chore, like cooking a good meal or repairing a faucet, and how often they expressed acceptance or affection. The social scientists doing the study used a feminized definition of love. They labeled practical help as "instrumental behavior" and expressing acceptance as "affectionate behaviour," thereby denying the affectionate aspect of practical help. The wives seemed to be using the same scheme; they thought their marital relations were pleasant that day if their husbands had directed a lot of affectionate behaviour to them, regardless of their positive instrumental behavior. But the husbands' enjoyment of their marital relations depended on their wives' instrumental actions, not their affection.[32] One husband, when told by the researchers to increase his affectionate behavior towards his wife, decided to wash her car, and was surprised when neither his wife nor the researchers accepted that as an "affectionate" act.

The masculine perspective is clearly expressed by a working-class husband discussing his wife's complaints about his lack of communication: "What does she want? Proof? She's got it, hasn't she? Would I be knocking myself out to get things for her – like to keep up this house – if I didn't love her. Why does a man do things like that if not because he loves his wife and kids? I swear, I can't figure what she wants." But his wife, who has a feminine orientation to love, says: "It is not enough that he supports us and takes care of us. I appreciate that, but I want him to share things with me. I need for him to tell me his feelings."[33] Many working-class women agree with men that a man's job is something he does out of love for his family.[34] But middle-class women and social scientists rarely recognize men's practical help as a form of love. Indeed, for upper-middle-class men whose jobs offer a great deal of intrinsic gratification, the belief that "I'm doing it for my family" seems somewhat self-serving.

Similar differences in men's and women's styles of love emerge in relationships between two persons of the same sex. Compared with homosexual men, lesbians are more likely to have stable relationships; they place a higher value on tenderness and verbal self-disclosure and engage in sex less frequently. In friendships also, men value sharing activities, while women emphasize confiding their troubles and establishing a supportive emotional attachment.[35] Thus men specialize in certain kinds of loving activities, but except for sex these activities are usually not recognized as love.

The relation between sex and love is unclear. Men separate sex and love more than women, but sexual intercourse seems to be the most meaningful way of giving and receiving love for many men. A 29-year-old carpenter who has been married for three years said that after sex, "I feel so close to her and the kids. We feel like a real family then. I don't talk to her very often, I guess, but somehow I feel we have really communicated after we have made love."[36]

Because sexual intimacy is the only "masculine" way of expressing love that is culturally recognized in our society, the recent trend towards viewing sex as a way for men and women to mutually express intimacy is an important challenge to the feminization of love. However, the connection between sexuality and love has been weakened both by defining sex as a form of casual recreation, and by emphasizing rape and incest, and viewing male sexuality as a way that men dominate and punish women.[37]

A final, somewhat surprising feature of men's style of love is that men have a more romantic attitude toward their partner than women. Men were more likely to select statements like "we are perfect for each other," in Reedy's study. In a survey of college students, 65% of the men, but only 24% of the women said they would not marry someone that they were not in love with, even if the person had all the other qualities they desired.[38] The usual sociological explanation for men's romanticism is that women are more dependent on men for money and status; therefore women are more realistic or mercenary. However, the hypothesis of mercenary wives is inconsistent with women's greater concern about self-disclosure and emotional intimacy. Perhaps men are more romantic because they are less responsible for "working on" the emotional aspects of the relationship, and therefore see love as magically and perfectly present or absent. Women in contrast, may assume that love varies and depends on their own efforts.

Except for romanticism, men's style of love fits the masculine role of being the powerful provider. The qualities judged most important in being a man, according to a large national survey, are being a good provider, having strong views about what is right and wrong, and being concerned with a woman's sexual satisfaction – qualities that are emphasized in the masculine style of love.[39]

POWER AND STYLES OF LOVE

It is striking how the differences between men's and women's style of love reinforce the power of men over women. Men's style of love involves giving women important resources that men control and women believe they need, and ignoring the resources that women control and men need.

Thus men's dependency on women remains covert and repressed, while women's dependency on men is overt and exaggerated; and it is overt dependency that affects power, according to social exchange theory.[40] The feminine gender role intensifies this power differential by encouraging women to think they have a great need for men's love and protection, as feminists have pointed out.[41] In fact, evidence on the high death rates of unmarried men implies that men need love at least as much as women.

Sexual relations can also reinforce male dominance insofar as the man takes the initiative and intercourse is defined either as him "taking" his pleasure or being skilled at "giving" her pleasure, in either case giving him control. The man's power advantage is further strengthened if the couple assumes that the man's needs can be filled by any attractive woman, while her sexual needs can only be filled by the man she loves.

In contrast, women's preferred ways of loving involve admitting dependency and sharing or losing control. The intimate talk about personal troubles that appeals to women requires a mutual vulnerability, a willingness to see oneself as weak and in need of support. The intense emotionality that is supposed to characterize women also seems inconsistent with being in control. Finally, the feminine style of love emphasizes reciprocal, equal exchange of confidences and emotional support, and not the unequal exchange that leads to power over another. It is true that a woman, like a man, can gain power by providing her partner with understanding, sex, cooked meals, or other valued services, and motherly nurturance and care can slide over into controlling the other person. But a woman's potential power over a man is usually undercut because the services she provides are devalued and his need for them is denied. The couple may even see these services as her duty or as her response to his requests and demands.

Men's power advantage over women will decline if they adopt an androgynous style of love and become more expressive, vulnerable, and openly dependent, while becoming more androgynous will increase women's power. Therefore, men probably resist a change towards androgynous love more than women. The hostility of many men towards the human potential movement and talking about their feelings may be part of this resistance; they may sense that if they become more aware of their feelings of dependency and their need for care, their power over women will diminish.

In sum, men are not as uninvolved and unskilled in love as the feminine perspective suggests. There is a distinctive masculine style of love focused on help, shared activities, and sex, but it is usually ignored by scholars and the general public. Recognizing it would undercut our traditional gender roles, which are based on identifying women with expressive love and weakness and men with competent achievement and power.

THE COSTS OF FEMINIZED LOVE

The feminization of love intensifies the apparent differences between women and men in several ways. Firstly, defining love as expressive leads to a false opposition between women's love and men's work. It obscures the loving aspect of the male provider role and the competent, active component of women's love. A major way that women are loving is by actively caring for others and doing physical, productive (but unpaid) work for their families. Nurturing children or a husband consists largely of instrumental acts like preparing meals, washing clothes, or providing care during illness. But because of our focus on the expressive side of love, the work of caring for another person is either ignored or is redefined as expressing feelings; doing is redefined as being.[42] Thus, from the feminized perspective on love, child care is a subtle communication of attitudes, not work or an instrumental form of love. A wife washing her husband's shirt is seen as expressing feelings, while a husband washing his wife's car is seen as doing a job.

The feminization of love also lowers the status of women and reinforces the power difference between the sexes. Our culture tends to glorify achievement, while emotional expression is disparaged as sentimental, foolish, and unrelated to the serious business of the real world.[43] Defining love as purely expressive demeans women, since love is in their sphere. It also leads men to see love as "sissy" or humiliating behavior that threatens their status, something they should avoid. Finally, love is devalued by being restricted to the sphere of women. Studies of the prestige of occupations show that jobs lose status once they become women's work.[44]

Psychological theories of human development illustrate the simultaneous devaluation of women and love. In these theories, a healthy person develops from a dependent child to an autonomous adult, and the upper-middle-class male is taken as the ideal. Self-development is equated with masculine independence, as Carol Gilligan has shown, and women who emphasize attachment are judged to be developmentally retarded.

The pervasiveness of this perspective was documented in a study of mental health professionals who were asked to describe mental health, femininity, and masculinity. They associated both mental health and masculinity with independence, rationality, and dominance. In contrast, qualities such as tact, gentleness, or awareness of the feelings of others were associated with femininity and not with mental health.[45]

The feminization of love also legitimates impersonal, exploitative relations in the workplace and among men. It is part of the ideology of separate spheres that reserves love and personal relationships for women and the home. Men, in this ideology, should be judged by their instrumental and economic achievements. For example, Daniel Levinson's conception of development for a man centers on the Dream of glorious achievement in his occupation. Attachments are subservient to the goals of becoming an autonomous person and attaining the Dream; if relationships impede progress towards the Dream, they must be renounced. Thus a man who has not progressed towards his Dream by mid life should break out of his established way of life by "leaving his wife, quitting his job, or moving to another region."[46] This concept of self-development not only discourages men from close relationships; it also defines men without challenging careers (which means most men) as failures, and implies that if a man is poor, it is because he has failed in his personal development.

The feminization of love contributes to overspecialization and unequal power between the sexes, implying that women need love and marriage much more than men and are much more skilled at love. Women are encouraged to become overinvolved in attachments, while men become overinvolved in work. The cost of this overspecialization is sometimes a matter of life or death.

6
Illness and split gender roles

Men and women who are unmarried and friendless get sick more often and die younger than people who have close relationships. Hundreds of studies have shown that social isolation is strongly associated with suffering heart disease, cancer, depression, and almost every other illness. In addition to this objective relation between close relationships and survival, there is also a subjective link. When asked in surveys about their values and what they need to be happy, most people say that family relationships are extremely important. These studies of illness, values, and happiness provide strong evidence that humans need attachments to survive and develop. On the other hand, people also seem to need some independence and freedom to develop themselves. These are central values for Americans, especially in the middle class, and several studies suggest that moderate independence in close relationships promotes health and happiness.

Our system of overspecialized gender roles blocks people from attaining a balance of love and self-development, dependence and independence. Women tend to be too dependent and involved in relationships, and the feminization of love encourages this specialization. When they are unhappy, women usually think they need more love, but the objective evidence suggests that they need more independence. Men typically are too independent and too focused on achievement at work. They think they need more success, but studies of illness and death rates indicate that they need more close relationships. Thus overspecialized gender roles lead men and women to ignore and repress important parts of themselves, resulting in illness, unhappiness, and premature death.

THE NEED FOR ATTACHMENT

The need for attachment in infancy and childhood is clearly established. Infants who are institutionalized and have little human contact waste away physically and often die. Even among monkeys, infants seek close contact with another monkey or even with a terry-cloth substitute, if that is all they can find; and when they grow up, monkeys reared in isolation behave abnormally and refuse to breed. Human infants, too, need continuing contact to develop normally.[1]

Close relationships also have a powerful effect on the well-being of adults. A raft of studies have shown that social support from friends and relatives contributes to health, especially in stressful situations. For example, in a group of factory workers who had lost their jobs because of plant shutdowns, men who had positive relations with their wives, friends, and relatives and saw these people frequently had fewer severe physical and psychological problems than men without social support. They had less change in their blood cholesterol and fewer illnesses.[2]

Sometimes even the simple presence of a stranger will make a person feel better. Thus patients in coronary care units who seem to be unconscious show an improvement in their heartbeat after the human contact of having their pulse taken. And psychological experiments done with college students show that in stressful situations, the mere presence of another person produces a lower heartbeat and reduced anxiety.[3]

That people need attachment is also suggested by the illness and unhappiness that often result from losing a close relationship. The loss or threatened loss of a spouse, close friend, or relative, can result in the onset of cancer, asthma, tuberculosis, or other illness, especially if there is no outlet for expressing the feeling of loss. Many people seem to die of grief if their spouses die or leave them. One study followed 4,486 widowers aged fifty-five and up and found that 213, 40% more than expected, died within six months of their wives' deaths.[4] James Lynch's book *The Broken Heart* shows how the absence or loss of love leads to heart disease. In one of the many cases he presents, "a 52-year-old man had been in close contact with his physician during his wife's terminal illness with lung cancer. Examination, including electrocardiogram, 6 months before her death showed no evidence of coronary disease. He died suddenly of a massive cardial infarction the day after his wife's funeral." Lynch concludes that "all available evidence suggests that people do indeed die of broken hearts."[5]

The negative consequences of losing a close relationship have been demonstrated by innumerable studies on stress and health. Social stress is usually measured by showing people a list of stressful social changes and asking them how many of these events have occurred in their lives recently. In the list used in most studies, the Holmes-Rahe scale, events are weighted by degree of stressfulness. When this weighting system was being developed, researchers found that "death of a spouse" was the event judged to be most stressful, followed by "divorce," "marital separation," "jail term," and "death of a close family member." Thus the many studies showing that high stress is associated with mental and physical illness primarily demonstrate that broken attachments bring illness.[6]

Finally, most Americans believe they need love. The most important personal values of young Americans in the seventies included love, friendship, and family life, according to surveys by Daniel Yankelovich. A more comprehensive study of the quality of life directed by Angus Campbell and others asked over 2,000 people what was most imporant to their happines, and found that "a happy marriage" and "a good family life" were the most frequent responses. People who were married and had many social ties to friends and relatives also reported that they were happier; although the presence of young children reduced the level of happiness. Campbell found the highest levels of well-being among men and women who were married and childless or were married and had children over eighteen.[7]

In sum, there is very strong evidence that people need close relationships. Studies of the objective consequences of attachment show that close relationships tend to produce better health and lower death rates. Studies of subjective beliefs show that most people believe they need close relationships to be happy.

This evidence on the benefits of love should not blind us to its costs. Caring for others can be burdensome and stressful, as suggested by the association between unhappiness and the presence of young children. In addition, many close relationships produce more anger, domination, and anxiety than affection or social support. About a third of all murders in the United States are among relatives. Family relationships, especially with parents, are often viewed as the major cause of mental illness, and physical aggression between spouses is estimated to occur in one-third of all marriages.[8]

The finding that close relationships are beneficial also raises questions that cannot be answered: What qualities of close relationships are most beneficial and lead to well-being in different situations? What are the relative values of such aspects of love as instrumental help, emotional support, physical contact, and companionship?[9] It is clear, however, that close relationships are one of the major requirements for human health and happiness.

THE NEED FOR MODERATE INDEPENDENCE

Independence is a central value for modern Americans, yet there has been little research on its objective consequences within close relationships. Psychologists have argued that overdependency and powerlessness lead to mental illness, and they have demonstrated that people who *feel* independent or in control of their lives are less likely to suffer from depression or other mental illnesses. Sociologists have shown that independence vs. alienation in the workplace improves the mental and physical health of workers. For example, men and women who have jobs in which they are self-directed and able to use their own judgment and initiative are more self-confident, less anxious and rigid, and better able to solve intellectual problems. It seems likely that moderate independence in close relationships has similar effects.[10]

Most of the evidence about independence in close relationships comes from studies of women, and suggests that the traditional feminine role provides insufficient independence. Women, whether they are married or not, are much more prone to depression than men. While depression is not clearly understood, many researchers link it to dependency, powerless, repression of aggression, and overinvolvement in close relationships – all characteristics of the traditional feminine role.[11]

Research on the physical abuse of wives by husbands provides the most dramatic evidence of the dangers of being a traditional, dependent young wife. Women are more likely to be seriously injured by their husbands if they have children under five and if their husbands earn more than 75% of the family's income, making them objectively very dependent on their husbands. Women who are subjectively dependent and believe they will suffer more than their husbands if the marriage breaks up tend to be the targets of minor violence; their husbands slap them or throw things at them.[12] A similar pattern emerges in studies of marital satisfaction. Wives are most unhappy with their marriages when they have small children and are most dependent on their husbands for money and for adult company.[13]

The superior health of employed wives compared to housewives also suggests that wives need more independence. Working wives often feel that their jobs free them from the constraints of the house and the demands of the family. Their jobs certainly make them less dependent on their husbands for money and often for social contacts and skills in dealing with the world. The results of studies comparing the mental and physical health of employed women and housewives are contradictory, but the overall pattern seems to be that employed women have better mental and physical health if they are not overburdened with housework, child care, and financial worries.[14]

The experiences of recovering mental patients provide additional evidence on the dangers of overdependency. Their family home is often not the best place for them when they leave the hospital, because relatives try to do too much for the patient. According to several studies, these patients need supportive relationships, but only "those that can accept and encourage independent, responsible behavior."[15]

Extreme dependence is harmful, but so is extreme independence, which undermines committed relationships and leads to isolation. An intriguing comparison of kinship ties and mental illness among Mexican Americans and "Anglos" in California documents the importance of balancing independence and dependence. The Mexican Americans had strong ties with their relatives. They were expected to obey their elders and generally to put the family's interest ahead of their own. The Anglos had much less contact with relatives and associated mostly with the relatives they happened to like. For Mexican Americans, there was more mental illness among those who had stronger ties with their extended families; their well-being was threatened by too much attachment and not enough independence. For Anglos, there was less mental illness among those with stronger kinship ties; here the imbalance seemed to be too little attachment.[16]

MARRIAGE AND HEALTH

Marriage is the most important close relationship in our culture, the relationship in which most American adults, especially in the middle class, expect to find love and companionship. However, marriage has also been an unequal relationship that curtails the independence and self-development of women. The relation between marriage and health is thus critical for understanding women's and men's need for both love and moderate independence.

That married people are healthier and live longer than the unmarried has been proved beyond a reasonable doubt, but there is a disagreement about what this fact means. The suicide rate for single men between twenty-five and forty-four is twice as high as for married men, and for divorced men it is over five times as high as for their married age-mates.[17] The powerful negative relation between marriage and suicide was noted by Durkheim in 1897, and since then many researchers have shown that married people are healthier and happier than those who are single, divorced, or widowed.

Married people have substantially lower mortality rates for almost all causes of death than unmarried people of the same age and sex. This "protective" effect of marriage is strongest for causes of death that are most closely related to a person's psychological state and life style, such as suicide, accidents, tuberculosis, syphilis, pneumonia, and cirrhosis of the liver. But married people are also less vulnerable to premature death from heart disease and cancer, and a detailed analysis of all the deaths in the United States over a three-year period concluded that "there is no disease that kills impartially, that kills the married and the unmarried alike."[18]

Table 2 *Mortality and marriage: death rate of the unmarried divided by death rate of the married*[a]

Unmarried category	Age					Average ratio 25–64
	25–34	35–44	45–54	55–59	60–64	
Single						
Men	2.2	2.2	1.8	1.5	1.5	1.9
Women	2.3	1.9	1.4	1.2	1.1	1.7
Divorced						
Men	3.9	4.1	3.1	2.6	2.3	3.4
Women	2.9	2.0	1.6	1.4	1.3	1.9

[a] Data for U.S. Whites, 1960, taken from Walter Gove, 1973.

Table 2 gives the ratios of the death rate for single and divorced people divided by the death rate for married people. For example, the number 2.2 for single men age twenty-five to thirty-four in the upper left corner of the table means that the percentage of *single* men age twenty-five to thirty-four who died in 1960 was a little over twice as high as the percentage of *married* men that age who died. For men and women in all age groups the numbers are larger than 1, showing that the death rate is higher for the single and divorced than for the married. Widowed people, who are now shown on the table, fall between the single and the divorced. Thus marriage is associated with longer life for both women and men.

Most studies of mental and physical illness also show that married people are healthier. Single, divorced, and widowed people are more likely to say they are sick, to be disabled, to visit the doctor, and to be hospitalized. And, as I have said, studies of stress find that marital disruption tops the list of stresses that produce illness. However, the findings on illness are not as consistent as the findings on death, perhaps because the information on death is more plentiful and more accurate. Some studies find that married people, especially married women, are no healthier than the unmarried.[19]

Finally, married people consistently report higher levels of happiness than do the unmarried. When Americans are asked "How satisfied are you with your life as a whole these days?" being married is the best predictor of their feeling very satisfied. Having a high income, a good job, and good health are also related to happiness but usually not as strongly as marriage.[20]

Do these facts mean that marriage causes better health and happiness? Some researchers argue that the causal relation may be in the other direction; good health and happiness may cause people to get married and stay married. A selection process may be operating: the fit are selected as mates and are more competent in finding and keeping a mate; thus those who are left without a spouse are sicker, on the average, and have higher rates of premature death and illness.[21]

The causal relation probably goes in both directions. Health affects marital status through a selection process. Being married also affects health, as we can see by looking at the widowed and divorced; the loss of the marital relation causes illness and premature death among those who were "fit" enough to have been selected as spouses.

But what is it about being married that has this positive effect on health? A few studies have found that married people are healthier if they have satisfying relationships with their spouses, if they share their troubles and say they are happy with each other, but there is little direct evidence about the qualities of a close relationship that affect health and happiness.[22] Marriage has beneficial consequences, I believe, primarily because it meets people's need for love – for an enduring relationship that provides affection, practical help, sex, a dependable commitment, and a sense of being special. This interpretation fits the evidence that married people feel less lonely than the unmarried; they have more frequent sexual relations and more social contact with their spouse and others. Marriage typically produces a web of relationships – between his family and hers, between children and their parents and grandparents. Love or companionship is also a primary reason most people give for getting married.[23]

Other aspects of marriage besides love also promote well-being. The most important factor is probably income. Married people have a higher average income than the unmarried, and it is well established that people with lower incomes die younger and have more mental and physical illnesses. In a careful study of several thousand people in Chicago, married people were found less likely to be psychologically depressed than the unmarried, and the major reason was that they had higher incomes and therefore fewer economic problems. Married people also take better care of their health. They are less likely to smoke heavily or drive cars too fast and more likely to see the doctor and take their medicine.[24]

An ambitious study of 5,000 adults examined all these causal relations and concluded that love is a major reason that married people live longer, even though other factors are also important. In 1965 Lisa Berkman and Leonard Syme interviewed a random sample of men and women in Alameda County, California, about their social ties, their incomes, and their health practices. Nine years later they went back and found out which of these people had died. Taking into account the effects of income, education, health care, and state of health in 1965, a greater proportion of unmarried people had died. Even among the people who were poor, sick, overweight, and smoked a lot, those who were married had a much better chance of surviving. Married people are healthier, then, partly because their needs for loving relationships are being met; the positive association between health and marriage cannot be explained entirely by selection or by income and health practices.

Attachments to friends and relatives are also important in keeping people alive. The Alameda County study measured people's contacts with close friends and with relatives and found out whether people belonged to a church or other organizations. Each of these social contacts resulted in lower death rates, but only contacts with close friends and relatives had a strong effect. The death rates for the attached and isolated people in Alameda County are presented in Table 3. It shows the percentage of people that died between 1965 and 1974 among the married vs. the unmarried and among those with different degrees of contact with close friends and relatives. Since the death rate obviously rises as people get older, the data are presented separately for three age groups. The table shows that marriage has a strong effect on mortality, especially for men, and that close relationships with friends and relatives have a strong effect for both men and women. Moreover, ties to friends and relatives seem to substitute for marriage. Men and women who are unmarried but have many ties to friends and relatives have a lower mortality rate than married people with few friends and relatives. Married or single, people with many friends are healthier, and women especially benefit from having a trusted friend with whom they can talk about personal problems. [25]

GENDER, MARRIAGE, AND HEALTH

Marriage benefits men's health more than women's. There is a striking sex difference in the results of the Alameda County study: being married had a statistically significant effect on death rates for men but not for women. National mortality rates such as those displayed in Table 2 show the same pattern.

Contrary to the popular image, spinsters are less likely to die prematurely than bachelors. In fact, single women over forty-four are less likely than wives to die of several causes including diabetes, hypertension, and cirrhosis of the liver. A study of census data in the seventies concluded that "being married is twice as advantageous to men as to women."[26]

If we look at subjective needs – what people say they need – the sex differences are in the opposite direction. The popular myth is that love and marriage are more valuable to women, and that women try to trap eligible men into getting married. Surveys show that people tend to conform to these gender role stereotypes. When adults are asked what is

Table 3 *Mortality rates in Alameda County study: percent of people that died between 1965 and 1974*

	Age					
	30–49		50–59		60–69	
Marital status	men	women	men	women	men	women
married	3	3	12	7	27	14
not married	9	4	25	10	34	21
Contacts with friends and relatives						
high	3	2	11	7	22	11
medium	3	3	14	8	25	17
low	5	5	14	12	41	31

From Berkman and Syme, 1979.

most important in their lives, women emphasize marriage and family relations more than men, while men emphasize work more than women, as we have seen in the last chapter.

This contradiction between objective and subjective needs can be explained by overspecialized gender roles. The feminine role leads women to value marriage, to be skilled in intimacy, and to develop many close relationships. Therefore, women benefit less from marriage because they do not have a scarcity of close relationships. Objectively, women are usually less emotionally dependent on marriage than men because they have close relationships with friends and relatives, but subjectively women believe they need marriage more. Men, on the other hand, are encouraged to be independent and specialize in work, so they often become too isolated. Marriage brings them great objective benefits because of the scarcity of attachment in their lives. Subjectively, men tend to believe they need more independence and success when they are in trouble, but these are "false needs," to borrow Herbert Marcuse's term.[27] What most men really need is to develop their "feminine" side and become more focused on relationships, more emotionally expressive, and more comfortable with being dependent.

Research on the "Type A" personality or the "Coronary Prone Behavior Pattern" supports the hypothesis that men are overspecialized in independence and achievement. Men are much more likely than women to show this behavior pattern, which consists of being "work oriented, ambitious, aggressive, competitive, hurried, impatient and preoccupied with deadlines."[28] Men who behave this way are twice as likely to develop coronary heart disease, a leading cause of death for men. Their drive to be tough and independent also seems to make men less aware of their symptoms when they get physically and mentally ill and keeps them from seeking help. A large national survey of men's and women's visits to doctors showed that men were more often unaware of serious health problems; they delayed going to the doctor and hesitated to admit symptoms.[29] Finally, the large and growing difference between men's and women's mortality, regardless of marital status, suggests that something about the life style of modern males is deadly. In 1921 life expectancy was 54 for men and 56 for women; in 1970 it was 67 for men and 75 for women. Some of this difference may be genetic or biological, but one study estimates that about a third of the excess male mortality is caused by the tough, competitive, hyperindependent behavior required by our culture's concept of masculinity.[30]

Men need spouses because they have no other source of care, while women get less from their spouses and more from their friends. A survey in Chicago asked men and women: "When you are really sick, is there someone to help take care of you?" While both sexes received more care if they were married, more married women than men reported that there was no one to care for them when they were sick (14% vs. 3%); in contrast, among people living alone, more men than women were unable to obtain care (54% vs. 38%).[31]

Finally, women benefit less from marriage than men because the traditional organization of marriage makes women more dependent and submissive, reinforcing the restrictions of the feminine role. Husbands are usually the major breadwinners, and wives, whether they work or not, are still responsible for child care and housework. Embedded in the demands of their children and husbands, wives are often unable to experience themselves as separate persons. Marriage is bad for women, concludes family sociologist Jessie Bernard, because wives are often dominated by their husbands and their husbands' jobs, and are controlled by the daily needs of their families.[32]

The argument that women get sick from being overfeminine is supported by the recent improvement of women's mental health. Mental illness in women has declined since the middle of the fifties. While women still are more likely to be mentally ill than men, the difference between the sexes has decreased in all age groups.[33] The main reasons for this improvement, researchers conclude, is that more women are working; they are less dominated by their men, partly because of the women's movement, and less confined to their households.

In sum, women seem to be healthier when they have also developed their "masculine", side, when they have jobs and friends and are less dependent on men, while men are healthier when they are married and have close relationships to balance their commitments to work and independence. Other things being equal, the trend away from rigid gender roles and feminine love improves the quality of life.

7

Marital conflict over intimacy

The conflict between wives who demand more love and husbands who withhold it is one of the most painful costs of feminized love and overspecialized gender roles. Wives in traditional, companionship marriages often complain that they do not get enough attention from their husbands, clinicians report, while husbands complain that they feel trapped and suffocated. Pierre Mornell sees this conflict in his middle-class patients as a struggle between "passive men and wild women":

> The husband arrives around 7 o'clock exhausted from his day at the office ... He pays only token attention to his wife, maybe a little more (or less) to the kids, and then withdraws behind TV's Monday night football ... [But] most wives – at least a majority of those who seek my help for their troubled marriages – do want "something more" from their husbands in those hours when they come together.
>
> This need for "something" more is directly or indirectly conveyed to the man ... He, in turn, experiences her demands (for longer talks, or an honest expression of feelings, or spending more time with the kids or her, or his being more active in sharing the domestic load, or her desire for better sex) as MORE PRESSURE ... And in the face of that pressure, direct or indirect on his wife's part, he withdraws ... and she comes back at him with greater demands for "something he's not giving her."[1]

Working-class wives in San Francisco interviewed by Lillian Rubin also express unfulfilled longings for more communication and more emotional closeness. They push for change but are confused: "I'm not sure what I want. I keep talking to him about communication, and he says, 'Okay, so we're talking; now what do you want?' And I don't know what to say then, but I know it's not what I mean." The women feel frightened and unsure about their demands:

> I sometimes get worried because I think maybe I want too much. He's a good husband; he works hard; he takes care of me and the kids. He could go out and find another woman who would be very happy to have a man like that, and who wouldn't be all the time complaining at him because he doesn't feel things and get close.

The men are also unsure and afraid:

> I swear, I don't know what she wants. She keeps saying we have to talk, and then when we do, it always turns out I'm saying the wrong thing.
> I get scared sometimes. I always thought I had to think things to myself; you know, not tell her about it. Now she says that's not good. But it's hard. You know, I think it comes down to that I like things the way they are, and I'm afraid I'll say or do something that'll really shake things up. So I get worried about it, and I don't say anything.[2]

Sometimes it is the husband who wants more contact and the wife who withdraws. A 29-year-old housewife that I interviewed seems happy with her marriage to a sensitive and emotionally expressive carpenter but would like more space.[3] "Couples need a lot of time alone and also a lot of time together," she comments; "I am glad to get away from him sometimes." She would like another child, but he opposes the idea: she would like to visit with other couples more, but "he loves to keep us to himself." However, in most couples it is the wife who wants more closeness. When male engineers and accountants and their wives were asked how they would like their spouses to change, wives more than husbands wanted their spouses to be more responsive and receptive, while husbands more than wives wanted their spouses to be less emotional and create less stress. Researchers who observed forty-eight newlyweds found a similar pattern – wives used more emotional pressure while husbands were conciliatory and tried to avoid conflict.[4]

In a study I designed to find out what proportion of couples fit the pattern of demanding-woman/withholding-man, about half fit the pattern. Forty-eight married and living-together couples and fourteen individuals were surveyed (see Appendix I for details). A hypothetical situation was described to them, in which the first person wants to work on the relationship and needs more closeness, while the second person wants to let things be and needs more freedom. When respondents were asked if such situations came up in their relationship and whether they sympathized with the first or the second person, thirty-three women and twenty-five men identified with wanting closeness, ten women and seventeen men identified with wanting freedom, and nine women and twelve men said the situation never came up in their relationships and they did not sympathize with either person. The other significant sex differences in the survey also confirmed the pattern of demanding-woman and withholding-man. Women more than men valued talking about feelings as a leisure activity, and wanted their partners to be less busy and more available for intimate communication. Men more than women wanted their partners to be less emotional and to create less pressure for change.[5]

CAUSES OF THE CONFLICT

The conflict over intimacy is rooted in three aspects of traditional gender and family roles; the feminized definition of love, women's responsibility for the marital relationship, and the overdependency of wives on husbands. One reason that wives want "love" more than husbands is that love usually means feminine styles of attachment that women prefer, such as intimate talk. If love were defined as sexual relations, the tables would be turned, and husbands would typically seek more love while wives withheld.[6] As a working-class husband said, "She complains that all I want from her is sex, and I try to make her understand that it's an expression of love. I'll want to make up with her by making love, but she's as cold as the inside of the refrigerator." According to the wife, "He keeps saying he wants to make love, but it doesn't feel like love to me."[7]

Women are assumed to be more interested in love, and marital love is defined as part of women's sphere of responsibility, at least among couples that adhere to the Companionship blueprint. A 1966 *Reader's Digest* article argues that men give up more than women for marriage: what sacrifices a woman makes are "for *her* marriage, *her* home, *her* family. Rightly or wrongly, the average man believes that while his wife may belong to him, the marriage belongs to his wife."[8] Magazine articles on how to improve marriage are still directed primarily to women.[9]

Insofar as marriage is defined as the wife's "turf," an area where she sets the rules and expectations, the husband is likely to feel threatened and controlled when she seeks more intimacy. If the couple believes that love is shown through the activities that the woman prefers and in which she is more skilled, i.e., intimate talk as opposed to sex, his negative feelings will be aggravated.[10] Talking about the relationship as she wants to do will feel to him like taking a test that she has made up and he will fail. Blocked from straightforward counterattack insofar as he believes that intimacy is good and should not be opposed, he is likely to react with withdrawal and passive aggression.

From a woman's perspective, since marriage is in her sphere of responsibility, she is very highly motivated to have a succesful relataionship with her husband. As the same *Reader's Digest* article comments, "when a woman marries, her home, her children and her husband become the most important things in her life . . . She is at last taking on the task she has been aiming for since she first understood the difference between boys and girls."[11] A more contemporary statement of this situation may be seen in Lois Gould's novel *Final Analysis*. Several professional women in a consciousness-raising group are discussing the heroine's love affair with Dr Foxx when a woman explodes:

... all *we* do is sit around worrying about some nut named Dr Foxx! What about her *work*, damn it? What about ..."

"Oh, Laurie," sighed Wanda, "Who cares about work when their love life stinks?"

"*Men* do," said Tess. "Doris Lessing said she never met a man who'd fuck up his work for a love affair, and she never met a woman who wouldn't."[12]

When there are problems in a marriage, or a love affair, the woman wants to take steps to make things better. Her husband takes little initiative, beyond proposing sex, in suggesting ways to get closer; this is her sphere, and he is unskilled and ambivalent about dyadic intimacy. A passive woman may accept this situation and retreat into tearful helplessness. A more active woman is likely to propose solutions such as discussing their problem or taking a vacation, and he is likely to respond with passive resistance and act as if she were being pushy, demanding, and unfeminine. Thus she is doubly blocked from achieving one of the main goals of her life – a happy marriage. Not only is the relationship strained, but her efforts to improve the situation make her feel unfeminine and guilty.

The connection between love being in women's sphere and men withdrawing from love is supported by the contrast between courtship and marriage. In courtship, men are more in control of love, and they seem much less likely to withdraw. Until the seventies, there was a strong norm that the man should arrange dates, initiate sex, and propose marriage, and most couples probably still follow this pattern. In addition, the emotional state of "falling in love," which frequently exists during courtship, seems to create intense dependency and preoccupation with the relationship for both partners.[13] It is not until marriage that love becomes primarily a woman's responsibility, and this may explain why the conflict between demanding women and withholding men seems to be much more characteristic of marriage. A cartoon by Jules Feiffer captures the change.[14] After marriage, the woman takes over the position of the initiator, and the man becomes resistant – note his stubborn jaw. Then he turns away from her and eventually fades away, while she tries harder and harder to get a response. The cartoon captures the limited sense in which a woman's control of marital love leads to power. It is her turf and she gets to do the initiating. They are talking, as she wants to do, but since her goal is to get a response from him, he also has a great deal of control.

A woman's dependency on her husband for love, money, and her sense of identify is the third aspect of traditional gender roles that may lead a wife to want "something more" from her husband. She is not sure

MAN TALKS. WOMAN LISTENS.

WOMAN FALLS IN LOVE WITH MAN AND HIS TALK.

MAN AND WOMAN MARRY.

WOMAN TALKS. SHE HAS BECOME "WIFE."

MAN DOESN'T TALK. MAN DOESN'T LISTEN. HE HAS BECOME "HUSBAND."

TRIBAL RITE.

Figure 3 Courtship and Marriage, by Jules Feiffer. Copyright 1983 Jules Feiffer. Reprinted with permission of Universal Press Syndicate. All rights reserved

she could survive without his money and his ability to manage the world. She thinks she needs his love to fill her inner longing and to prove that she is a successful woman. As a result, she is more concerned with the relationship than he is. She needs to have him reassure her of his commitment by spending time and emotional energy with her and is jealous of his work and other interests. An extremely dependent wife may develop an insatiable need for attention and closeness much like that of a dependent child or a sick person; they often focus all their attention on whether they are getting enough from the person they depend on, and feel abandoned and deprived even when they actually are receiving a lot of care. Similarly, a husband very dependent on his wife, for example, because he is retired or unemployed, may develop an insatiable need for her attention.

Extreme dependency may also produce chronic anger, both because the husband will inevitably fail to meet some of his wife's needs and because her dependency implies that he has a great deal of power over her and that he is responsible for what is wrong with her life. The anger of dependent and powerless wives may explain Mornell's observation that even when a husband agreed to talk more or do what his wife wanted, she often rejected his offer and continued to criticize him for not being a good enough husband. It also explains the tendency of wives to blame their husbands for problems in the marriage while husbands tend to blame themselves.[15]

Coupled with the expressive, dependent wife of Companionship marriage is the instrumental, independent husband who has the responsibility to provide for his wife and children. In our individualistic system, if he fails as a provider, it is his fault; therefore, he is likely to feel burdened by his marriage and family.[16] Again, the system implies that if he is a real man, his wife will be satisfied. If she says she wants something more from the relationship, he may feel that he has failed, that he is being accused of not measuring up to a new test of his manhood. As a result, he will defensively reassert his masculinity and become more aggressive and rational; or if he believes that aggression and "intellectualizing" are wrong, he may close up and withdraw.

Husbands are expected to be more independent and powerful than their wives, and on the level of overt behavior most couples conform.[17] The fact that men and women usually prefer a marriage in which the man is older, smarter, better-educated, and better-paid, helps to ensure his considerable power advantage;[18] and the belief that women need love more than men reinforces the power imbalance. But on a less overt level, it is not clear who is more dependent and who needs whom the most. Married people with a strong attachment depend on one another, by definition; men who appear independent are probably covertly dependent on their wives. For example, a man in the play *I'm Getting My Act Together and Taking it on the Road* is married to an apparently helpless and neurotic woman. One of the ways he tries to keep her happy is to rent her an art studio – where she then meets her lovers. In a conversation with a feminist friend, the man says, "If my wife were strong like you I'd leave her." In other words, he is dependent on her needing him, and she has a lot of power in the relationship. But overt and covert dependency seem to have quite different consequences. It is overt dependency that undermines power and results in a preoccupation with the relationship and a desire for more closeness.

GOOD TIMES AND BAD

The conflict over intimacy is more frequent in some stages of the life cycle and in some social classes, and these variations clarify its causes. In the courtship stage of a relationship, as I have pointed out, the conflict seems infrequent. Something about marriage leads women to seek more closeness and men to withdraw, and I have suggested that it is women's responsibility for marital love and the dependency of wives on their husbands.

In the early years of marriage the conflict is often intense.[19] The husband is absorbed in work and the wife in childrearing or combining children with a job. This is the stage of life when couples of all social classes tend to be most unhappy with their marriages, the period when she is most dependent on him for money and emotional support.[20] In later years (if the marriage survives) the conflict may abate if the husband becomes less absorbed in work and the wife can focus on her own projects and develop a network of friends as the children leave home.

Men's preoccupation with work obviously depends on their social class. Working-class men who have tedious or insecure jobs usually do not identify strongly with their work; if they are unavailable to their wives it is more likely because they are anxious about supporting the family or numbed and exhausted by their work.[21] Middle-class husbands who provide a steady income but are not extremely involved in their work may have the best relationships, on the average, with their wives – they are successful providers but still have plenty of time and energy to devote to their families.[22]

It is in the upper middle class that the conflict between demanding wives and withholding husbands may be most intense. The husband's career becomes his first priority, and he has little time for his wife or any attachment. Morover, she becomes increasingly dependent on him as his earning potential moves far ahead of hers. He becomes obsessed with his work and she with her marriage.[23] If she also has career aspirations, she may feel not only rejected by her husband but also angry about her blocked ambitions and her conflicted and messy life compared to the focus and importance of her husband's career.[24] Ann Gerrard, a biologist, reflected on her unhappiness early in her marriage, when her career was floundering and her children were young:

> I was starting to get restless. I remember when we first went to Boston [where her husband had a job and she did not] just getting in the car and driving, thinking I'm just going to drive forever and I'm not ever coming back ... I thought there was something wrong with my husband because my life wasn't ... , I didn't like my life, so it must have meant there was something wrong with the marriage ... I thought what I needed was another man.

What Ann did with her "restlessness" was to press her husband to talk to her more and to have long arguments about their relationship. Her anger over her blocked career, which she blamed on her husband, was probably one of the reasons he withdrew from her demands for "more closeness." At the same time, she became less interested in sex and more allied with her children. After commenting that her husband was "not terribly involved" with the children when they were small, she added:

> I remember I kind of liked it that way. I guess it was my revenge.
> *You mean, this is mine, you have yours?*

That's right, something like that. I remember that our sex life turned kind of sour after David [her second child] was born. That was the same time that my career was the total pits . . . It wasn't what I had planned.

Controlling or attacking one's husband as a reaction to the burdens of the wife and mother role is also suggested by Lyn Gilmore, the woman described in Chapter 1, who has just returned to school after many years of being a housewife. "I think what it was before was I wanted control over everybody else's life without trying to control my own. Now that I have control over my life, the control over my children's and my husband's life has kind of floated away . . ." These changes in the course of the life cycle show the importance of the immediate social situation in creating the conflict over intimacy.

Enduring personality differences between men and women undoubtedly also play a role. The fact that girls but not boys retain their original attachment to their mothers contributes to the conflict, as Nancy Chodorow's psychoanalytic theory suggests. Theories of gender role socialization alert us to the many social pressures that direct girls' personalities towards close relationships and boys' towards achievement – the reactions of parents and peers, the toys they are given, the television programs they watch. These psychological explanations imply that men's and women's orientations to love become part of their personalities, built-in dispositions that are difficult or impossible to change in adulthood. In contrast, evidence that people change their orientations to love in different situations indicates that current social conditions can be more important than personality. Thus the conflict over intimacy can be alleviated by changing the underlying social conditions – the feminization of love, the assumption that love is in women's sphere of responsibility, and the imbalance of dependency between the sexes.

TALK TO ME: LYN AND TOMMY GILMORE

The Gilmores have been married for fourteen years and have a secure and lively relationship. Yet Lyn's desire for intimate communication has been a major area of conflict, and their marriage has been based on the split gender roles that create this conflict. Following the Companionship blueprint, she was the compliant housewife and mother of their three daughters, and he the dominant breadwinner. Lyn, and to a lesser extent Tommy, assumed that love meant talk more than sex and that she was responsible for maintaining a harmonious and intimate relationship between them.

Now the relationship is becoming more androgynous. Spurred by a period of depression after they moved to California last year, Lyn enrolled as a full-time college student and built up a network of friends. She is becoming more assertive about trying to improve communication with her husband, and he is participating more in housework and child care. She remains responsible for family relationships, however, and he still makes all the money and is the dominant partner.

To Lyn, love means communication, especially since she took a course on Carl Rogers, "A Helping Relationship," at the community college and had therapy with the instructor of the course. For several years she had felt that sex was the only channel of communication open in her marriage, "and I don't like that. It was enough for him, or so he said, but it wasn't enough for me ... And that's where some of our problems came in when I first started to get him to talk with me." Lyn stopped initiating sex and "turned off." In one interview, she considered whether she was withholding sex to punish Tommy for not talking. "I don't want to hurt him either, but it's a two-way street."

Lyn is the one who works on improving marital communication. She encourages Tommy to talk about his work at a chemical plant, where he has received several promotions and is now being pressured to move on to a managerial position. At first, Tommy says, he started talking about work because Lyn "expressed a desire to share more things like that ... and because she needed somebody other than the children to talk to." But now that their relationship is becoming more interdependent, he enjoys it more, and she seems to need it less. "There's less of a demand, less of a need to get into my work," he comments, "now that she has school and other contacts outside the house ... So I think that now I am starting to share more with her, there's less of a need for it. So it's almost like the boomerang came back and there's no one for it to hit, or now that it's come back the target's moved." His comments suggest his dependence on Lyn and his anger and sadness over being rejected by her in favor of new interests.

From Lyn's perspective, she is still the one who initiates most conversations, and he is rarely responsive or empathic when they do talk. In her first interview, Lyn described an incident the night before, when she was making supper while her children were under foot, and he came out to the kitchen: "I said, 'while I'm making supper, why don't you unload the dishwasher and talk to me, just stand here and chat.' And he proceeded to tell me what had happened with his day, then said 'I'm tired' and went in to lie down, and I never got to share my end of it." An interview six months later revealed that the conflict over communication is persisting. Lyn reported mentioning to Tommy that she missed their old routine of talking together every evening, "looking at each other and listening, and he said, 'yeh, I've missed it too.' I almost dropped dead, because a year ago he never would have said that ... and I said one of the reasons we haven't done it is that I got tired being the 100% initiator of it."

In other aspects of love besides talking, Tommy is far from withdrawn or resistant. Lyn reports that he was quick to change when she asked him for help with "physical" and not "emotional" things, like "help me with the kids, help me with the shopping; at one point he used to do the shopping every week . . ."[25] Tommy apparently has always been more interested in sexual intimacy than she, and in the past few years she has rarely taken the initiative. When he recently bought the book *How to Make Love to a Woman*, she was delighted that he was interested in "something besides just the physical end" and was willing to admit that he didn't know everything. But when he suggested that she read *How to Make Love to a Man* her reaction was a vague "I might." Both Gilmores seem to accept a feminized definition of love according to which it is Lyn, not Tommy, who is deprived of the kind of love they want. Thus Tommy's response when asked how he would like to change the relationship was: "make her laugh more. She takes everything so seriously" and "have more time together. I look forward to that as the kids get older." He made no reference to sex. Lyn's response was: "I'm working on changing our intimacy level."

The Gilmore's tendency to treat their emotional relationship as Lyn's domain is probably reinforced by their belief that Tommy is a rational "loner," who is focused on work and doesn't need much love, while Lyn is a "feeling person" who is skilled at close relationships and needs them.[26] Lyn has several close friends; Tommy has none and even reports getting "real itchy" at work when he has to be "one on one talking to people." Lyn seems to have a good relationship with her daughters and tries to be attuned to their unspoken troubles and needs. Tommy seems uncomfortable with his children, and Lyn says he is an "authoritarian" father.

The imbalance of power and overt dependency in their marriage also contributes to their conflict. Lyn not only is completely dependent on Tommy financially but believes she could not survive economically without him, even though she was a registered nurse before marriage. She often expresses her fear about "what could happen if anything ever happened to him." As Tommy says,

> It seems to be an underlying thought that she always expresses, "If you die, I'm not going to have any way to take care of the kids." I don't think she is so much afraid of my dying as she is of fending for herself in a situation like that . . . So right now she's expanding and she's trying to move out into a self-sufficient, stand-by-herself type person.

Except for the sphere of intimate communication, Lyn defers to Tommy's authority. Before returning to school last year, she reports,

> I used to just care about what he thought, not what I thought . . . I was just a housewife, mother, Mrs Gilmore . . . never Lyn, a person, and I allowed

that and never did anything about that. I never said "hey pay attention to me, I'm a human being," and when I would get put down in different ways, I would just go around and be depressed periodically.

She still seems fearful about confronting her husband directly. Thus, to get him to agree to be interviewed, she thought about how to approach him for a few days. Then one evening, she says, "I said something like, 'Boy, you've really given me so much support. I have a friend who is doing a study comparing people who give each other support and some who don't . . .' Then I presented him with the questions, . . . and dropped it." This is her usual strategy for persuading him to do something. To avoid threatening him, she has learned to "just bring it up, mention it, and drop it. And when he's ready he'll bring it up again or maybe I'll wait a week and if he hasn't mentioned it, I'll bring it up again."

Lyn is also cautious about trying to change the division of labor at home, and Tommy seems successful in resisting primary responsibility for housework or child care, although he does a lot of the work at home. For example, he has agreed to do the shopping but insists that she make up the shopping list. Lyn describes what happened recently when Tommy was in charge of the children:

> Monday night, I came in from here and found Loren had a 102 fever, and he felt terrible because he hadn't realized it. Then he asked me what classes I have on Tuesday. I told him one class from 11–12 . . . and he said well I'll come home from work. I'll babysit Loren so you don't have to miss your class. I mean I said, "oh you doll'" I complimented him, I try not to be too gushy with the compliments because that turns him off . . . He was a real doll about it when I was a little nervous about how he'd accept it.

While Lyn's interviews convey her deference to her husband and "nervousness" about his reactions, Tommy talks as if there were no power imbalance. In fact, he complains about her attempts to dominate him by getting him to do more around the house: "She tries to put bounds on me that I don't see myself putting on her," and tries to set up "a dominance type thing" instead of a "sharing balance." But when asked how he handles her attempts at dominance he says, with a laugh, "I just ignore it," suggesting that at some level he is aware of his power.

Lyn's dependency on her husband probably intensifies her need to get emotionally closer to him and improve their communication. Her powerlessness may also lead her to suppress her feelings of being overburdened at home, producing underground anger that comes out in periodic fights with her husband. Lyn describes a "really bad argument about communication":[27]

> It happened right in the middle of the restaurant and I ended up leaving the restaurant. What really bummed me out, was that he said "When all you

think about is yourself . . ." and that was all he needed to say . . . I had just spoken to him about that I make sure every day before I leave for class that all the children are taken care of . . . I write notes to the sitter and to the kids about what to do, and usually the dinner is set out, and five hundred other things . . . and all he has to do is take care of Tommy and leave . . . and then he calls me only thinking of myself.

This fight seems to have been triggered by Tommy's jealousy about Lyn's best friend, Ellen. The fight began when Lyn tried to change the family's plans so she and Ellen could have their weekly breakfast. Tommy is quite dependent on Lyn – perhaps just as dependent as she is on him – but his dependency remains covert, hidden from both himself and his wife, so it does not undermine his power.

Despite these strains, the Gilmores have a strong attachment that will probably survive this stressful period of their lives in which they are adjusting to Lyn's new self-assertion and are pressured by the demands of children, his career, and her school. Lyn remains eternally hopeful that their communication will improve. "I think it will get easier especially if we both sit down and talk, just a little bit every night, and practice some of these things we both need to work on." Tommy loves to watch her develop, "in spite of its being aggravating at times." "She's coming into her own," he observes, "growing beyond the confines of responding to other people's needs into responding to her own needs." For him, "it's like watching a new person blossom. And I'm excited for her, as much as I am for us." Tommy himself is showing signs of "blossoming" recently and has just enrolled in the course, "A Helping Relationship" at the Community College.

III
Androgynous love

8

Self-development through androgynous love

Feminized love creates conflicts over intimacy and reinforces overspecialized gender roles. Androgynous love provided an alternative based on interdependence and the integration of love and self-development for both sexes. Most scholars have dismissed androgynous love as a workable guide to enduring relationships, and the implicit message in their criticism is that we should return to traditional family and gender roles. But their criticism rests on a misinterpretation of androgynous love and the popular search for self-development.

Two blueprints of androgynous love can be distinguished, as I have shown. The Independence blueprint emphasizes expressing one's needs and feelings, and implies that the self can be developed without committed relationships or shared norms and obligations. The Interdependence blueprint emphasizes mutual support and implies that self-development requires committed relationships. Most scholars consider only the Independence model, and criticize it as a selfish, hyper-individualist perspective that undermines close relationships. The positive aspects of the trend to self-development evident in the Interdependence blueprint have been largely ignored.

Confusion about the meaning of self-development partly explains the negative bias of academics. They link the search for self-fulfillment with extreme independence and self-indulgence, and do not seem to understand how self-development can foster love and mutual dependence, even though psychoanalytic theories explain the connection.[1] Popular conceptions of self-development contribute to the confusion, mixing individualistic notions about releasing the natural self within, with more social notions about constructing a self through intimate relations. Lacking a clear social theory of the self, sociologically-inclined scholars often dismiss the whole enterprise of self-development as another destructive, misleading product of capitalism or American individualism.[2]

The theoretical perspective on the self presented in this chapter shows how committed relationships contribute to self-development. This perspective explains why committed relationships have persisted in the past decade, as the search for self-development became more popular. It also clarifies the kinds of close relationships that promote self-development, and the extent to which therapy is a useful model of love. Psychological studies of the content of a developed self suggest that self-development is promoted by relationships that are androgynous and encourage a broad range of behavior. Psychoanalytic theories suggest that self-development requires a secure, loving relationship that moves from dependence to interdependence.

COMMITMENT IN CONTEMPORARY RELATIONSHIPS

In the contemporary ideal of marriage, the woman and man openly communicate their feelings and work on the relationship so they can both develop themselves. According to several studies, this blueprint has become dominant in the middle class and is increasingly popular in the working class. Researchers generally agree that a more androgynous blueprint of love focused on self-development has emerged since the sixties, along with the diffusion of therapy and the ideas of the human potential movement. My disagreement with most researchers centers on whether this blueprint is compatible with enduring commitment and mutual support.

Several studies show that enduring commitment has persisted as an ideal and has not declined as a reality. In the massive study, *American Couples*, Philip Blumstein and Pepper Schwartz found that "an intimate enduring relationship" remains a central aspiration for Americans. The married couples they interviewed, as opposed to the more independent cohabiting couples, told them that marriage meant "making the total commitment" and that in a good marriage, both partners should "give more than you take" as well as "talk and be open."[3] My survey in 1980 showed that being "supportive and caring" was the second most frequently mentioned quality in a good marriage, following "good, open communication."[4]

Even the authors of *Habits of the Heart* acknowledge that permanence and interdependence are part of the new "therapeutic" image of love, although the main point of their book is that individualism and the human potential movement are undermining social bonds. Bellah *et al.* point out that "96% of all Americans held to the ideal of two people sharing a life and a home together," (in other words permanent marriage) according to surveys done in 1970 and 1980; and they acknowledge that "the satisfactions of marriage and family life have been increasing." Moreover, unrestrained independence was far from the ideal among the couples they interviewed. In fact, many of them "speak of sharing –

thoughts, feelings, tasks, values, or life goals – as the greatest virtue in a relationship."[5]

Trends in behavior also suggest that commitment has persisted in the last decade as the search for self-development spread. The divorce rate gradually declined in the early eighties, after reaching an all-time high at the beginning of the decade. Americans were also happier with their marriages in the seventies than in the fifties, according to large national surveys, although they also recognized more conflicts in their relationships.[6] Apparently, committed relationships were *not* seriously weakened when self-development became more valued.

There are two opposing explanations of how self-development is related to this persistence of committed relationships. I argue that the trend to self-development has strengthened committed relationships. Others maintain that the persistence of commitment is a survival of traditional family and gender roles, and view the search for self-development as undermining committed relationships.[7]

For Bellah *et al.*, the image of love as a permanent commitment is supported by a "traditional view of love and marriage as founded on obligation," a view that emphasizes "will and action" rather than feelings, and accepts "a version of the traditional distinction between the sphere of men and the sphere of women." The new therapeutic ethic of self-development is slowly eroding this cultural foundation of commitment, and replacing it with "a relentless emphasis on self-interest." The traditional view of enduring family obligations is giving way to a new model of relationships based on therapy, a model that "leaves every commitment unstable."[8]

Other observers, who ignore the persistence of committed relationships, are more extreme in their criticism of self-development. Historian Sheila Rothman concludes that the new ideal of a woman as a self-developed person is turning family life into "a zero-sum game" of competing individual interests, "a battleground among members, each trying to gain his or her own personal victory."[9] Christopher Lasch charges that the therapeutic ethic has accelerated the decay of the family, producing an "ideology of non-binding commitments" in which the distinctions between marriage and an affair "have become increasingly immaterial."[10]

These critics argue that self-development conflicts with committed love while I maintain that self-development strengthens commitment. Our disagreement stems from different interpretations of self-development and therapy, and different readings of contemporary close relationships. There is no conclusive evidence to settle this argument, no systematic comparisons of commitment in Companionship vs. Interdependent marriages, or large scale studies of how commitment changes after a couple becomes involved in therapy and personal growth. In the absence of evidence, I will support my position by examining our interpretations of self-development and therapy, and presenting cases that illustrate how enduring love and self-development can support each other.

THE NATURAL AND THE SOCIAL SELF

The critics believe that self-development, in popular culture, means releasing one's natural self from restrictive social bonds and rules, and spontaneously expressing one's needs and feelings. They assume that self-development means independence not interdependence. Both views of self-development exist, but the critics attend to only one of them.

The 1966 bestseller by Eric Berne, *Games People Play*, illustrates the ideal of the natural, independent self. Berne defines the attainment of personal autonomy or self-development as "the release or recovery of three capacities: awareness, spontaneity and intimacy." Awareness "requires living in the here and now" and being able to see and hear events in one's own way; spontaneity "means option, the freedom to choose and express one's feelings," and "intimacy means the spontaneous, game-free candidness of an aware person, the liberation of the . . . uncorrupted child," unrestricted by parental rules.[11] We do not need close relationships for self-development, Berne implies, since a developed self already exists within each individual, waiting to be released from artificial constraints.

Shared rules and values are usually harmful, according to Berne, although he includes parental rules and habits as an important component of a developed self. Berne advises us to be spontaneous and express our feelings, offering no criteria for choosing what feelings and desires need to be expressed. His image of self-development tends to be "empty" and "impulsive" as the critics charge, free of the social bonds, values, and rules that constitute and limit an individual's choices and give them meaning. For Berne, the criticism of Bellah *et al.*, is appropriate: "Ideas of potentiality (for what?) tell us nothing of which tasks and purposes are worth pursuing . . . Why should we do one thing rather than another, especially when we don't happen to feel like it or don't find it profitable?"[12]

Therapy fits this vision of an independent self, according to critics like Bellah, and teaches people to be independent and focused on their own needs and feelings. "Needing others in order to feel 'O.K.' about oneself is a fundamental malady that therapy seeks to cure."[13] Therapy, according to Bellah *et al.*, is typically "a contractual relationship" that teaches patients to deal with the troubles of emotional interdependence "by distancing from it and manipulating it through intellectual/verbal discussion, interpretation and analysis." The temporary, emotionally-limited relationship between therapist and patient provides a new model for intimacy that "leaves every commitment unstable." People learn to test every claim by others against the "giving-getting" calculus: "Are they getting what they want? Are they getting as much as they are giving?"[14] With these interpretations of therapy and self-development, critics like Bellah obviously conclude that the therapeutic ethic is undermining enduring love, and that the persistence of committed relationships can only be the result of surviving traditional beliefs.

A different conception of the self that emphasizes social bonds and interdependence is also popular, exemplified in Carl Rogers's very influential writings. Self-development for Rogers depends on a particular kind of close relationship – a therapeutic or "helping relationship" in which a person is "dependably real and caring." A helping relationship requires being sensitive to the other person's needs and providing support and empathic understanding, even when one doesn't feel like it. Self-development also includes Berne's themes of being "fully open" to the complexities of internal and external experience, and doing what "feels right" instead of relying on external principles and codes.[15]

Many followers of the human potential movement incorporate something like Rogers's helping relationship into their idea of self-development, forming what I call the Interdependent blueprint of love. They believe that mutual support and care are an important part of love, as the research described in Chapter 3 shows, and they implicitly or explicitly assume that a developed self is a social product, constructed not by oneself but by participating in committed, loving relationships.

Most theorists in psychology and psychoanalysis also assume that the self, or personality, is built up out of close relationships that are taken in or internalized, and become part of us. This is the assumption of Freud, who argued that the ego and super-ego grow out of real and phantasied interactions with others, primarily one's parents. Similarly, sociologists like George Herbert Mead and Charles Horton Cooley theorized that a person develops a "looking glass self" through attending to the reactions of "significant" others.

The model of therapy that usually accompanies this concept of a social self emphasizes the warm, trusting relationship that develops between therapist and patient. Gradually the patient internalizes the therapeutic relationship, as I will describe below, resulting in a more developed self that is more capable of participating in loving relationships. Psychiatrist M. Scott Peck presents this perspective in his recent bestseller. Intensive therapy, according to Peck, is "a process of genuine love," and "any genuinely loving relationship is one of mutual psychotherapy."[16] Peck's view of the similarity between therapy and marital love is extreme, but Freud himself said: "Psychoanalysis is in essence a cure through love." The distinguished psychoanalyst, Bruno Bettleheim, prefaces his recent book with this definition.[17]

Scholars like Bellah seriously misrepresent intensive therapy when they portray it as a cool, contractual relationship that undermines love. It is true that the emphasis on the patient's needs and feelings may weaken commitment and conformity to others, as the critics charge; but what they ignore is that the love and trust that patients typically develop for their therapist makes it more likely that they will love others.

If self-development is seen as a process of internalizing relationships with others, especially loving relationships, then love and self-development are mutually reinforcing, not conflicting. Therapy, from this perspective, contributes to self-development by providing a loving relationship that can be internalized.

In contrast, the idea that each person has a good, natural self that is blocked by social constraints, implies a conflict between self-development and enduring love. It implies that therapy is primarily a process of freeing the patient from attachments and obligations to others. While both perspectives are influential in popular culture, most psychologists and therapists seem to accept the perspective of a social self. Because they ignore this perspective, critics like Bellah conclude that the search for self-development is undermining committed relationships.

THE CONTENT OF A DEVELOPED SELF

The connection between self-development and love is the key to understanding and evaluating the Interdependence blueprint. The idea that the self is social and is based on internalizing relationships with intimate others is a first step towards clarifying this connection. The next step is to examine the meaning of a "more developed" vs. a "less developed" self, and the process by which a relationship becomes part of one's self. Building on psychological and psychoanalytic studies, I will define a developed self, describe the process of internalization, and identify the qualities of a loving relationship that contribute to self-development. This interpretation provides a theoretical basis for accepting some popular conceptions of personal growth, and criticizing others.[18]

Freud's structural theory defines a well-developed person as someone who integrates id, ego, and super-ego – someone who combines a child's vitality, sensuousness, and capacity for pleasure; an adult's perception of reality and ability to make choices; and a parent's discipline and commitment to a meaningful world view. The id and ego concepts include many

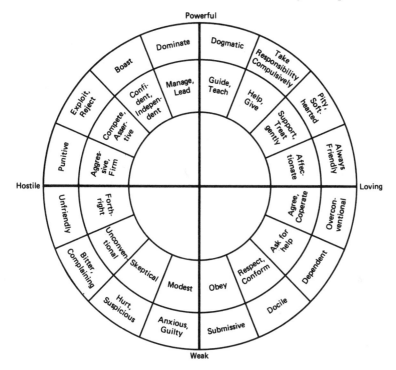

Figure 4 The circle of the self: sixteen ways of relating. From Leary, 1957, p. 65

of the ideals of the human potential movement: to know and express one's feelings, to be vitally alive and enjoy physical experiences, and to seek both love and meaningful achievement. The super-ego concept points to the necessity of moral codes, although psychoanalysis rejects rigid codes that are very constraining and guilt provoking.[19] A person is more self-developed, from this perspective, if they can integrate or balance spontaneity and feelings of pleasure with effective achievement of personal goals and socially responsible behavior. A loving relationship that encouraged self-development would help both partners to develop and integrate these general qualities.

Psychological research on the categories of interpersonal behavior suggests a more specific definition of a developed self that highlights the negative impact of rigid gender roles. The work of Timothy Leary is especially useful. He identified sixteen categories of behavior that describe all the "adaptive" and "pathological" ways of interacting with others (see Figure 4).[20] His original purpose was to help evaluate patients in mental hospitals; the healthier the patient, the more they would engage in all sixteen adaptive behaviors. But his approach is also useful in defining self-development, and captures the ideas of "developing one's full potential" and becoming more "whole." It also incorporates values that discriminate between good and bad potentials, or adaptive and maladaptive behavior.

The sixteen categories of behavior in Leary's scheme were identified by asking students, psychiatrists, and others to judge the similarity among hundreds of words describing behavior, such as "dominate," "agree," "pity," "love." They represent the major clusters of ways of relating to others. Categories placed close together in the diagram are those that have been judged similar in meaning. Words in the inner circle describe moderate, "adaptive" ways of relating, while words in the outer circle are more extreme and unacceptable (thus "dominating" is an extreme and unacceptable form of "leading"). The dimensions that best predicted the judgments of similaritiy are shown by the two lines intersecting the circle.[21] Leary's category system is incomplete; it leaves out, for example, being playful, sexual, or creative, but it moves us towards a more precise definition of a developed self. Describing the self as a composite of ways of relating to others also highlights the connection between self-development and social relationships.

Using this system, well-developed people can be defined as those who can comfortably engage in all the sixteen ways of relating in the inner circle. They can ask for help and also be independent and assertive; they can be affectionate as well as angry. And because they are not threatened by different ways of relating, they can empathically respond to others engaging in many types of behavior and thereby help them to become more developed or more "whole." In contrast, a less-developed person is overspecialized in a few ways of relating, or relates in unacceptable ways.

This definition of self-development clarifies the negative effects of rigid gender and family roles, and implies that well-developed people are androgynous. The two basic dimensions of the diagram – power vs. weakness and love vs. hostility – are clearly related to gender roles and the split between the family and work.[22] Thus the positive end of the "loving" dimension describes the ideal for women and the family while the negative end describes unfeminine characteristics to be avoided in women. Similarly, the positive end of the "powerful" dimension is the ideal for men and the workplace, while the negative end describes how to be unmasculine or "sissy." Thus men who are restricted to "masculine" behavior and women who are restricted to being "feminine" are very limited in their self-development. A relationship that promotes self-development, from this perspective, will help both partners become more comfortable and skilled in new ways of relating, including behaviors associated with the opposite sex.

THE PROCESS OF SELF-DEVELOPMENT

Psychoanalytic theories explain how a loving relationship can foster self-development. Object relations theory, as presented by Harry Guntrip and others, is especially useful because it emphasizes relationships very strongly, and focuses on dependence and interdependence – concepts that are crucial to my analysis of love and gender.[23]

Our selves are constructed out of past social relationships, and are maintained or changed by present relationships, according to object relations theory. Disturbed relations of dependency in childhood cause us to repress or split off parts of ourselves. On the other hand, secure, supportive relations in adulthood can help us re-experience and reclaim split-off ways of relating, making us more developed.

Childhood relationships are especially important in forming the self. As infants, we begin life in a relation of intense dependency on our mothers or other caretakers, especially if we are raised by one woman in a small, isolated family. Psychoanalytic research suggests that the child feels merged with his mother – in his experience and in reality he cannot survive without her. His needs are all-important, and he has little sense of mother as a separate person with her own needs and desires. Feelings are intense partly because children are so dependent on others for their survival, partly because children live in the present moment and are very aware of their bodily reactions (in contrast to adults, who often live "in their heads").[24]

Self-development entails transforming the dependency of early childhood into a more mature capacity for interdependence, according to Guntrip. The dependency of the infant involves an "oral incorporative" or "taking in" attitude, but mature dependence "is characterized by full differentiation of ego and object" and "therewith a capacity for valuing the object for its own sake and for giving as well as receiving."[25] A child develops interdependence by participating in a secure and supportive relationship with his mother or other caretakers. His experiences in the relationship teach him that he can trust others to meet his most pressing needs. He begins to learn that he is a separate person by experiencing the conflict between his needs and her actions. Gradually he realizes that he is not totally dependent on the person he loves but can survive on his own, and he begins to venture out on his own projects. As his need for his mother becomes less intense, he can tolerate being frustrated by her without becoming enraged or terrified. With time, he becomes aware of himself and her as two separate people who have different needs and who are mixtures of gratifying and frustrating qualities. His own self-development improves his ability to have a satisfying, loving relationship of mutual dependency.

Moving beyond childhood dependency, for Guntrip, does not mean denying the need for close relationships. "The independence of the mature person is simply that he does not collapse when he has to stand alone. It is not an independence of needs for other persons with whom to have relationship."[26] In other words, a developed person can be described as separate from others, rather than independent. He is aware that he can survive the loss of any particular relationship and can distinguish between his own needs and feelings and his partner's, but he is also overtly dependent and aware that he needs close relationships.

Most people, says Guntrip, fail to attain mature interdependence. The child becomes frightened of experiencing his intimate relationship with his mother because of frustration or punishment from her, or rage from within. The child then represses or splits off his dependency, and part of his development becomes frozen at that point. He may deny his needs for help and intimacy and withdraw from close relationships, or he may rigidly and unconsciously repeat infantile dependency. Thus, an interdependent love relationship can be a goal to work towards but not an actuality for most adults. Conflicting feelings of approach and withdrawal, dependence and independence, will persist, although they will diminish as the couple becomes more self-developed.[27]

Gender roles encourage women and men to repress their childhood dependency in different ways. Men tend to withdraw from intimacy and become rigidly independent on an overt level, while women tend to repeat childhood patterns and be rigidly dependent on an overt level. Both sexes repress certain ways of relating, and both will have conflicting feelings about intimacy, contrary to the common assumption that women are unambivalently drawn to love.[28]

To illustrate this perspective on self-development, we can sketch the development of an imaginary boy, Douglas. As an infant, Douglas had a gratifying relation with his mother until his younger brother was born. Then Douglas became much more angry and demanding, and his mother responded by ignoring him and getting extremely upset a few times when he hit his baby brother. As a result, he became terrified that his mother might leave him and that he might injure his brother. This led him to repress that part of himself that was a dependent, angry, and frightened child and develop a conscious self that was strong and self-reliant. Since repressed parts of the self do not change and develop, he was unable to progress from childhood dependency, in which immediate satisfaction of needs seems necessary for survival and safety. His dependency, split off or projected onto others, appears only in dreams and in distorted, rigid ways of behaving that are not integrated with the rest of his conscious self.

In sum, the development of our adult self is shaped by earlier relations of dependency, and by our ability to give up childhood relations of asymmetrical dependency for mutual relations of interdependence. Let us now consider how our adult self effects current close relationships, in psychoanalytic theory, and how these relationships can change our self.

In intimate relationships, most people repeat old ways of relating that maintain their old self. A person who has split off his dependency (because of disturbed relations in the past) will create a similar disturbed relationship in the present. For example, when Douglas becomes intimate with a woman, he probably will be intensely dependent, on an unconscious level, and will feel ungratified and rejected, as he did with his mother. Whatever the women does, she will probably fail to satisfy his longing to be cared for, because it is so intense and so hidden. Moreover, he may search for signs that she is failing him just as his mother did, and behave so as to discourage her from gratifying his dependency needs, for example, by always appearing strong and in control. When she does fail to care for him, he is likely to feel that his survival is threatened, as he felt in childhood, and become terrified and angry. Douglas thus creates a negative cycle, maintaining his old pattern of relating and his limited self. He distorts reality and pays most attention to responses that fit his childhood expectations of rejection and deprivation, experiencing her not as a separate person with her own concerns and needs, but as an actor in his internal drama from the past. His behavior also encourages his partner to reject him or leave, reinforcing his expectation of future rejection.[29] Their relationship will include a great deal of hurt and anger, and little mutual support and trust.

A "good" relationship – one that helps a person reclaim the repressed, split-off parts of himself – can break this negative cycle. Within a secure, supportive relationship with a spouse, friend, or therapist, we can relax the fear that maintains the repression, experience a new response to our old needs, and develop a more gratifying and flexible pattern of relating to others. A good relationship will increase our self-development, which will improve our capacity to have good relationships in the future, in a positive cycle. From this perspective on the process of self-development, the Interdependence blueprint of love seems quite reasonable. The quest for self-fulfillment can foster love, not selfishness and isolation.

The major weakness in this approach to the self is that it overemphasizes intimate relationshps, not that it undermines them. Relationships at work and in the community should be given more emphasis in conceptualizing the content and process of self-development. Even when these relations are limited, they may promote self-development by allowing a person to experience a new and important way of relating to others. Thus for many wives, relations with co-workers and acquaintances are critical to becoming more confident and less dependent on their husbands, and young adults often learn to be competent and effective through relations at work or at school. A college senior described how the boss at his part-time job was enabling him to improve his self-confidence: "He's been letting me develop skills. I work in a law office and I'm the bookkeeper, the only bookkeeper there . . . And it's really building up my confidence, they're really putting their trust in me." A variety of experiences in everyday life can enhance or retard self-development. But experiences in intimate relationship with our "significant others" are probably most important in changing the parts of our selves that were formed in childhood.

THERAPY AND LOVE

What kind of close relationship promotes self-development? An interpretation of self-development based on Freud, Leary, and Guntrip suggests a preliminary answer. Firstly, developing oneself requires a secure, supportive relationship, since fear is the underlying cause of rigid behavior and splitting off parts of the self – fear that the other person will abandon or attack us, and fear of our own unrestrained passion and rage. Secondly, the relationship should give us the freedom to explore diverse ways of relating instead of restricting us to rigid roles or old patterns of behavior. Finally, the relationship should move towards interdependence, so we are separate enough to accurately perceive our partner's responses, and to tolerate some frustration of our needs, and also dependent enough to care about our partner and continue the relationship.

Intensive traditional therapy, when it succeeds, is one model of a close relationship that reclaims the split-off parts of the self. For example, if Douglas were to work with a psychoanalytically oriented therapist, he would be encouraged to re-create or transfer his early dependent relation with his mother onto the therapist and re-experience the intense neediness, anger, and fears of early childhood. The therapist would attempt to create a relationship that was different from his past, and to help him experience this difference – a relationship that gave him more reliable support and acceptance, and more encouragement to be a separate and valuable person. The therapist would be reliably present at a set time and would dependably provide attention and acceptance. She would resist Douglas's attempts to put her in the role of the rejecting mother (or the perfect, all-giving mother). Thus, when he became demanding and hostile, she would not get angry and withdraw, as his mother had. Through her behavior and interpretations she would show him that his transference was unrealistic and that she was more trustworthy and caring than he perceived. Her acceptance of his childish needs and fears would encourage him to accept this part of himself, and her warmth and confidence in his worth would help him to value himself.

Insofar as he could overcome his fear and trust her enough to experience this new kind of relationship, he would gradually become the person he saw mirrored in her response to him.[30] He would become more self-developed and more capable of love as he moved beyond the intense, merging dependency of childhood and experienced himself and his therapist as two separate and complex people. In his outside relationships as well, he would become more interdependent, experiencing a broader range of desires within himself, and perceiving more accurately what his partner was doing in the present, rather than fearfully waiting for the past to repeat itself. Instead of the earlier internalized (but repressed) image of a rageful, bad, abandoned child and an absent, rejecting mother, he would develop a more conscious image of a lovable and needy child and a reliably present mother who would often care for him. As his dependency became more conscious, his childhood vitality and connection to his body might also re-emerge, since they are often repressed along with infantile dependency.[31]

Although traditional therapy contains many of the qualities that encourage self-development, it is a limited model for an Interdependent marriage because it is so asymmetrical and limited.[32] The relationship provides security and support for the patient and focuses on his needs while the therapist has the authority but rarely expresses her feelings and desires. She receives payment in exchange, not care. Because of this asymmetry in power and dependency, the patient can experience an extraordinary degree of security, responsive attention, and freedom to express a wide range of reactions, and dramatic personal changes can occur. But in "real world" relationships, both partners want care, attention, and power, and both are distracted by external and internal pressures.

Therapy is also much more limited and structured than real world relationships. Interaction occurs in scheduled, fifty-minute periods, and is restricted to talking about the patient's experience. The instrumental, cooperative actions that make up so much of a couple's life together do not occur, actions like preparing a meal, taking a child to the doctor, or arguing about when to schedule different activities. If instrumental activities were included, it would be very difficult for the therapist to put aside her own interests and needs, and focus only on the patient. In sum, the limited range of activities in traditional therapy together with the asymmetry limits its usefulness as a model for love.

Newer forms of therapy are more symmetrical and are more often used as models of good relationships. Carl Rogers's concept of the "helping relationship" has been especially influential. Therapy, for Rogers, consists of providing clients with a relationship that helps them to develop themselves. Like traditional therapists, Rogers's view of this relationship emphasizes establishing a secure, supportive relationship, encouraging a broader range of feelings and actions, and moving towards interdependence. But unlike the traditionalists, he also stresses clear communication of feelings by both therapist and "client," and seems to aim for a more equal relationship between them.

Rogers's helping relationship is characterized by security and support. The therapist should be acceptant, avoid behavior that will be perceived as a threat, and have a warm regard for the client as a person of value no matter what his condition. He should sensitively and empathically understand "the client's feelings and communications as they seem to him at that moment." In addition, the therapist should be aware of his own feelings and communicate them clearly and congruently in both words and behavior. The client is also encouraged to develop diverse ways of relating to others, by the therapist valuing and understanding him, and accepting the fact that he is changing. If such a relationship can be established in therapy or in other contexts, Rogers argues, the other person "will experience and understand aspects of himself which previously he has repressed"; he "will be more able to cope with the problems of life;" and "will be more understanding, more acceptant of others."[33]

The importance of these qualities fits the psychoanalytic view of self-development. They are also consistent with the way people describe the kind of relationship they want. Honest communication, caring, acceptance, and understanding are the qualities of a good marriage that are most often mentioned in surveys. In a study of 180 couples in Indiana, for example, wives and husbands of all social classes preferred their spouses to be "contactful," that is, to disclose their feelings and intentions verbally and to be open and respectful towards their partners' views, and interested in what their partners had to say.[34] There is also some evidence that these qualities do, in fact, promote self-development. Most of the research looks at this process from the negative perspective and shows how being rejected, devalued, and ignored produces a closed, hostile orientation to others, lower self-esteem, and rigid behavior.[35]

Therapy is a questionable model of love, not because it lacks affection and commitment, but because it is asymmetrical and is limited to talking. It is unrealistic to expect one's partner in everyday life to be as consistently supportive and understanding as a therapist, and to make so few demands. Even if it were obtainable, in the long run, a relationship of such unmutuality would not encourage the development of either partner. Therapy can be a useful guide to good relationships, but only if both partners take the role of therapist to the other, and if the range of activities is broadened.

SELF-DEVELOPMENT AND CONSTRAINT

The final controversial feature of therapy as a model of love concerns the necessity of security, self-discipline, and rules. A feeling of security is essential to the patient's self-development in therapy, as object-relations theory makes clear, because fear maintains old, rigid ways of relating. This idea explains, on a personality level, why social changes that create insecurity – such as the Great Depression – lead to rigid roles. It also implies that relationships that promote self-development need to include rules, obligations, and long-term commitments so as to provide a sense of security.

Therapy is structured by many rules and professional norms that contribute to patients' feelings of security. In particular, there is the rule that the therapist will provide empathic attention at the appointed hour, whether she feels like it or not, a rule that helps patients feel more secure about the relationship and less frightened of experiencing dependency or other feelings that are usually repressed. Other rules encourage change by setting limits. For example, patients are able to express split-off sexual feelings that frighten them because of the pro-hibition on sexual relations in therapy. Thus the behavior of therapists that encourages self-development requires conformity to rules, obli-gations to others, and self-dicipline, as well as spontaneity and self-expression.

However, in their writings and explicit messages to patients, therapists tend to ignore these rules and obligations, as critics like Bellah have pointed out. They often counsel patients to focus on their own needs and feelings, and give out the message: "Do what I say, not what I do." Fortunately, I believe, many patients ignore this message and incorporate the caring, rule-bound behavior of the therapist into their model of a developed person.[36]

Carl Rogers, for example, fails to incorporate the empathic, disciplined love of a "helping relationship" into his conception of a developed self. Sensitive concern for the other is a major part of his description of a helping relationship, but he barely mentions concern for others in describing the fully developed person, focusing instead on living fully in each moment and doing what feels right. He does not face the potential conflict between doing what feels right and helping one's partner, as, for example, when a man feels like attacking his wife. Rogers, like many others in the human potential movement, gets around this conflict by assuming that qualities such as altruism and self-restraint are natural and will be expressed when the person has become his or her "true self."[37] Even if it were true that people have a natural, virtuous self, constraining rules would be necessary to encourage helpfulness until the natural self was uncovered.

Marriage, like therapy, requires rules and obligations if it is to provide the security that fosters self-development, according to my interpretation of the self. The rules Interdependent couples adopt, as we will see in the next chapter, necessarily differ from therapy, because the situations are so different. For example, always listening empathically may be a useful rule for a therapist, because the relation is limited to brief periods of talking. Partners who share their daily lives tend to have rules about listening empathically in certain situations or when one of them signals that they need attention.

Rules are also needed to regulate the expression of intense feelings, since people tend to transfer their early dependent relations onto their spouse or lover, just as they do in therapy, and re-experience the neediness, terror, and rage of childhood relationships. Shared expectations and the rituals of daily life can limit disruptive feelings and can encourage both partners to be supportive, and to tolerate difficult times when their needs are not being met. Thus, the role expectations in Companionship marriage limit the wife's needs for more attention with norms about avoiding "nagging" and being a cheerful wife, while the husband's need to withdraw is tempered by norms about weekends being family time. Family roles often produce the security and support that is necessary for self-development. That is why relationships that are rigidly bound by traditional roles sometimes produce more self-development for both partners than a freer relationship in which hostility and thoughts about leaving are openly expressed.

However, the rules and structure that create security also may restrict self-development. Family roles usually emphasize hierarchy and gender differences. They restrict the behavior of both sexes and limit the possibility of integrating the sensual spontaneity of childhood into adult relationships, as Eric Berne argues. When family roles are internalized, many people become overly self-critical and develop unrealistic expectations for themselves and their partner.

In a marriage of Interdependence, this dilemma is partly resolved by developing flexible, androgynous roles that fit the couple and their network of friends. Shared rules are seen as created by the couple and their network, and changeable by them; they are not seen as the natural, "one right way" to behave. But rules limit us, even if the rules are chosen. The freedom to develop oneself paradoxically requires giving up some freedom from constraint.

EVALUATING THE THERAPEUTIC ETHIC

The idea that self-development can be combined with a commited relationship is obviously sound, given the interpretation of self-development I have presented, and the therapeutic relationship is a better model of love than many critics judge it to be. Intensive therapy usually involves a kind of committed love by the therapist, structured by professional norms and obligations. To become a useful model for close relationships, the asymmetrical helping role needs to be transformed into a symmetrical, equal relationship where both partners help each other develop. Another limitation of therapy as a model of androgynous love is that it is restricted to talking about feelings. Masculine styles of love such as providing practical help, sharing physical activities, and sex are excluded, and the material basis of the relationship is often obscured. Taking therapy as its model, the Interdependence blueprint shares the same failings and neglects material interdependence.

The institution of therapy and the feminization of love produce some of the same biases in our conception of intimacy – an overemphasis on talking and feeling, a mystification of the material basis of attachment, and a tendency to ignore physical love and the practical aspects of nurturance and mutual assistance. A major goal in androgynous love is to help both partners develop their potential by providing a secure, supportive relationship where split-off or undeveloped parts of the self can be expressed and shared. This goal cannot be achieved if the relationship ignores some of the most important human capacities – productive work, physical activity, and physical care of others.

9
Androgynous love in marriage

Self-development within marriage is the goal of a growing number of Americans who follow the new blueprints of Independence and Interdependence. To promote self-development, a relationship should provide security and support, freedom to develop new ways of relating, and encouragement to become separate and interdependent, according to my analysis of the self. Within marriage, security is usually easier to achieve than freedom or interdependence. Married couples are pressured to stay together, and their lives are structured by a myriad of rules and expectations about how they should behave and feel. Emotional and material exchange and sharing also contribute to the security and commitment of marriage. Married couples usually live together, pool their money, have children, make love regularly, and share their meals and much of their leisure time. But the rules and exchanges that provide security often restrict freedom and channel men and women into rigid, overspecialized gender roles. On the other hand, couples that live together without being married often lack the security and commitment that is necessary for self-development and for maintaining the relationship. Case studies of several couples show the problems and possibilities of balancing security and freedom, and illustrate the perspective on love and self-development presented in the last chapter.

BECOMING INTERDEPENDENT

Interdependence is the cornerstone of a relationship that helps both partners develop an expanded, androgynous self. Both partners will have to move beyond the merging, demanding dependency of childhood – which is usually overt in women and covert or repressed in men. As they feel more interdependent and separate, they will be able to tolerate situations in which their immediate needs are not met without collapsing in fear or becoming angry or withdrawn. They will experience themselves as powerful and in control within the relationship, at times, as well as weak and dependent, and will be able to empathically accept a broader range of their partner's self. The process of breaking out of rigid gender roles and becoming interdependent is well described in Lois Gould's novel about the love affair between a psychiatrist and his former patient, *Final Analysis*.

At the beginning, the woman was overtly very dependent. In her eyes, he was a man she desperately needed to be close to but one who would surely abandon her. He was overtly independent and treated her as a weak and burdensome child who might engulf him. "The thought that he might also have some need never occurred to either of them."[1]

Gradually he became more and more dependent on being with her, but he could not bear to admit it to her, or to his own consciousness. He "forgot" his keys and his papers at her apartment and was constantly phoning about them or dropping by to retrieve them. He began to spend the night but no longer made love. Instead he sat in bed reading medical journals while she silently cried because she needed him so much and he was ignoring her. "Then he turned off the light, and reached around her to cover her breasts with his hands, like a child playing Guess Who . . . He always fell asleep like that. First."[2]

She tried to set up meetings with him and wept when he explained how busy he was:

> Once he called and said 'Hey, come meet,' just like that. And she walked to him through the night streets, four miles, she walked, as if on hot coals, like a human sacrifice . . . 'Hi,' he said to her softly, instead of scolding her for walking alone . . . it was so strange that he should be anywhere at all, waiting for her . . . They danced together clinging, but saying nothing. Then he didn't call her for a week.[3]

At the beginning, she saw only her needs and how he failed to meet them, and ignored the signs of his neediness and incompetence in caring for himself – his drug addiction and inability to manage his finances or maintain his apartment. Her letters to him described her needs, her history, and her inadequacies. He saw only her emotional problems and demands and did not notice that her career in writing was floundering.

The turning point came when, encouraged by her friends in a women's consciousness-raising group, she left town for a month on a writing assignment. He became involved in a risky financial venture without telling her; "that would show her who needed who," he thought. "She had walked out on him, hadn't she? Like everybody else."[4] When the venture collapsed, he became sick, and she took charge and cared for him, a process that made them aware of his dependency and her strength. Then they both began to change. Her letters started to describe the world outside her as well as herself. He helped her spend some months alone, writing, and when he was late for their reunion because of an accident (caused by his incompetence) she comprehended that he was not rejecting her.

Finally, she began to call him by his first name instead of Dr Foxx, signifying their equal dependency and power, and he told her he loved her and needed her. Then they made love. "Fitting her body to his, over it; he held her where she wanted to be, high, riding now, posting, a blue-ribbon rider feeling the wind, the sun, the double rhythm . . . She felt him sigh, and then the rush of him inside her, the way a child sobs, she thought, in spite of itself."[5] Then after a while, when he had gone to sleep, she got up and returned to her writing.

Similar themes emerged in many of the intensive interviews. Friends and satisfying work helped many women become less dependent on men, and an interdependent love relationship often increased men's awareness of their needs for intimacy. Work, friends, and associations in the public sphere often have an important effect on self-development. The women's movement made it easier for many affluent couples to move towards interdependence by strengthening the bonds among women and leading both sexes to value women's careers and their independent interests. The human potential movement also helped people move away from polarized gender roles, encouraging men as well as women to attend to their needs and feelings.

The development of greater interdependence in the marriage of Ann and Michael Gerrard illustrates these themes.[6] Ann (who was discussed in Chapter 7) is a 42-year-old biologist and has been married to Michael, a hospital administrator, for nineteen years. They have two sons in high school. Ann's best features in Michael's eyes are "energy and enthusiasm" and "honesty and integrity, I mean I respect her." Ann values Michael's "physical attraction . . . it isn't just being sexy, it's also being very alive and strong but not frightening . . . it's just sort of there in his body . . . I respect him a lot." What she values most in her marriage is

> the sex, the house, the life, it's a whole life. I think of doing fun things together. I think of someone to hang on to when I get scared. I feel grounded. It makes me feel located and challenged. I mean nothing like trying to get close to someone to find out who you are.

Ann described the slow process of becoming less desperately dependent on her husband and more separate and able to share with him. Ten years ago Ann was unexpectedly fired from her part-time job with a large corporation. For several years, she had been working, raising her sons, and worrying about her marriage. "I was doing it all and being pretty successful . . . I was this macho, achieving, brilliant, tough person . . . But I felt somehow restless and boxed in. I thought it was something wrong with Michael, something he wasn't giving me." She joined an encounter group and had frequent meetings with a new woman friend, breaking her habit of spending all her time away from work with Michael or the children. She also had long arguments with her husband, reminiscent of the Gilmore's fights, in which she would pressure him to change, to come to the encounter groups with her, to talk with her more.

Then she was fired and unable to find another job. "My world crashed down around me" – her world of being a successful person, overtly independent but covertly very dependent on her husband, following a stereotypically masculine pattern. At her friend's suggestion, Ann entered therapy; she developed an intense bond with her therapist and slowly began to experience and integrate the dependent, split-off part of herself. Over the next four years, "all the creative, feminine parts, all that came out," and Ann began to play the harp and write poetry as her mother had done.

> *Why was it so tough to let that side out do you think?*
> Part of it is I didn't trust anybody. And because I learned to trust my therapist, I was able to not live my life as if I was a fortress constantly under siege.
> *You didn't trust Michael?*
> No, not that much. It was very hard. I was tense around him a lot. I always expected that anyone I was really close to was going to leave or betray me.

Ann developed a close friendship with two women, joined a feminist support group for women biologists, and eventually found a good new job. As she became more intimate with others, more aware of her own need to be taken care of, and more confident, she and Michael became less angry with each other and less dependent. "Now we're more separate and not as umbilically tied to each other . . . for all those years we were so tied," Ann comments. "I spent so much time thinking about him, and he spent so much time thinking about me, and lots of times it was a very angry thing, but we're very involved, passionately involved, even when it's awful." Michael describes how it used to be:

> She wanted to be working in the garden, I didn't want her in the garden. Why wasn't she paying attention to me? I wanted to watch a football game and she'd say why aren't you with the family? That kind of stuff, so we were giving each other incredibly little space.

Michael remembers how he began to feel more independent when he realized he could survive without Ann.

> I can remember in one of our particularly bad periods, being afraid of breaking up, and I was working with a counselor at this particular time and

this was one of those dramatic experiences, realizing that I could do it. Because you get married and you kind of define yourself in terms of the relationship and you can't imagine yourself not being in it, ah, so it was really nice to know that I could do it, that is, I felt perfectly OK about the possibility of living alone and my own life.

"Michael and I started giving each other some room," Ann remembers. "I started like not being home every weekend and every evening. I started having my own friends and doing things, and not hating him if he watched TV. Now we don't have to eat each other up all the time." Her struggles for independence and self-development are supported by her friends. "I go off and essentially take vacations by myself and trips by myself, and go out with friends, including sometimes men, and like that's really neat. I feel very free to do things." Michael admits to being jealous of her friends at times: "I have certainly been jealous of her male friends, but we're both smart enough about relationships not to get into trouble blindly [have affairs]."

In Ann's words

> We trust each other more . . . I don't think it's so frightening any more. I can afford, we can afford to let each other get angry. We can afford to get out of touch, but we don't do that as much any more either . . . Just let go and the more you let go the closer we get.

Michael and Ann now share more at the same time that they spend more time apart. Michael has discovered that he likes to cook, and they enjoy making dinner for each other and discussing cooking techniques. Ann more often joins Michael in complaining about work – she no longer needs to be the master of every situation. And when their travels separate them, they can share their feelings of fear and sadness and phone each other. Their old pattern was to deny their fears about being apart, never phone, and have fights about some other issue before and after each trip. Michael and Ann seem less afraid that they will be rejected or controlled by the other and therefore less angry and demanding, and more able to support each other. They express more of their feelings, a style of relating that is supported by their circle of friends. "I'm still involved in this whole culture of human potential stuff." Ann comments, "all my very close friends are into this way of talking."

Ann still seems more dependent on the relationship than Michael, and she worries about becoming too separate. When asked if there was something she would like to change about the marriage, she said,

> . . . We could confront a little bit more. We had this long period of confronting so much that I think we both just got burnt out. Then we had several years of peacemaking. And now . . . we're a bit too careful. We tend

to say, let's wait until tomorrow ... you both go off in your separate directions, and cool off. It gets kind of chilly, distant.

Marriages such as the Gerrards' that have moved from Companionship to Interdependence seem traditional in many ways. Like couples in their parents' and grandparents' generations, Ann and Michael aspire to a life-long marriage, they are committed to support each other and to share their money and daily life. What makes this a modern, androgynous relationship is that both partners are responsible for maintaining the relationship; their balance of dependency and power is close to equal; and they are dedicated to developing themselves, working on their relationship, and communicating openly.

STAYING INDEPENDENT

Couples dedicated to Independence not Interdependence come closer to popular conceptions of the modern relationship. They emphasize their own freedom more than security or mutual support. Focusing on an independent couple clarifies how different the Independence blueprint is from the majority of long-term relationships.

For men and women who live together for many years without marrying, independence "is the most consistent theme of their relationship," conclude Philip Blumstein and Pepper Schwartz, after interviewing forty-eight cohabiting couples.[7] One of the couples was Lauren, thirty-nine, a speech pathologist in the city school system and Blair, thirty-eight, a social worker at the same school. They met seven years ago at work.[8] "I was impressed ... by the way she was able to verbalize feelings and attitudes about education and social relationships," says Blair. "I just thought he was a fox," comments Lauren, "and then I found out he was married and decided that was too bad." Lauren, who was divorced and had two children, did not want an involvement with a married man, but Blair was unhappy with his wife, and the structure and commitment of marriage. "I was dissatisfied being married 'cause I didn't like that contract ... The overriding feeling of commitment was something I really didn't want ... My wife was a homebody. I wanted more freedom."

Blair and Lauren fell very much in love and one night had sex together. Ten days later, Blair spent several nights at Lauren's house, and he never left. Blair explains the almost casual way he ended his marriage and began a new commitment "for a while." After a few days at Lauren's

there was kind of the next decision which needed to be made, which was: "I think I have to go home and get some more clothes." So I remember that day as being an incredibly intensive emotional day, 'cause I knew then what

I was really doing – which was moving out of my marriage. I knew at that point I was making a commitment.

He went home "with every intention of packing my stuff and sitting down with my wife and telling her that I'm getting out for a while." But his wife "didn't show up." Then "it started raining and there was no waiting around, so I hopped in the car and left. And got back here, and it was clear then – almost unspoken – that I was going to be here for a while."

From the start, Lauren and Blair tried to avoid permanent commitments and mutual dependence. They were both "just sure it was love," Lauren explains, but they didn't expect their bond to last very long, even after they had been living together for three years.

> We just sort of said, "This is the neatest thing that has ever happened to me. I place no limits on it. It may be over tomorrow and I'm not going to worry about it. I'm just going to enjoy it for what it gives right now." And love was used every other word.

Feelings of love and a willingness to communicate and work on the relationship are their positive bonds. "The neatest thing for me is that he is willing to work on the relationship," says Lauren. When a problem comes up, they talk about it until it's resolved. "We never quit till it's over if that means staying up all night ... I don't feel insecure bringing anything up that bothers me, 'cause we can always work it out." Blair shares the value on communication, praising Lauren for being "incredibly out-front about all her feelings."

They also share the task of raising Lauren's two children, even though they have serious arguments about his standards of discipline, and they enjoy playing tennis and doing leisure activities together. Sexual exclusiveness may be another bond. After a "bad time" when Blair had sex with other women,, "we have agreed on an exclusive intimacy" according to Lauren. Blair's version of their agreement on sex with other people is vaguer, following his pattern of avoiding definite commitments: "we agreed to sort of write it off" and tell the other person unless it's "a one-time sort of thing that may happen as a result of getting really stoned sometimes . . ." If one of them decided they would like sex with someone else, Blair says, "we have made a commitment to discuss that interest with the other before it is consummated, and the appropriate steps will have to be taken at that point – which may mean that we will have to break for a while."

Other parts of their lives they keep separate and equal. "We maintain very separate financial records," Blair explains. "I essentially make all the decisions about what I do with my money. She makes all the decisions about what she does with hers." "We keep all of our finances as separate as we can," Lauren agrees, and even when a friend gives one of them a gift, "if it's an *us* gift and it comes from my friends, it's mine, even if it's to both of us." They also attempt to divide housework equally, but Lauren "probably does a little bit more," Blair admits.

Staying independent, separate, and equal are primary goals for both of them partly because of problems in the past. When she was married, Lauren recalls, "I went through three years of psychotherapy thinking I was crazy for not being happy"and "that affects why I don't ever want to marry anybody again." With Blair she intends to remain more independent: "I know if Blair were to walk out and get hit by a truck, I would be devastated but I would be okay. I would make it, and I'd raise my kids and I'd still have things to do, and I lost all of that in marriage. I was either tormented or I was tormenting."

Blair feels he has learned from the failure of his marriage "to talk openly about problems as they occur rather than sandbagging" and to give each other more freedom to pursue separate interests. The key elements in making his new relationship work, he thinks, are "dealing openly and honestly with conflict" and "allowing each other space." Blair believes "the best relationships probably are made by people who don't really need them, just want them; don't have to have it, but since it's around I'm sure going to take advantage of it." And Lauren agrees, "if you ever need me, we're going to be in trouble."

Couples like Lauren and Blair avoid emotional and material inter-dependence to such an extent that it becomes almost impossible to have a committed, enduring relationship. Many of the cohabiting couples that Blumstein and Schwartz studied were more committed – about 85% of them were still together when they were recontacted eighteen months later, and couples that shared their money were especially likely to endure. Blair and Lauren were still "involved" when they were recontacted, but living in separate homes and exploring relations with other people.

SELF-DEVELOPMENT AND SUPPORT

Couples in an Interdependent relationship try to combine more mutual dependency and more commitment than Lauren and Blair have, with a great deal of freedom to develop themselves. The Gerrards illustrate some of the possibilities of developing an androgynous self at mid life, within the constraints of a stable marriage. A young engaged couple shows how an Interdependent relationship can foster self-development during the transition to adulthood.

Greg, twenty-four, and Lisa, twenty-two, have been dating for five years, and plan to get married soon, if they can overcome the objections of her family.[9] They both describe their relationship as a combination of secure nurturance and freedom to develop themselves. What Greg likes best about their relationship is that "she's always there no matter what, no matter what kind of mood I'm in or how bad a day it's been – she's always there to talk to, to help me, and over the years she has domesticated me a lot – she's made me into a more grown-up type person . . ." Greg describes himself as "the baby of the family" and is very close to his father – "I've always been under his wing." He has many friends including a best friend whom he sees every day, and who describes Greg as "outgoing, honest, funny and boisterous." When Greg met Lisa he had graduated from high school and was working in a gas station. "I had hair down to here (his shoulders). I was wild, crazy, into doing all kinds of stupid things," and Lisa helped him be "more grown-up." For example, she helped him conquer his bad temper. "She has developed that out of me, because for a while there I used to be the type that when I got mad I would see only red . . . I was uncontrollable, but with her around I am able to control my emotions." Now he has settled down, with some reluctance, into a job as a technician in a computer company, and has signed up for their management training course.

Lisa also has developed new ways of relating to others. "She has always been very sheltered" Greg said, "and I introduced her to a lot of fun things in life and she introduced me to a lot of responsibilities . . . Also she's just a damn awful lot of fun to be around all the time." With Greg, Lisa for the first time went water skiing, jet skiing, motorcycle riding, innertubing the rapids, and backpacking. "I'm a school principal's daughter, I was home every weekend. I have a very protective family. I mean it was a big deal to go to the grocery store alone! I have learned so many new things, and so many fun things . . ." With Greg's encouragement she is overcoming her internal restrictions. "I'll give anything a try, even though sometimes I get this radical fear that sweeps through me – I just have to put it out of my mind."

Lisa goes to college part time, works as a clerk, and has just started her own business, selling the ceramics she makes. Her best friend describes her as "outgoing, positive, understanding and very ambitious." Both Greg and Lisa say that they share equally in making decisions, but Lisa used to carry most of the responsibility for being emotionally supportive. "I'm not one that expresses my problems," says Greg, following the typical masculine pattern, and "she gets mad because I'm not as open with her as I should be." But mostly, he adds, "if there's ever anything that's bothering me or her inside or any problem we're having we can more or less bring it out and just talk to each other about it – problems about anything – that's why our relationship goes so well." From Lisa's perspective, "the first year or two I gave more, but now he gives more. I think with everything I'm doing – going to school, opening a shop – he's being the emotional support which I need, and he's just really behind my decisions and my goals." They seem to be moving towards more androgynous gender roles, and there is a high level of mutual emotional dependence between them.

They are also financially interdependent, making joint investments in recreational equipment and in savings for their marriage. When Lisa was asked about her goals in relation to Greg, she answered with a mix of fifties familism and eighties consumerism:

> Marriage. We want a home and to be able to afford children and give them the best. We like a lot of toys and we like to do things like water ski and ride and we'd like to be able to afford to do these things. We are working really hard now, and hopefully it will pay off in the future.

Along with their mutual dependence, Greg and Lisa also seem unusually separate and autonomous for their age. Lisa describes herself as "a private person. I set aside time for myself every day . . ." Greg comments that "When we really disagree we'll say so, 'no, I don't want to do that.' And we can talk about it and work things out . . . We don't have to worry about stepping on each other's toes because even though we're coming together as one, we are still separate entities and there's always going to be times when we'll disagree."

Part of their separateness is that they have many other important relationships. They both live with their families and describe themselves as very close with their fathers and with their friends, and they both occasionally go off on a weekend trip without the other.

They also seem very much in love, especially Greg. "Normally when I'm my happiest is when I'm with her. Sometimes when I first appear around her, I'm a jerk to her . . . and she just takes it all in stride and gives it back in love, and that's the time when I can be as happy as I can be." His gratitude is remarkable and so is his mature recognition that he is "normally" happiest with her, not "always." "I can feel her when she's there and I don't need her to touch me or anything . . . I enjoy her presence even when we say nothing. She's very soothing to me."

STRIKING A BALANCE

Interdependent couples try to strike a balance between opposing forces – to have a relationship of equality unconstrained by traditional gender roles and still depend on each other for emotional and material support, to be free to develop new capacities and still maintain a secure, committed relationship. Greg and Lisa, and Ann and Michael come close to achieving this balance. The material and emotional dependency between the woman and man is much more equal than many couples, such as, for example, the Gilmores, although the traditional pattern of the woman being more emotionally and verbally expressive is still evident. Lisa supports herself economically, and Ann makes a good income at a prestigious job. Both women are energetic and ambitious and seem to have developed their "masculine" side more than the average female. Neither of them seems to think of herself as less competent or less powerful than her partner, nor do they express their individuality vicariously; each one is involved in her own projects. Moreover, the women have many other close relationships, which further decreases their dependency. The men also show few signs of supermasculinity. They do not deny their emotional needs, nor do they undermine their partners' moves towards independence and success. Greg seems more androgynous – more emotionally expressive and concerned with intimacy – than Michael, perhaps because he is younger, perhaps because he is not committed to a job that encourages him to be impersonal and competitive. Finally, it is probably significant that neither couple has young children. In the early childrearing years, the burdens of marriage and parenting are so great that most couples probably have little energy to focus on developing their selves or their relationship.

A less expected similarity among the couples is the way they describe their love in terms of a reassuring physical presence. In Greg's words, "I enjoy her presence even when we say nothing." Their words are reminiscent of the attachment between mother and child and the reassurance that a child feels from the physical presence of his mother or primary caretaker.[10] They suggest that transferences from early relationships work in positive as well as negative ways, and that part of the somewhat mysterious bond that keeps some couples together while others separate is an unconscious conviction that they are connected and safe with their partner as they once were with their mothers.

These four individuals illustrate how self-development and enduring love can be mutually reinforcing in a relationship that balances security and freedom. The rules and expectations that make their relationships secure and supportive are relatively unconstricting. Instead of adopting the roles of Companionship marriage, they have developed their own more flexible codes, so that Ann can have male friends and Lisa and Greg can go off with other people during the weekend. Each couple also belongs to a network or subculture that supports their rules for combining commitment and freedom, such as Ann's encounter group and Greg's family and friends.

Some conflict between developing oneself and marriage remains. As Ann comments "the bad part is it's limiting. Sometimes I'd like to go try somebody else, sort of, and you can't. I mean I don't because I don't want to run the risk . . . You don't know the road not taken and that's the cost of marriage."

But couples that choose Independence, like Lauren and Blair, seem to limit themselves more, cutting themselves off from the possibility of enduring love and the self-development that can come from love. Given the alternative ideals in our time – Interdependence, Independence, and Companionship marriage based on polarized gender roles – Interdependence is the best blueprint for many couples.

10
Friends and relatives

Our culture increasingly emphasizes the couple as the major close relationship for adults; the very word "relationship" has come to refer to heterosexual and homosexual couples. But Americans are spending a smaller proportion of their adult life in a stable couple relationship, as divorce increases, the age of marriage rises, and the years of widowhood lengthen.[1] "Love in America" includes friends and relatives as well as couples.

Bonds with friends and relatives also can be instructive models of an Interdependent relationship. Unlike married partners, friends of the same sex do not have to overcome restrictive family and gender roles. Friends must create their own culture, their own expectations of commitment and support, in order to create an enduring intimate relationship. Those that succeeded are often excellent models of how love and self-development can be mutually reinforcing. Extended families, especially among the working class, provide models of emotional and material inter-dependence among a network of people instead of an isolated couple. The close family ties of men who are not preoccupied with their careers also show how involved men can be in close relationships, when their jobs do not push them towards independence.

BEST FRIENDS

Committed friendships are models of a secure relationship without restrictive and hierarchical roles.[2] Compared with marriage, there are few social rules about how to behave, and people are free to make and break friendships with little public notice. Thus among middle-class women, the current rules about close friends include an expectation that they will confide their troubles, give first priority to their husband and children, and avoid sexual contact. Within these limits, the rules of friendship can be minimally oppressive because they are created and changed by the immediate participants. Equality is also easier to attain in friendship than in marriage because friends are usually similar in age and social background and are the same sex, so their relation is not structured by the pattern of females being weak and dependent on males.

The self-created character of friendships also has disadvantages. It is hard to maintain commitment to a relationship and the rules that structure it when only two people are involved – the entire structure can collapse if one person "forgets" or has a change of heart. In other ways, encouraging self-development in a friendship involves the same issues as in marriage: being interdependent instead of extremely dependent or independent, sharing a broad range of expressive and instrumental activities, and establishing a supportive and secure bond.[3]

"We have never said straightly out that we love each other in the friendship sense . . . we are afraid that people would take it the wrong way." Chris and Jenny, two women of twenty who have one of the most loving, interdependent relationships I have encountered, express their feelings indirectly.

Chris and Jenny grew up in the same small town in southern California and have been close friends for five years, since junior high school.[4] They took all their classes together and studied and played together. On the weekends, Chris explained, "a lot of times we do something physical and we really enjoy that, you know . . . ride our bikes for hours." Chris feels closest to Jenny when they are working on something together. "I like to be doing something we both enjoy. It is a good time to talk. Even when we don't talk you can feel the harmony."

They also share their families:

> We are kind of adopted by each other's family. Jenny is considered like a sister by all my brothers and sisters and I'm considered part of her family. We just walk into each other's house anytime . . . My two youngest nieces think of her as much of an aunt as they do me. She participates in all the family events surrounding them like birthdays, christenings, pictures. They even call her auntie.

Chris is twenty-one years old, the youngest of six brothers and sisters, and currently "in limbo" about where she is headed. Her older siblings have left home; her parents are busy. "Everybody is involved in something special and I am not." Jenny, according to her mother, "has always been shy" and has always had one best friend. "She is the perfect image of her father" and has an especially close bond with him:

> They both have similar hobbies. Jennifer really likes sports and can talk about them with her dad as good as any guy. When they are together they hardly ever really talk about serious things like I do with her sometimes . . . They can work on something for hours and never say anything, but you can just feel they are sharing and communicating.

Jenny and Chris's friendship combines the "masculine" style of instrumental help and wordless harmony while doing something together, with the "feminine" style of emotional support and talking about personal experiences and troubles. "They seem to read each other's needs," Jenny's mother said, and give without being asked. "Chris picks up on the subtle clues I give off," Jenny commented, and gives me "silent support, something you can just feel." When Jenny used to be studying in high school and would get "bogged down, I would hear the phone ring and it would be Chris wanting to know if I wanted to hit some tennis balls around. I know a lot of times that she had better things to do." When Chris was upset because her married brother moved back home, Jenny would leave her homework and "just stop by, maybe put her in the car and we would go for a drive or go get yogurt."

Providing help is not associated with domination, as it often is when men help women, because the help is reciprocal, and both friends acknowledge their mutual dependency, and tend to give help only when the other wants it. As Chris comments, "I like to have Jennifer with me when I just need someone there for moral support like when I'm going for a key job interview or when I am enrolling in college. Jennifer not only knows more about that stuff, she only intervenes when I ask her to."

Love rarely conflicts with freedom and self-development, in this relationship. Instead, the two friends support each other's independent development with encouragement and sometimes criticism:

> I use Jenny as a mirror. I see myself in her through her reactions to what I am doing . . . She has made me more aware of what is good about myself and what I have to offer to the world. I have learned from her that I don't have to mold myself to everyone else . . . Jenny has taught me to find my own limitations and not let anybody else tell me what they are . . . She lets me know when I veer off the track or when I take a big step forward.

For example, one time Chris studied hard for an exam and acted as if it weren't very important when she got an A, and Jenny came and congratulated her for being so disciplined and studying hard and took her out for yogurt. "She doesn't make a lot of it," Chris explains, "but you know she's in there rooting for you. Always. Everyone should have their own personal fan, don't you think?" And Jenny describes how her self-development has been helped by Chris. Chris

> has given me the confidence to go after my degree . . . she told me I could do anything I wanted academically . . . She was also the main force in me starting to really take care of my body . . . She swims and I run but we encourage each other. It gets hard to get out there everyday and do it, sometimes you are so tired and you ache all over. We support each other on these days. I count her laps and she rides the bike along with me if I need a little extra motivation. We help each other get to where we want to be.

This fall, at the age of twenty, Jenny left home to go to college in San Francisco. The two friends are determined to keep their special bond in spite of their separation. "There just aren't many people who would give you the total support and unconditional love that Jenny does," says Chris. "I will work as hard as I can to keep what we have through marriage, our own families, jobs, and old age." Jenny has been homesick and unhappy at college, but "Chris is behind me all the way and keeps me in line. When I talk of giving this up [quitting school] she tells me 'do the work the way you always have and you will be fine, and quit ragging on all the bad things.' . . . I needed someone who I trusted to give me a kick in the butt."

Last weekend Jenny called from college, Chris recounted: "I kind of heard something in her voice, I think, so I offered to come down that night. Well I could tell she was glad so I just forgot my previous commitments and left." They went to visit Jenny's aunt, and the aunt said "she hadn't heard Jenny laugh like that since we stayed with them this summer." Chris's visit seemed to help. "I think it was good for Jenny to show me where she lived and goes to school. It made us feel that we were each a part of it, her doing the actual work and me standing invisibly behind her even though I wasn't there."

The combination of commitment and freedom from constraint in this relationship is remarkable. They are loving without much jealousy or possessiveness. They can count on each other to give support, even when it is very inconvenient, without holding each other to rigid expectations. Chris's encouragement of Jenny separating from her and going away to college is an impressive example of how love can free the other person to develop, an example that few marriages can match. Even if a married couple were personally able to overcome their jealousy and neediness, social expectations about marriage would make it difficult to encourage one's spouse to strike out in new directions the way Jenny and Chris encourage each other.

"Their friendship is the envy of many people of all ages," says Jenny's mother. "People just enjoy being around them when they are together . . . One thing that really amazes me is the way they can each have boyfriends and spend a lot of time with their guy and neither one of them gets bent out of shape or seems to feel left out." But despite their families' support for their friendship, Chris feels uneasy about how other people will interpret their intimacy. She fears they won't understand that two people can be so close "and not have a sexual interest, which there is none, and I hope this [interview] makes people realize the fact that it does exist and that it can be wonderful."

There are problems in the friendship. A small problem is that Jenny sometimes gets drunk. Then "she changes into a totally different person, a real obnoxious loud drunk," but it happens rarely, says Chris, and "I just pack her up and take her home when it does." A bigger problem is Jenny's distress at leaving her family and Chris. "I don't want to depend on anyone," says Jenny. "You get disappointed, that's what always happens. It is much easier to just count on yourself, then when you move away or something you don't have this much trouble adjusting to leaving your friends. I still miss Chris all the time. I have to stop." She realizes that Chris is actually being very supportive, but the pain of separation is making it difficult for her to perceive Chris realistically and to express her own vulnerability and dependency. Instead, she feels angry and betrayed, and considers denying her need for Chris. "I feel deserted sometimes and it hurts . . . I blame Chris when I miss her a lot. She could be here. She could listen more closely to what is bothering me now." Sometimes Jenny fears that their friendship will end, "now that we are both taking different paths and that we don't have the daily things in common any more," and "in the bad moments," she considers breaking off the friendship before this happens, to avoid the pain. Jenny is also curtailing her social life at college for fear of making Chris jealous of any possible new friends. "I am just concentrating on not losing what I had instead of building up anything new . . . I am treating this thing like a summer camp; just hang on and survive and it will be over soon. My goal now is Thanksgiving."

This extraordinary friendship may not survive the strains of being apart, of Jenny's internal conflicts, and of social pressure to follow the "normal" path and focus on love with a man. Jenny says she looks forward to the day when she will have "everything I want," and that turns out to be "a man who loves and respects me . . . like what my parents have in their relationship, and also to be a terrific teacher, have a career and a family, be a good mother." And, she adds later, "I hope that Chris is still a part of my life."

Jenny and Chris's friendship shows that it is possible to create a secure, committed relationship without restrictive social roles. Some outside legitimation for the relationship may be crucial – in this case, the families of both women support the relationship – but it is not necessary to have an elaborate set of expectations that is widely shared throughout the society, like family and gender roles before the sixties. Their relationship integrates love and self-development, giving each of them dependable affection, encouragement to try new activities, and freedom to change. They also model an androgynous love that combines "feminine" expressiveness and verbal disclosure with "masculine" physical activities and practical help.

Such a friendship is obviously rare. In fact, most people in our society probably do not have a close bond with someone who is not their lover, spouse, or kin. When a random sample of northern Californians were asked to name the people they turned to for advice, sympathy, money, and other kinds of support, only 23% of those named were friends, while 42% were relatives. None the less, friendship is an important social bond for many people, providing companionship and support, and fostering their self-development.[5]

FAMILY NETWORKS

Many Americans look to the family, not the couple, for their closest relationships. Sixty percent of Americans visit a relative at least once a week, according to a 1978 survey, and the bond between parents and their adult children is extremely important in providing material help and emotional support.[6] Especially in long-term crises, such as extended illness or periods of unemployment, people of all social classes turn to their kin. Among working-class people and ethnic minorities, people's primary attachments throughout their lives are often with their parents and their children, and the collective welfare and economic security of the family tend to be valued more than the intimacy of the couple or the development of the individual.

This emphasis on material interdependence among a network of kin sometimes leads to happier marriages and more self-development than the middle-class, couple-centered way of life. Under the right circumstances, a working-class kinship network can foster more androgynous, interdependent relationships than a middle-class marriage. Masculine styles of love, like giving practical help, are more appreciated, which makes it easier for men to participate in close relationships, as long as they have enough economic and psychological resources to enable them to provide help. Many of the services that are bought by more affluent families are provided by kin, such as house painting, carpentry, help in moving, or babysitting. "Our families are like a large council," said one man. "If this one knows more about legal problems, we talk to him, if another knows more about cars, we talk to him."[7] What probably is lacking in many working-class families is the feminine style of love – empathic communication, and verbal affection and encouragement. But families that appreciate emotional support as well as instrumental help have a more androgynous image of love than most middle-class families.

Another reason that working-class men are often more involved with their families is that they are less preoccupied with individual success in their careers. These differences are reflected in the reasons people give for moving to another town. Working-class families typically say they are moving to get away from troublesome relatives, while middle-class families say they are moving to advance the husband's career.[8] Middle-class men typically are very committed to a job that rewards them for focusing on their independent achievements and for being impersonal and competitive with people at work. Men who have such jobs may be unable to experience mutual dependency and intimacy in their private lives. (This probably happens less frequently with women, since they are not so identified with their work.)[9]

The conflicts between public and private roles were described by a group of single professional men. "If I weren't successful, most of the women I know would lose interest in me," said a divorced stockbroker, "but success is difficult, and you pay a high price for it. If I am successful, it's because I'm dedicated, competitive, and driven . . . but then they want me to be a totally different person with them" "Society just doesn't allow you to be emotionally integrated," a Chicago lawyer explained.

> Something has to give. Either you end up being too soft at work, or else you're too tight and controlled at home . . . But women . . . seem to be searching for some kind of androgynous man, a man who has all the qualities and sensitivities of a woman. I think they want some new kind of species that hasn't evolved yet.[10]

There are some examples of this "new species" among working-class men with jobs that are not too consuming or competitive, yet give them a sense of accomplishment and enough money to feel that they are good providers.

Working-class life also encourages more equal dependency between husband and wife in some respects. Men lack the high incomes and respected careers that give middle-class husbands a considerable power advantage over their wives, and women's ties with relatives make them less emotionally dependent on their husbands.[11]

These positive features of a working-class family-centered way of life are often outweighed by the negative effects of poverty and rigid traditions. The lower the income, the more likely that family relations will be undermined by the constant worry about paying bills, the fear of unemployment and other disasters, and the husband's sense of economic failure. Fear strengthens personal rigidities and failure may lead men to withdraw from family life. To maintain their dignity, the men often fragment different areas of their experience and keep work and home separate, as Mirra Komarovsky observed in her study, *Blue-Collar Marriage*. "To talk about what matters most – the bills, the fear of sickness and of the uncertain future – is only to intensify the anxiety," so these concerns are suppressed, and the suppression spreads, severely restricting the possibility of intimate communication and personal development.[12] Traditional family and gender roles, which are more prevalent in the working class, can also be very restrictive, and the value on family solidarity can preclude developing oneself as a separate person. On balance, the average working-class family is probably less successful than the middle-class family in providing the conditions that encourage self-development: security, freedom to behave in diverse ways, and interdependence. However, some working-class families like the one I will now describe are rare models of androgynous love.

INTERDEPENDENCE IN A WORKING-CLASS FAMILY

John Blaine is thirty years old and has been married for eight years.[13] He has a high-school education and has found his vocation as a truck driver, enjoying his work immensely, as well as making a good income. The most important people in his life, he says, are his wife Carol, who works in an office, his five-year-old-son Brian, and his mother-in-law. John and his own mother are not on speaking terms, and he has only recently established "a very close relationship" with his father, but he is very involved with Carol's relatives, who come from the rural South.

Both John's and Carol's families have been marked by many disruptions. John was in jail several times before he joined the navy at seventeen, and Carol's mother has had three husbands and was married to an abusive alcoholic during most of Carol's childhood. In contrast to stable working-class families who emphasize security and conformity to traditional values, the Blaines are "hard-livers"; they often experience unemployment, alcoholism, violence, and desertion, and value freedom and self-expression over security.[14]

There were many deaths in Carol's family in the six years before the Blaines were interviewed: Carol's father and stepmother died in a fire, her uncle died of alcoholism, her brother was killed in Viet Nam, and her great-grandfather died. John is impressed with all the mutual aid among kin during these calamities. When Carol's great-grandfather died, relatives came from Texas and all over California and helped pay the funeral expenses.

> If you needed anything, all you had to do was ask. If you didn't ask, it was being done for you.
> *Did they help each other financially or materially?*
> Financially, really never, no one looks at it that way. Not in a dollars and cents kind of way. It's just help. It doesn't matter if it's my money, or your money – it's *our* money. Materialistic things are not so profound on my wife's side of the family. They're a very basic, down-to-earth, help-your-fellow-human-being kind of people.

Since her great-greatgrandfather's death, Carol and her family have taken care of her 92-year-old great-grandmother. Carol takes her to the grocery store and the doctor, and helps her stay active. "Right now I'm helping her out because she's making a quilt for my mom, for my mom's birthday ... So I went over to Sears and got a sheet for her for the backing. Last week she needed some of the padding, so I went over to Penney's and grabbed some ... and took that over and had lunch." As Carol's mother explained, "I think you thrive on a family ... A family feeds upon each other. I mean give each other something. We just know that when everybody else deserts you, your family won't. Sometimes they'd probably like to."

John and Carol's daily life is shared with Carol's mother and stepfather, and the two couples are bound together by a great deal of material sharing as well as affection. "My mother-in-law is a great person," John explains. "She's really into Brian. So's my father-in-law. They're like friends. We spend more time with them than with anybody else." Although the couples live in separate houses, they seem like one family:

> They came over here this morning to show us their new car. Carol's going over there now. And I was over there earlier. They have the keys to our house and we have the keys to their house. If I'm over there, I'll check out the place, have a cup of coffee. If he's over here, he'll come on in. They'll pick up Brian and come over and play for a while. We have a big back yard here; he has none. My father-in-law and I own a jeep between us. And a trailer. And I have three dogs. We're a big family here. My father-in-law and I keep things here in my back yard. We're always changing things back and forth and giving things to each other.

The material interdependence within this extended family fits previous accounts of working-class life, but their emotional interdependence and androgynous gender roles are unusual. John is very androgynous in his close relationships, combining a masculine interest in giving practical help with a feminine ability to talk about personal experience and be sensitive to others' feelings. He describes the "immediate rapport" he had with one of his best friends. From the first moment it was "like we've always known each other. It's just overwhelming. We talk about everything between each other. To me that is trust that you can't have with anyone but your best friend or two." And he continued in the interview with a long and subtle description of his relationships, in contrast to the shorter, more impersonal responses of most men.

John is also very involved with his son and his marriage. When he was asked about his goals in marriage, he answered:

> I just like to see my wife happy ... I go about my business in life, making my wife happy. And Brian. I love Brian. Brian's great. If I'da known I was gonna have a boy like Brian, I'da wished for twins or more. Really, he's fantastic. That and trucks. Trucks is it. I've always been fascinated by trucks.

Every night, John says, he talks to Brian about what he learned at nursery school. "He'll tell me what he learned and I'll throw a couple of other things at him . . . He understands completely what I say to him. That's the kind of rapport we have. I talk to him and he understands – it's like talking to a midget." Carol's mother comments, "As far as John is concerned, that child's name is Jesus Christ." And Carol mentions John's attraction to other children and his protectiveness towards animals. For a man, he is unusually focused on relationships and children, and protective of the weak.

His sensitivity to his wife's moods is also unusual. He describes her as "a very loving, warm, dependent human being. To me she radiates easiness. We've been really happily married for eight years. It's so easy." But when she's upset:

> She's quiet, there's no glow to her face . . . She snaps at Brian sometimes and gets a little short-fused. That's a sign that something's wrong . . . You let it go for a while; maybe it'll go away, maybe she's just got a headache. If it's something that goes on from day to day, and it's more than three or four days, I start looking for the problem. I'll ask her . . . how's it going at work. Get her to talk to me about what's on her mind . . . You've got to talk about it or it's not going to get any better.

Although John does not use the jargon of the therapeutic ethic, he believes in the value of communicating about personal problems.

Carol appreciates his sensitivity and skill in helping her feel better, and admits that she has more difficulty in self-expression than he does, reversing the typical gender roles. When asked what she would do if she had any personal problems, she says,

> I'd hold it in. No, really, it depends. There's a girl at work that I can talk to, if I need to talk to her. We're pretty good friends. I'm learning to share my problems with John, but he has to sort of pry it out of me. He can always tell when something's wrong with me.

Carol and John's marriage seems loving and secure, but less intense and self-consciously worked at than the other relationships I have described. For both of them, their marriage is one connection in a larger web of relationships that includes her parents and their son.

This network of loving, interdependent family relationships has helped John develop from a dominating, insensitive young man into a warmer, more androgynous person. "When I first met him, he was, you know, 'This is the way it is. This is the way it's going to be,'" Carol said.

> It didn't matter if it affected me or Brian or what. And I told him "I can't live that way because it does affect me and Brian . . . You gotta start thinking about other people, and not just you," because that's what he's used to. Because he sort of brought up his own self. He didn't have a mother to bring him up and give him the love, and all the things that I had. And the

thoughtfulness of other people, besides your own soul. His own self [was all he had].

The lack of loving relationships in his childhood explains John's limited development at the beginning of their marriage, Carol believes, and she implicitly uses a social theory of the self.

Carol's mother describes how John was changed by becoming part of her family:

> When Carol started with John, I thought I'd die . . . He was a smart-ass little brat was what he was . . . And he's saucy, he tries to rule, run everything. We have to tell him where, what he can run and what he can't run . . . But it really has gotten better . . . He's a very warm person, and he didn't used to be . . . And I think that it's because he has seen how . . . a family operates and a family does care.

At first, John was emotionally distant with Carol's family, following the patterns in his own family, in which each person was "off on their own, doing all their own things." For Carol,

> My family is my *life* . . . And he didn't understand that. And each time the family reunion would come up . . . he'd always go off to the side of the room and sit there and read the newspaper [as his parents had done when he was a child] . . . Now it's completely different. He jumps at the idea of having dinner . . . He's closer to my family than he is his. And it helps me to love him more, when he is sort of conforming to *me*, too.

John's attachments to his wife, his son, and his in-laws are helping him develop the dependent, trusting, and sociable parts of himself. He probably remains much more tense and fearful than he realizes; his inability to admit any problems in his marriage – "it's so easy" – and his unrealistic conception of his son as a miniature adult suggest that there are many parts of external and internal reality that John cannot allow himself to see without anxiety. Hopefully, he will have time to consolidate his personal gains before he has to cope with a serious crisis like unemployment or a major problem with Brian.

Carol has also developed new parts of herself, largely as a result of confronting John and getting a job. She is described by herself, her mother, and John as a warm, accepting, and dependent person. As she says, "I need to rely on people because they've always been there. They've felt like they've always needed to be there for me. I was the baby of the family." But she has learned to be able to stand her ground since the earlier years of her marriage. "In the very beginning of our marriage I did all the giving."[15] When he was angry he wouldn't talk to her for days, and that, Carol said, "would drive me crazy." Now,

> I don't let him run my life like I did in the beginning of our marriage. And this all stopped when I went back to work. We did have a little tiff about me

going back to work. He thought that my place was at home raising Brian, and doing all that. And I tried to get it across to him that Brian and I are at a point where we're bored with each other ... So finally I decided to come out and say, "I'm going back to work. and that is that." He needed help financially, you know, in our financial state ... and now everything is fine. He doesn't mind me working anymore.

After eight years of marriage, Carol concludes, "I feel myself stronger in my personality and my own feelings ... he's just become more sensitive and I've become more aggressive." In spite of their troubled childhoods, they are both becoming more androgynous, developed people.

Their family ties benefit their relationship and their individual development. Her mother and stepfather help care for Brian and would give them financial assistance if they needed it. John seems to have found the warm home he never had, helping him to become warmer and more connected to others, and Carol's move towards self-assertion may have been encouraged by support from her mother and by the power she has because John depends on her family. Kinship also restricts them. Their dream of moving to the northwest has been postponed because they feel obliged to stay and care for Carol's great-grandmother. They are also limited by lack of money – they would like to travel to visit their friends and relatives, but they cannot afford it.

The friendship of Jenny and Chris and the family ties of the Blaines extend the current conception of Interdependent relationships. Both relationships integrate emotional support and practical help and encourage participants to move away from restrictive gender roles. In addition, Jenny and Chris demonstrate the possibilities of creating a secure relationship that is not based on constraining roles and as a result fosters a great deal of change and development in both partners.

Carol and John, who are older and much more enmeshed in the demands of childrearing, family and work, show how experiences outside the intimate dyad can contribute to self-development. Their jobs have been very important to their development. Carol's growing independence was supported by going to work, and John is able to combine masculine and feminine qualities partly because he has a job that gives him pride and an adequate income, yet leaves him time and energy for his family and does not pressure him to be impersonal and independent. Carol and John are also more interdependent with their relatives than the other marriages we have considered, more successful at bridging the gulf between the intimate couple and wider communities. Their relationship suggests new images of love that more fully integrate what has been split apart since the nineteenth century: material production and personal relationships, masculine and feminine, public and private life.

Conclusion

11

Current trends and future possibilities

Interdependent relationships combine enduring love and self-development. Contrary to the critics' charges, the "therapeutic ethic" is in many ways a useful guide to committed relationships. Psychoanalytic theory explains how a close relationship that is interdependent and secure, and encourages a broad range of behavior, can foster the kind of androgynous self that many Americans desire. The particular cases described in the last chapters give concrete illustrations of the process.

The trend from role to self has been negatively evaluated by most scholars because they focus on the theme of independence in contemporary conceptions of love and self, and ignore the importance of interdependence. While both themes are influential, my assessment is that interdependence predominates in the language and behavior of married people and committed couples.

The Independence blueprint is an unworkable guide to self-development and committed relationships, as Lasch, Bellah, and others have argued. A stable self is a social product that develops out of enduring relationships, and shared beliefs and values. An independent individual cannot create his or her own self, contrary to what some popular psychologists suggest. Two independent individuals, like Lauren and Blair, who are committed only to openly communicate their feelings and needs, are unlikely to achieve either enduring love or self-development.

The Interdependence blueprint, in contrast, views self-development as the product of intimate relationships, often using the therapeutic relationship as a model. Greg and Lisa's description of how they have helped each other grow up exemplifies this perspective. Their relationship is androgynous in two senses: love is the responsibility of the man as well as the woman, and it includes "feminine" emotional support and expression, as well as "masculine" material assistance. They have a relationship of fairly equal interdependence, instead of reverting to the roles of dependent woman and independent man; they encourage each other in diverse experiences and ways of relating, instead of restricting each other with rigid roles, yet they have developed their own rules and expectations to establish trust and security.

The Interdependence blueprint also has its faults. Unlike the couples in the previous chapters, communication and emotional interdependence often seem to be overemphasized, while material interdependence is ignored, and the importance of constraining rules is overlooked. Interdependence between two people also fails to link the couple to the larger society. It leaves the gulf between private and public life intact and may even reinforce it by directing so much energy to intimacy and self. But changing the relation between public and private life probably depends much more on changing our economy than our close relationships.

Compared to the alternative blueprints of love in contemporary society – Independence and Companionship marriage – Interdependence is a step forward. Independence leads neither to self-development nor to enduring relationships, according to most social science research and theory. The ideal of Companionship marriage can provide a blueprint for a fairly stable, family-oriented way of life, as it did in the fifties, but the cost is high – both sexes are constricted by overspecialized roles that undermine health, limit self-development, and create chronic conflicts over intimacy.

STABILITY AND CHANGE

The historical trend is from role to self, from Companionship marriage and feminized love to Interdependent and Independent relationships and androgynous love. But many of the social conditions that favour polarized gender roles and Companionship marriage show few signs of changing. Thus we can expect the Companionship blueprint to persist for many decades, along with newer blueprints.

There is much more stability in family patterns than many observers realize. For over a century, Americans have had exaggerated visions of the imminent collapse of the family. It was 1859 when a contributor to the *Boston Quarterly Review* warned: "The family, in its old sense is disappearing from our land, and not only our free institutions are threatened but the existence of our society is endangered."[1] Despite these predictions of the death of the family, most Americans still get married and have children, and most children are raised by their biological parents.[2] Thus in 1984, 76% of white women between thirty-five and fifty-four years old were married and living with their husbands. Married couples also continue to value monogamy. Eighty-five percent of the couples in a large recent study were strongly committed to monogamy and would not allow sex outside marriage under any circumstances. And living together without being married is rare – 96% of heterosexual couples that live together are married.[3]

Polarized gender roles also continue, along with many features of the nineteenth-century division of labor and imbalance of dependency. The division between the feminine, loving home and the masculine, impersonal workplace persists. Despite the enormous increase in women's labor-force participation, women continue to do almost all the child care and the regular housework. Husbands of working wives in the seventies spent an average of only ten minutes more per day on child care and housework than husbands of non-working wives. Most wives are still financially dependent on their husbands, as women remain segregated in low-paid occupations and receive wages that are a third lower than men's.[4] Many women also feel emotionally dependent on men and fearful of dealing with the outside world on their own; the thesis of the 1981 bestseller *The Cinderella Complex* is that women are held back by a conflict "between wanting to be free and wanting to be enclosed and protected."[5] With the continuing imbalance in dependency, husbands continue to dominate their wives in making decisions, and the primacy of the husband's career remains strong.[6] Gender role stereotypes have also remained surprisingly stable. Women are still expected to be emotional, concerned about others, and weak, while men are expected to be powerful, independent providers.

The stability of traditional family and gender roles in the midst of change was expressed by undergraduates from several prestigious colleges who were surveyed in 1981. Ninety-five percent expected to get married, and almost all the young women and men also anticipated getting advanced degrees and having prestigious careers in medicine, business, and other professions. When asked about their life priorities in twenty years, both women and men said their highest priority would be "to spend time with my spouse," followed by their career and spending time with their children. But 80% of the women and only 30% of the men expect to stay home or work part-time while their children are pre-schoolers.[7] This persistence of traditional roles indicates that something like Companionship marriage will continue to be an influential blueprint for many decades.

There are also many social changes that challenge Companionship marriage and encourage people to adopt the Interdependence or Independence blueprints. As more women work for wages, the balance of economic dependency in marriage is becoming more equal, although there will be an imbalance as long as women's wages are lower. An economic shift towards "comparable worth" or equal pay would be a powerful force towards more androgynous gender roles. The long-range trend towards valuing self-development will probably continue, especially if economic conditions are good and levels of education rise. The trend to more flexible family and gender roles is also continuing, part of the long-term trend towards tolerance and the spread of feminist ideology. These trends towards androgyny and self-development, coupled with the persistence of marriage, support the Interdependence blueprint. The current interest in images of "the whole earth," and the connections of human and ecological systems also contribute to the popular appeal of interdependence.[8]

Other social changes undermine committed relationships and lead to the Independence blueprint. Extreme independence is encouraged by our competitive, free-market economy and our individualistic ideology. The ideal of independence often leads to the reality of isolated individuals and impoverished mother–child households. Given the current rate of divorce, there is only a 50% chance that any marriage will endure. Most men rarely see their children after divorce and do not pay child support. In 1984, 26% of all American families with children were headed by one parent (compared with 13% in 1970), and in only 3% of these families was the parent the father. Moreover, an increasing proportion of children have no legal father, since 18% of all births were illegitimate by the early eighties. A growing proportion of American children are being raised in poverty by women without the help of a man – 35% of the families maintained by women are below the poverty level, compared with 10% of families maintained by men.[9]

Thus all three blueprints are likely to remain influential and couples will follow some version or mixture of these blueprints in their private lives. However, as the long-range trend from role to self continues, the blueprint of Companionship will recede leaving us the alternatives of Independence and Interdependence.

FUTURE POSSIBILITIES AND UNANSWERED QUESTIONS

Interdependence clearly is the better alternative insofar as couples are seeking enduring love and self-development. The critical questions then become: How can interdependence be encouraged, both as an image of ideal relationships and as a workable blueprint for daily life? How can extreme independence or individualism be discouraged? To answer these questions we need a better understanding of the causes of interdependence vs. independence; we need to compare societies and groups that vary on this dimension and identify the social, cultural, and psychological factors that seem to make a difference.

My analysis suggests that the American ideal of extreme independence is primarily caused by our capitalist competitive economy and the beliefs in the self-made man and meritocracy which justify this economy. The social history of love and gender in America shows how independent achievement became the hallmark of masculinity in the nineteenth century. In the twentieth century, the focus on the self spread to women and the private sphere and contributed to a different ideal self that was more androgynous and interdependent, and was expressed in intimate relationships, not economic achievement. But the old ideology of the self-made man persists, in the contemporary ideals of the self-actualized, self-created person, or the tough but successful business executive.

Encouraging Interdependence over Independence thus depends on changing our economy and the masculine role. Economic relationships would have to shift from "free market" to more socialist ideals and practices, emphasizing the collective responsibility of all citizens to provide for each other's material and social needs, and establishing a welfare system that would guarantee a secure minimum level of living. This economic and ideological change would probably produce a change in the masculine ideal from independent achievement in competition against others towards cooperative achievement with others. Such changes would greatly reduce the split between public and private life, because interdependence and caring for others would be emphasized in both spheres. Other concrete benefits might include greatly expanded public expenditures for the care of children, and policies to improve conditions for single mothers and other disadvantaged groups. Emphasizing material interdependence in the public sphere might also lead people to pay more attention to material interdependence in intimate relations.

Another less desirable scenario for strengthening Interdependence would be to weaken the identification of men (and to a lesser extent women) with their economic roles. The split between public and private life would remain, but private life would be the main focus for both sexes. The management of community and national affairs would be left to a ruling elite, and the democratic and equalitarian aspects of American society would decline. There are signs that such a change is occurring as men and women increasingly focus on their private lives. At the same time, local involvement in political affairs seems stronger than ever, although it is concentrated on single issues like abortion, nuclear disarmament, or ecology. Perhaps we are evolving a new way of life focused on close relationships, private consumption, and a few public issues of immediate concern. The future is uncertain, as always, but the future that many Americans desire includes a more humane, interdependent public sphere and interdependence in private relationships.

The separation of the home and workplace in the nineteenth century created a conflict between love and self-development, especially for women. The Interdependence blueprint resolves this conflict better than any existing alternative. Instead of looking back to traditional gender roles or way ahead to the distant possibility of revolutionary change, we should recognize and cultivate this positive development in American styles of love.

Appendixes

Appendix I
Study of close relationships in southern California

Between 1980 and 1983, I conducted two surveys and several intensive interview studies on close relationships. These studies were done by undergraduate and graduate students in my research seminar, at the University of California, Irvine, in Orange County, southern California. Respondents for these studies were not randomly selected, but were selected by each student, usually from among their acquaintances. Each student interviewed a particular "sociological type" of person, such as single professional men, or Mexican-American middle-aged housewives, and located five to nine individuals of this type to interview. The seminar as a whole tried to include a broad diversity of types. The majority of the respondents are from Orange County (which is not as affluent as many people assume and includes many working-class and middle-class people, and many Mexicans and Asians). About a quarter of the respondents were from Los Angeles and San Diego counties. The names and identifying characteristics of respondents who are described in detail have been changed to protect their anonymity. The respondents for each study are described below.

Students were trained to interview for about a month, and the class was limited to fifteen students so I could closely supervise their work. I prepared the questions or interview guide.

I. SURVEY OF CLOSE RELATIONSHIPS

The sample consisted of 133 adults with a median age of thirty. Ninety were male and forty-three were female. Forty-seven of the respondents had fathers with only a high-school education. The sample is very skewed towards young single males. The youth of the respondents probably created a bias towards emphasizing self-development and androgyny, but the over-representation of males probably created a bias in the opposite direction.

To determine the qualities that the respondents thought were most important in good marriage or love relationship, two research assistants, Clynta Jackson and Ann Wysocki, coded the responses to the open-ended questions listed below. A system of twenty-four categories was developed by reading through the interviews, identifying the most frequent responses and redefining and regrouping them until the researchers reached a 90% level of agreement between them in coding a particular interview. Each interview was assigned a maximum of three codes. The researchers started with the response to question 1, below, and proceeded through the four questions until three codable responses were identified.

Responses to the following four questions were analyzed: (1) "What qualities are most important for a good marriage or love relationship?"; (2) "Think of the best marriage that you have seen at close hand. It could be yours. What made that a good marriage?"; (3) "Think of the worst marriage you have seen at close hand. It could be yours. What made that a poor marriage?"; (4) "How about your (marriage, relation with lover, boy or girl friend)? What are the major strengths and weaknesses in that relationship for you?"

2. COUPLES SURVEY

106 individuals were surveyed about their couple relationship, focusing on the extent to which they had conflicts in which the woman wanted more attention or more intimacy, and the man wanted more "space" and less pressure. The respondents included forty-six couples, in which both partner was interviewed, plus fourteen individuals whose partners were not interviewed. Homosexual couples were excluded from this study. There were fifty-two males and fifty-four females, and sixty-nine of the respondents were married. The mean age was thirty-seven, and twenty-one of the respondents had fathers with no more than a high-school education.

The following questions were used:

QUESTIONS FOR COUPLES SURVEY

1. I'd like to talk to you about how you spend your time when you're not at work (or at school taking care of your children or family). What are some of your favorite ways of relaxing and enjoying yourself?
2. How about the last two weekends? What did you do that you enjoyed?
3. How about after work. What do you like to do in the evening during the week?
4. How about the last two weeknights. (Mention the two weekdays.) What did you do when you came home?
5. If you could have done anything you wanted to on (mention days) evening, what would you have done?
5a. How do you feel about what you actually did?
6. Do you get together with friends during your leisure time? About how often, once a month or once a week or less often?
7. How do you feel about the amount of time you have to spend with friends? too much time _____ about right _____ too little time _____
8. How about people that you talk to about your feelings and experiences. If something happened that really hurt you or worried you, is there anyone you would talk to about it?
    male friend (#) _____ female friend (#) _____ lover _____
    mother _____ father _____ relative (x) _____
9. How about if you accomplished something that made you especially proud of yourself, is there anyone you would talk to about it?
    male friend (#) _____ female friend (#) _____ lover _____
    mother _____ father _____ relative (#) _____

10. How do you feel about the opportunities you have to talk about your feelings? more than you need _____ about right _____ not enough _____

11. Now let's talk about your (husband, wife, current relationship). What do you value the most about (him, her)?

12. When do you feel most comfortable or happy with _____? Think of a time in the past few weeks when you felt most relaxed with _____, what were you doing?

13. Here is a list of things that many couples like to do together. Please put a "1" before the activity that you personally enjoy the most, a "2" after the one you enjoy next most etc.
    _____ being alone together quietly, reading, or watching T.V.
    _____ being with our friends at a party, or restaurant
    _____ physical love making
    _____ being alone together and talking about our feelings and experiences
    _____ being with our children, friends, or relatives at home

14. What qualities in (your husband, wife, partner) don't you like? What about (him, her) causes the most problems in your relationship?

15. When do you feel most uncomfortable or unhappy with _____? Think of a time in the past few weeks when you felt most unhappy, what were you doing? (Try to get record of several interchanges.)

16. Here is a list of things that many people would like to change in their spouse or partner. Which of these changes would be most important to you, if you could change one thing about your (spouse's, partner's) behavior? (place a "1.") Which change would be next most important? (Place a "2.") Which Next? (Place a "3.")
    _____ be less busy with work or outside interests
    _____ be more interested in physical love making
    _____ be more responsive and receptive when we talk
    _____ less over-reaction and emotionality over own problems and my problems
    _____ take more initiative in planning activities to do together
    (Comments on most important changes)

16a. How about the things that keep you together with _____. Many couples split up these days. What are some of the main reasons you stay together with _____?

17. Here are some samples of arguments that couples often have. I would like to know your reactions.
    First person: I need you to work on our relationship.
    Second person: I work all week. I don't want to work on weekends. Why can't you understand that?
    First person: I do understand. But we need some ground rules for Saturday and Sunday.
    Second person: I hate ground rules. Can't we let the rules develop naturally?
    First person: They've developed so naturally I never see you anymore.
    Second person: I need my freedom.
    First person: I need some closeness.

17a. Has this kind of argument ever come up in your relationship? (If no, ask which person respondent sympathizes with more?)

17b. (If yes) Did this kind of argument come up when you first met _____? When did it start?

To finish up the interview, I want to ask you about your work (school, family responsibilities) and then get some background information.
18. Please describe your job (school work, family responsibilities). (Note level of involvement and enjoyment.)
19. On the average, how many hours a day do you spend at work (school, childcare, and housework).
weekday _____ weekend _____
20. How important is your work (school, family) to you, compared to your relationship to _____ ?
_____ it is a lot more important than my relationship
_____ it is a bit more important
_____ it is the same in importance
_____ it is less important
21. Background information
Age _____ Sex _____ Marital status _____
Do you live alone? yes _____ no _____
If no, how many people do you live with _____ (give relation of residents to respondent)
Children: sex and ages

Parents and spouse	residence	when last seen	occupation	education
Father				
Mother				
Spouse				

Current job (or school if student) _____

Education (last degree earned) _____
Years married (or couple) _____
22. Is there anything important that we haven't talked about in our discussion? For others to understand your ideas about leisure time and close relationships, is there something else that would be helpful for them to know?
23. A major purpose of this interview is to find out if many couples have a problem where the woman wants more closeness and more time together, and the man wants more space, or more time for himself. Do you think this problem comes up with many couples?
24. What are your reactions to this interview? Do you have any suggestions for how it could be improved?
Interviewer's comments (observations and additional information)

3. INTENSIVE INTERVIEWS

Thirty-two individuals, and their spouses, relatives, and close friends were intensively interviewed. These interviews were done by three groups of students, and each had a slightly different focus. One focused on friendship, and produced the case study of Chris and Jenny by Nancy Broomfield. One focused on intimacy and self-development, and produced the case study of Ann and Michael by Eileen Pinkerton. The third one focused on a comparison between apparently good and bad relationships, and produced the case studies of the Gilmores, interviewed by

Eileen Pinkerton, Greg and Lisa by Kim Thompson, and the Blaines, interviewed by Kitty Rowley; these cases were selected as exemplifying a good relationship. Each case included four to eight open-ended interviews that lasted an hour or longer. In addition to interviewing the individual and their spouse or most "significant" other, an effort was made to interview the other two or three people who were closest to the individual. In most cases the individual was interviewed twice. The interviews were spread out over two or three months, sometimes longer, and throughout this period the interviewers discussed the case with me and the other students, identifying gaps and major themes. This technique of interviewing the personal network of one individual yielded very rich material. The cases included in this book are those that yielded the richest, most convincing material on issues relevant to my argument.

Interviewers followed a guide that I prepared, but were encouraged to deviate from this guide and follow the respondent's lead. The interview guide varied somewhat from year to year; the one used for the study of good and bad relationships is presented below.

INTERVIEW GUIDE

Topics

A. Structure of relationships

1. *Types and number of important relations*: lover or spouse; children, parents and relatives; friends, co-workers
2. *Activities and exchanges*: eat together, watch T.V., confide, give money and services, give advice or support, etc.

Sample questions

I'd like to know about the people that are important in your life now. Tell me about a typical day (week). Who would you be with that was important or close to you? How about people at work? Do you get together with anyone from the office after work? When was the last time? Is there anyone you share your personal troubles with? How about the last time you were in a difficult situation? What happened? Did you talk to anyone about it?

B. Qualities of relationships

Freedom and self-development

1. *Self-directed*: sense of control over relations; respect for desires and worth of self and other
2. *Aware*: knowledge of feelings and goals of other
3. *Open to growth*: welcome new experiences, new relations, change
4. *Zestful*: joyful
5. *Intimate*: involved, share self with other

What are some of the things about your relation with X that you like best? What would you like to change about your relationships? Have you ever tried to change anything in your relation with X? What happened? How do you make decisions about (where to live? vacations?). The last time you and X had to decide where to live what happened? What are some of the most important things on your mind these days? Have you talked to (spouse, friend) about it? Do you often feel trapped or caged in? Have you started any new activities in the past year? Made any new friends?

Commitment and security

1. *Accepted* and warm, feel connected to others, not isolated
2. *Nurturant*: give and receive care
3. *Enduring*: long-term relationship
4. *Practical*: help in providing shelter, food, healthcare, childcare, skills
5. *Integrated*: sense of wholeness, of meaningful way of life

Where do you feel safe and at home? When you're feeling sick, is there someone to take care of you? What happened the last time you were sick? How do you think your relationships will change over the next few years? Will X still be your friend (lover)? What are your major goals in your relation with X? How do you combine the demands of work and family?

C. Causes and contexts of good vs. bad relationships

1. *Supportive subculture* vs. isolation or conflicting and confusing values; friends, books, minister, therapist that support life style.
2. *Childhood experience* and personality: pattern of relating learned in childhood; model of family and friendship; capacity to trust and change based on early experiences of deprivation or gratification.
3. *Previous relations* as an adult.
4. *Resources*: money, skills in communicating and relating, access to satisfying work, quantity and quality of relatives.

D. Background data

(Form similar to question 21 on Couple survey questionnaire)

Appendix II

Trends in magazine articles on marriage, 1900–1979: number of articles supporting traditional vs. modern themes

Traditional [T]	Modern [M]	1900–1909		1910–1919		1920–1929		1930–1939		1940–1949		1950–1959		1960–1969		1970–1979	
		T	M	T	M	T	M	T	M	T	M	T	M	T	M	T	M
Self-fulfillment and flexible roles																	
1. self-sacrifice com- vs. promise	self-fulfillment indi- viduality	7	1	4	3	5	1	7	2	10	0	11	0	7	7	5	2
2. togetherness shared vs. activities vital	privacy is important	1	0	2	2	2	1	4	1	2	0	8	3	4	5	2	4
3. rigid female role vs.	flexible female role	10	7	14	4	8	10	11	7	8	9	13	5	8	10	6	13
4. rigid male role vs.	flexible male role	9	7	13	3	7	9	9	7	8	9	13	5	9	10	7	12
5. divorce is not vs. acceptable	divorce is acceptable	5	0	0	1	5	5	5	2	4	0	3	2	3	1	1	4
Intimacy																	
6. avoid conflict keep vs. up a front	communicate openly confront problems	1	2	2	0	3	2	5	3	4	0	4	6	4	8	3	10
7. sex not important vs.	sex is important	0	0	0	0	0	5	1	4	0	5	0	9	1	4	0	9
8. romance is vs. immature	romance, passion, impulse and fun are good	3	1	2	1	3	3	7	1	5	2	4	5	4	4	3	7
Percent of modern themes		33%		27%		52%		35%		38%		38%		55%		69%	

Appendix III

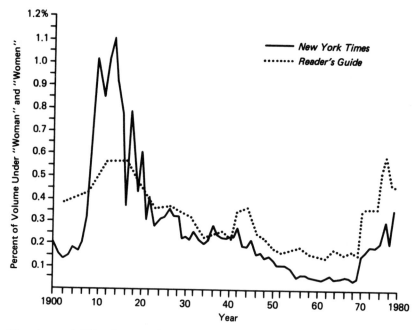

The rise and fall of women's movements in the twentieth century. From Cancian and Ross, 1981, p. 14

Appendix IV
Biology and gender

Only women can bear children. Only women can nurse – until recently the primary, safe way of feeding infants. These biological facts, along with some other innate sex differences, seem to rule out the possibility of a society where men and not women specialize in child care and love. On the other hand, the relation between biological sex and expressive and nurturant behavior varies a great deal among individuals and societies. This variation implies that men and women could be almost equally involved in attachment, given the right social and cultural conditions.

Three kinds of evidence would demonstrate the inevitability of women's being the providers of attachment: absence of variation in these arrangements across culture and time; experimental evidence that changes in the quantity of a sex-linked biological substance such as hormones produce significant changes in attachment behavior; or evidence that violation of these "natural" patterns has major negative effects in terms of individual unhappiness or social disorganization.[1]

Americans tend to assume that the natural, universal pattern of human attachment is the affectionate nuclear family, with the wife focusing on internal family relationships and the husband being the breadwinner and leader. In fact, although the bond between mother and infant may be a "natural" pattern, the relationships among mother, older children, father and other relatives vary enormously in different societies and historical periods. Love between husband and wife is no more "natural" than an attachment between uncle and nephew.

The expectation that husband and wife will love each other and be each other's main companion is a modern idea that first became popular in Europe and the Americas only in the eighteenth century. In other areas of the world, the closest relationships of husband and wife are typically with relatives of their own sex, not each other, and in many societies children are sent to other homes to be raised or to work. Even in Europe and the United States in the twentieth century, a woman's ties to her mother are often more important than her ties to her husband in working-class and poor communities, while in the upper class a man's ties to his relatives may take precedence over those to his nuclear family.

On the other hand, there are good reasons for connecting the concepts of "love" and "the family." The bond between mother and child is near universal and is usually the strongest attachment there is. Sharing a household and pooling resources will normally produce strong attachments, and so will cultural rules that define two people as related fairly permanently and publicly. Therefore, strong bonds are likely to develop in a "family" or group of people that includes mothers and children, that lives together, and that is culturally defined as permanent. Such a "family" is the (most likely) basis of attachment. But the "family" would not have to be nuclear or based on heterosexual love.

The pattern of love being a feminine speciality is much more widespread than the affectionate nuclear family. Throughout the world, males tend to be more aggressive and females more nurturant. Females are *not* more expressive in the sense of showing their feelings more; rather, they are more nurturant and give more emotional support and instrumental help.

When children in six societies including the United States were observed, girls on the average gave more help and support to others, and boys were more aggressive. In the United States, the girls were more loving and nurturant, but the size of the difference was not large; most girls and boys fell into the same middle range. There was no significant sex difference in aggression.[2]

Adult family roles in societies around the world also identify women as more nurturant. One researcher studied fifty-six societies and found that in forty-eight of them the mother was expected to be more affectionate and indulgent to the children, and family members were "emotionally attached" to her. In contrast, the father was expected to be the boss in the family economic enterprises and the "final judge and executor of punishment"; family members had a constrained, reserved relation with him.[3] These findings were interpreted to mean that a stable nuclear family requires that the mother be "expressive," while the father is "instrumental." In fact, they show that women are expected to have closer attachments to young children than men and that men are expected to be more powerful than women. Hundreds of psychological studies, done mostly in the United States, point to the same conclusion: females are more nurturant and males are more aggressive both physically and verbally.[4] There are almost no consistent differences in any of the other kinds of behaviors that psychologists measure.

There seem to be both biological and social causes for the universal link between gender, nurturance, and aggression. The male hormone, testosterone, increases aggressive behavior in both animals and humans, but no biophysiological substance that produces nurturance or affection has been clearly identified.[5] Insofar as being aggressive is incompatible with nurturance, there is a biological tendency for females to be more nurturant than males. On the other hand, social and cultural factors can overcome biological differences. Dramatic evidence of this possibility comes from humans who appear to be males when they are babies because of their external genitals and are raised as males but are biologically females in terms of internal genitals, chromosomes, and hormones. These people are generally found to behave like other males, and the same pattern appears for humans who are socially and externally female but biologically male.[6] Their social gender identity, not their biological sex, determines their behavior.

A more complex cause of gender differences is the combination of the biological fact that only women bear children and nurse with the social and cultural fact that even in modern societies women provide almost all the care of infants. It is possible that human infants have a built-in tendency to become attached to the person who cares for them during their first few months; if this is true, women's care for infants would produce a lifelong tendency for a person to bond with women. Child care by women, not men, also probably contributes to women's desire for intimacy and men's fear of it, as Nancy Chodorow's theory clarifies. In addition, people throughout the world socialize girls to be nurturant and curb their aggressiveness to prepare them for their future roles as mothers.[7] In our own society, girls are expected to play with dolls and stay close to home; they are rewarded for being considerate and are encouraged to work as babysitters – all of which trains them for nurturance.

The experience of taking care of infants during childhood is especially important in fostering nurture. In an African society in which boys often take care of infants, there is no significant difference in nurturant behavior between boys and girls, and young boys are slightly more nurturant than girls. And in the United States, where neither boys nor girls usually take care of infants, girls score lower on offering help and support than girls in any other of the seven societies examined, although they are more nurturant than the boys.[8]

A final source of evidence on the "naturalness" of women's specializing in attachment comes from studies showing the terrible consequences for the child if it is not attached to its mother. The best-known of these studies, by René Spitz, showed that institutionalized infants who were isolated from their mothers *and all other social contact* often failed to survive. Studies like this are often cited to "prove" that every child needs a full-time mother in order to develop. In fact, what they show is that infants need to be cared for by someone. Many researchers have investigated the effects of child care by one mother vs. several caretakers vs. institutionalized child care. Their findings are sometimes contradictory, but on the whole they show that children need responsive care from a small number of people; there is no clear advantage to having one caretaker as opposed to three or four, nor is there a clear advantage to having the mother as caretaker rather than another woman or man.[9]

In sum, there is strong evidence that the affectionate nuclear family based on expressive, feminized love is *not* the natural, universal pattern of human attachment. Females are more nurturant, a behavior that combines instrumental help with emotional support or expressiveness; they do not necessarily express feelings more.[10] There is no universal pattern of women being strongly attached to their husbands or heterosexual lovers; it is the bond between parent and child that usually is primary. There is also fairly convincing evidence that males have a biologically based tendency to be more aggressive than females. Thus there is some unchangeable biological basis for women specializing in love. However, there is a great deal of room for change, because the size of the difference between the sexes is small and because a substantial part of the difference between the sexes is based on gender role socialization.

Notes

1. Love vs. self-development

1 Two recent social histories conclude that individualism and self-development for women are incompatible with family bonds: Degler, *At Odds*, 1980; and Rothman, *Women's Proper Place*, 1978.
2 The history of love is examined in the next two chapters.
3 The list is taken from Broverman *et al.*, 1972. More recent, similar, findings are reported by Ruble, 1983. Unfortunately, these studies include only college students.
4 See Derlega and Chaikin, 1976; also David and Brannon (eds.), 1976.
5 Supporting evidence is presented in Chapter 5. Also, see Stockard and Johnson, 1980.
6 Gilligan, 1982, pp. 12–13.
7 Bakan, 1966, p. 15.
8 My distinction is quite similar to Simone de Beauvoir's contrast between masculine transcendence and feminine immanence. Unger, 1975, has analyzed social theories and philosophies since the seventeenth century and concluded that modern thought has been dominated by the split between desire and reason, fact and theory, and the particular and the universal.
9 The Gilmores (a fictitious name) were interviewed by Eileen Pinkerton. Appendix I describes the methods used in these intensive interviews.
10 The term "androgyny" is problematic. It assumes rather than questions sex-role stereotypes (e.g., aggression is masculine); it can lead to a utopian view that underestimates the social causes of sexism; and it suggests the complete absence of differences between men and women, which is biologically impossible. None the less, I use the term because it best conveys my meaning: a combination of masculine and feminine styles of love, or a combination of parts of the self identified as masculine or feminine. The negative and positive aspects of the concept "androgyny" are analyzed in a special issue of *Women's Studies* 2 (1974), edited by Cynthia Secor. Also see Bem, 1983.
11 These changes are documented in Veroff *et al.*, 1981, and in other studies discussed in Chapter 3.
12 See Bellah *et al.*, 1985.
13 This paragraph typifies the views expressed in Bellah *et al.*, 1985; and Lasch, 1978.
14 Peck, 1978, p. 168. This was largely ignored when first published. It became a bestseller when republished in 1985.
15 See Veroff *et al.*, 1981; also Yankelovich, 1974 and 1981.
16 Typical examples are Jacoby, 1975; Lasch, 1977 and 1978; Bellah *et al.*, 1985.

17 Clecak, 1983, p. 115.
18 Zaretsky, 1976, presents a very useful, partly positive analysis of the human potential movement. Other positive books are briefly mentioned in Lasch, 1984, Chapter 1.

2 The feminization of love in the nineteenth century

1 This historical description, which focuses on the white middle class in New England and the other eastern states, is based primarily on the work of Ryan, 1979; Cott, 1977; Welter, 1966; Degler, 1980.
2 Demos, 1979.
3 This description of family and gender roles in the colonies draws heavily on Ryan, 1979.
4 For example, the puritan minister, Cotton Mather, warned that "sloth and idleness in husband or wife are sinful and shameful." Ryan, 1979, p. 12.
5 *Ibid.*, pp. 23–4.
6 *Ibid.*, pp. 24–5.
7 Ryan, 1981. See Stone, 1979, on the transformation in England, and also Goode, 1963; and Shorter, 1975.
8 Ryan, 1981, p. 33.
9 In a typical court case, the Oneida County Court ordered a man to support his aging father, to avoid expense for the town. Ryan, 1981, pp. 24 and 39.
10 *Ibid.*, pp. 9.
11 *Ibid.*, pp. 44.
12 Johnson, 1978, p. 43.
13 *Ibid.*, pp. 46.
14 *Ibid.*, pp. 57.
15 Demos, 1974, p. 433. Also see Johnson, 1978.
16 Johnson, 1978, p. 7. Degler, 1980; and Ryan, 1981, describe childrearing in the nineteenth century, and for an incisive analysis of mother–child intimacy and its relation to Freudian theory, see Poster, 1978.
17 Ryan, 1981, p. 102.
18 Both Degler, 1974, and Cott, 1977 conclude that this ideology was widely accepted in different social classes.
19 See especially Welter, 1966; Cott, 1977; Degler, 1980; Ryan, 1979; also Rosenberg, 1975; and Demos, 1979. An interesting analysis of how the ideology was created in female religious groups in the early nineteenth century is presented by Ryan, 1981.
20 Quoted in Cott, 1977, p. 64.
21 *Ibid.*, pp. 64–5.
22 Welter, 1966, p. 325.
23 Degler, 1980, p. 31.
24 Quoted in Welter, 1966, p. 326.
25 Lantz *et al.*, 1975.
26 Some historians argue that the separation of spheres increased women's status; see for example, Cott, 1977; and Degler, 1980.
27 Welter, 1966, p. 325.
28 The quotes are from Ryan, 1981, p. 147; and G. J. Barker-Benfield, in Gordon, 1978, p. 374.
29 Demos, 1974. The quote is from Rosenberg, 1980, p. 229. Historians tell us less about the masculine ideals in the nineteenth century because there is as yet no male equivalent to the feminist-inspired research on women's roles.
30 Rosenberg, 1980, p. 237.
31 Gordon and Bernstein, 1970.
32 Fiedler, 1966. See also Swidler, 1980 for a discussion of male aversion to domestic love in

our culture. Wahlstrom, 1979, shows how this image persists in contemporary mass-media portrayals of men. The psychoanalyst Erik Erikson has also noted that American myths and folksongs glorify the womanless, unattached man without roots.

33 See Bane, 1976, on marital dissolution, and Degler, 1980, p. 155, on household composition. Around 1870, 1 out of every 6.6 white families had servants. Taking in boarders was a popular way for a woman to bring in income, and about 20% of urban households had lodgers.

34 This discussion relies on Ryan, 1979; Degler, 1980; and Flexner, 1974.

35 Thernstrom, 1964.

36 Calhoun, 1917, p. 74.

37 Degler, 1980, pp. 131, 136.

38 Quoted in Cott, 1977, p. 160.

39 Douglas, 1977, p. 149.

40 Cott, 1977, p. 186.

41 Women's reform activities are well described by Ryan, 1979, and Rothman, 1978.

42 See Ryan, 1981, for a description of the domestic work of women in the nineteenth century and men's devaluation of this work. Douglas, 1977, also describes the increasing invisibility of women's domestic work in the nineteenth century.

43 Cott, 1977, p. 60. See Braverman, 1975, for a description of increasing discipline and alienation at work.

44 Cott, 1977, p. 168. Smith-Rosenberg, 1975, and Faderman, 1981, describe women's friendships.

45 Cott, 1977, p. 185.

46 Faderman, 1981.

47 Quoted in Rothman, 1978, p. 86.

48 *Ibid.*, pp. 85.

49 From Ryan, 1979, p. 124.

50 Goldman, 1931, p. 23.

51 Historians who take this position include Ryan, 1979; Demos, 1974; and Douglas, 1977. A related change in the nineteenth century was that children became more dependent on their parents as schooling increased and apprenticeships declined; see Kett, 1977.

52 Quoted by Rose, 1982.

53 For example, see Jacoby, 1975; Marcuse, 1964.

54 Johnson, 1978, p. 7.

55 *Ibid.*, pp. 138 and 141.

56 Stone, 1979, pp. 172–3.

57 *Ibid.*, pp. 151 and 155. Stone avoids clear causal arguments and does not assert a necessary connection between individualism and affect (see chapter 6 of his book). For other evidence on the rise of individualism and a concern with the self and psychological perspective, see Lyons, 1978; Zweig, 1968.

58 Goode, 1963. Goode labels this the "conjugal" family system. Another sign of affective individualism is romantic novels, which were extraordinarily popular in American in the middle of the nineteenth century, while in England they became very popular at the end of the eighteenth century; see Zaretsky, 1976; Ryan, 1979. The religious revivals which swept over the Northern States, in the 1820s and '30s might also be considered as a sign of affective individualism.

59 Bellah, *et al.*, 1985, pp. 33–4.

60 It is possible that intimacy increased as patriarchal authority based on the family farm declined, as the family no longer functioned as a productive, formally organized work group, and as the values of freedom and individualism spread. Degler sees the family of this period as characterized by affection and respect between spouses along with an increasing separation of men's and women's spheres, a growing focus of women on

childrearing, and a decrease in family size. See, for example, Parsons, 1954; Goode, 1963; Degler, 1980; Shorter, 1975.
61 Cott, 1977, p. 190.
62 Gordon and Bernstein, 1970.
63 On the decrease in the marriage rate, see Degler, 1980, p. 152; Stone, 1979; Goode, 1963. On the decline in husband–wife affection, see Ryan, 1979; Barker-Benfield, 1976; Demos, 1974. The increase in intimate friendships among women also suggests that women may have been missing something in their relations with their husbands; such friendships were rare for wives who had very affectionate marriages according to Degler, 1980, Chapter 7.

3 *From role to self*

1 Fixing the date of these periods is only approximate, and is based on the sources quoted in this and the previous chapter.
2 The Civil War occurred in the middle of this period, but, surprisingly, most historians do not attribute great social consequences to it. Eleanor Flexner's history of women is an exception.
3 O'Neil, 1978, pp. 143–4.
4 Chafe, 1972, p. 49.
5 Fass, 1977.
6 Rothman, 1978.
7 Fass, 1977; Newcomb, 1937.
8 Quoted in Rothman, 1978, p. 43.
9 For a poignant description of how respectable but poor married women had to hide the fact that they were working see Rothman, 1978, Chapter 2. Single life was not unattractive, given the close bonds among women, especially for the privileged few with a college education. The women born between 1865 and 1874 "married later and less frequently than any group before or since," and by the turn of the century "nearly one in five married women was childless" (Ryan, 1979, p. 142).
10 Ryan, 1979, p. 140.
11 Many of its supporters and opponents believed that women's winning the vote would change their role in the family and drastically alter electoral politics. The large amounts of money spent by the liquor industry and urban political machines to fight women's suffrage are an indication of the importance they attributed to it. On the high hopes of many suffragists about the changes that would occur after women got the vote, see Flexner, 1974; and O'Neil, 1978. O'Neil documents the conservative and occasionally racist rhetoric of the suffrage movement.
12 The eight-hour day became common during World War I and the forty-hour week was mandated by New Deal legislation in the thirties (Harris and Levey, 1975, p. 1,511). On the declining masculinity of work, see Hantover, 1980, pp. 285–302, and also Filene, 1974.
13 For a supporting argument, see Zaretsky, 1976, and for supporting evidence see Pleck, 1985; and Veroff *et al.*, 1981.
14 On the economic changes, see U.S. Bureau of the Census, 1976, pp. 164–5. On the relation of security and self-development, see Maslow's theory of the hierarchy of needs, 1970.
15 The quotation is from Lynd and Lynd, 1937, p. 80. For a description of this period, also see Chafe, 1972, and Rothman, 1978.
16 Educated people, according to many studies, are more likely to believe that they control their lives and to question authority and traditional rules. See Kohn, 1969.
17 U.S. Bureau of the Census, 1976, pp. 379 and 380. In 1924 B.A.s or first professional

degrees were awarded to 55,000 men and 28,000 women, an increase since 1900 of about 200% for men and 500% for women.

18 I am indebted to Thomas Kemper for this observation.

19 Quoted in Lasch, 1977, p. 31.

20 These quotes are taken from Rothman, 1978, p. 180.

21 Quoted in Lynd and Lynd, 1937, p. 116.

22 See the thought-provoking analysis of magazines from 1921 to 1940 by Johns-Heine and Gerth, 1949.

23 Lynd and Lynd, 1937, p. 118.

24 Newcomb, 1937. In contrast, the Lynds report that high school students in Muncie became more accepting of premarital sex and women's working between 1924 and 1935. This may be an instance of a lag in changes among working class and provincial people compared to college students.

25 Chafe, 1972, Chapter 4. The proportion of college teachers who were women began to fall in the thirties and continued to decline until the late fifties.

26 Chafe, 1972, p. 105.

27 Quoted in Chafe, 1972, p. 105.

28 Elder, 1974, analyzes the effects of the depression. Virtually all researchers find that middle-class people tend to be more modern. They value companionship between husband and wife more and having children less, and place more emphasis on self-fulfillment, tolerance of diversity, and flexible gender roles. This pattern confirms the hypothesis that economic security, prosperity, and education promote the shift from role to self. The classic study of class and child-rearing values is Melvin Kohn's *Class and Conformity*, 1969. The preference of middle-class people for self-actualization and esteem, and working-class people for belonging and security, is shown in an interesting British study using Abraham Maslow's theory of the hierarchy of needs by Gratton, 1980. Duncan *et al.*, 1973, document the greater importance of job security for working-class people. Also see Gurin *et al.*, 1960; Mason *et al.*, 1976; Gecas, 1979; and Rubin, 1976.

29 U.S. Bureau of the Census, 1976, p. 133.

30 Cherlin, 1981.

31 Chafe, 1972, p. 208.

32 *Ibid.*, p. 178.

33 For a similar interpretation, see Rothman, 1978, p. 218.

34 For an example, see Hicks and Platt's widely quoted and basically sound review of the literature on marital adjustment, published in 1970. Even Komarovsky (1962), usually very sensitive to issues of gender, took for granted the superiority of Companionship marriage. She criticized the blue-collar pattern of restricted communication and separate social activities for husbands and wives as a form of "social disorganization," failing to see that the husband's buddies and the wife's close ties with relatives and friends might provide a valuable counterbalance to the tendency of women to be overdependent on their husbands in Companionship marriages. Evidence on the role of relatives and friends in limiting wives' dependency on husbands comes from a study of British working-class families by Michael Young and Peter Willmott. They found that wives became more dependent after they moved away from their old community into a suburb.

35 Evidence of the discontent of college educated wives with their marriage is presented in Campbell *et al.*, 1976. Also Pahl and Pahl, 1971.

36 See Cherlin, 1981, for data on changes in women working and an analysis of how the fifties interrupted many long-term demographic and family trends. For quantitative data on the postwar boom, see U.S. Bureau of the Census, 1976, and Lebergott 1976. Generation and politics may explain the unusual familism of the 1950s. Perhaps the

generation that raised their families in the fifties had too many frightening memories of depression and war to feel secure, despite their new prosperity. And perhaps American politics of cold war and McCarthyism diminished people's sense of self-direction and the importance of their personal lives by enhancing the significance of government actions and patriotic values.

37 The phrase "from role to self" was suggested to me by Almond's essay (1977) on the transitions from character to role to self since the nineteenth century. Also see Turner's influential paper (1976).

38 For more detailed information on these trends see Cherlin, 1981, and U.S. Bureau of the Census, 1982. The survey on premarital sex is reported in Zelnik and Kantner, 1980.

39 Several studies document substantial shifts of public opinion towards personal liberation and away from the standards of the Companionship family between the middle of the sixties and the middle of the seventies. See, for example, Yankelovich, 1974. Cherlin, 1982, also suggests that the acceptance of divorce accelerated in the late sixties and early seventies.

40 For a history of the women's movement, see Carden, 1974; and Hole and Levine, 1971. Freeman, 1975, gives an excellent account of its legislative victories. For an analysis of media coverage of the movement, see Cancian and Ross, 1981.

41 Degler, 1980, p. 471.

42 See Friedan, 1963, on the conservative message of Freudian and other therapists in the 1950s.

43 See, for example Osmond and Martin, 1975.

44 Luker, 1984.

45 Clecak, 1983, reviews this criticism. Christopher Lasch's book, *The Culture of Narcissism*, 1978, is the critical book that had the greatest impact. On the need for commitment, see Yankelovich, 1981.

46 Kidd, 1974 and 1975. Zube's study (1972) of changing concepts of morality in the *Ladies' Home Journal* from 1948 to 1969 comes up with an interpretation similar to Kidd's. Her quantitative analysis shows a clear shift from values oriented to the future and active "doing," to values oriented to "being" in the present.

47 Bellah *et al.*, 1985, pp. 93 and 100; and Swidler, 1982, pp. 7–8. Similar findings are reported by Quinn, 1982, who did intensive interviews with eleven couples in North Carolina.

48 Harris, 1979.

49 Bellah *et al.*, 1985, p. 101.

50 See Appendix I for more details on this survey.

51 Here is more detail on the methodology. The high circulation magazines that were included were taken from a list in Kidd, 1975. In the early decades, I also selected articles listed in the *Readers' Guide* from *Harper's* and *Atlantic*. Because of the ease of obtaining articles from *Reader's Digest*, I randomly selected four articles from *Reader's Digest* and four from other magazines, after *Reader's Digest* began publication in the early 1920s. The coding system was originally developed to study changes in magazines between 1950 and 1970, therefore the categories are progressively less applicable as we move towards the beginning of the century, and the earlier articles receive fewer codes in any of the categories. The categories about gender roles are an exception; every article was coded as traditional or modern on these categories. A few articles contained very contradictory messages and were "double-scored" or counted as both traditional and modern on some categories; however, double-scoring was avoided whenever possible. The category system was refined until I reached a criterion of two coders agreeing on 85% of the coding for a particular article. This method of measuring changes in popular images of marriage has several problems. The intended audience of the magazines seems to come from a higher social class in the earlier decades, and the content of the articles partly

reflects the policies of editors and advertizers and the attitudes of the writers. None the less, the magazines seem to provide a fairly valid measure, since my findings are consistent with the other sources of data described in this chapter.

52 *Harper's Bazaar*, September, 1909.
53 Vahanian and Olds, 1978.
54 Maurois, 1940.
55 Lederer and Jackson, 1974.
56 Miller, 1925.
57 Easterlin, 1980, emphasizes the changing size of birth cohorts. He sees very little change in family blueprints and gender roles since World War II. What has changed, in his view, is young people's income relative to the standard of living they grew up with. When their income was relatively high, they lived according to their family ideals, and wives stayed home and had many children as happened in the fifties. When the baby boom generation (or cohort) reached the labor market in the late seventies wages were relatively low because the cohort was so large that wages were depressed. As a result, they were unable to live according to their ideals and had fewer children. When their children reach the labor market, their income will be relatively high because their cohort is so small, and the cycle will repeat. The relative merits of his theory and mine will be clarified by changes in the family during the recession that began in the seventies. Easterlin predicts a decline in family attachments as relative income declines. I predict a rise because hard times lower people's aspirations for freedom. See Cherlin, 1981, for an excellent analysis and critique of Easterlin. Although I agree with Easterlin that the changes in gender roles are often exaggerated, he exaggerates the stability. For evidence of major changes in women's goals since the late sixties, see Parelius, 1975; Roper and Labeff, 1977; Duncan *et al.*, 1973; Thornton *et al.*, 1983. Cherlin argues that the pattern of family change is not cyclical; rather there have been gradual changes since 1900 interrupted by the peculiar fifties. Another explanation sociologists have developed is the marriage squeeze argument advanced by Oppenheimer, 1973, and others. They argue that, because women marry men about three years older than themselves, it will be difficult for women to find attractive husbands in historical periods following a rise in fertility, since there will be more younger women on the marriage market than older men. This situation occurred in the seventies, following the baby boom. According to Heer and Grossbard-Shectman's interpretation (1981), the unfavorable marriage market for women in the seventies helps explain why a growing proportion of women did not marry, why they turned to employment instead and became involved in a women's movement to improve their situation at work.
58 The few reversals are in the thirties and the fifties. My method was to check all issues of the *American Sociological Review*, the *American Journal of Sociology*, and the *Journal of Marriage and the Family*, from 1960–1980, as well as current books on social change in the twentieth century, and the references cited in these sources, searching for studies with quantitative data on family and gender for at least two points in time.
59 Veroff *et al.*, 1981, p. 529.
60 Yankelovich, 1974, pp. 21–2. For example, 51% of college youth said they would welcome stronger traditional family ties in a survey in the early seventies compared with 61% of non-college youth. Both groups also showed an increasing acceptance of sexual freedom and a declining concern with economic security, saving money, working hard, religion, and patriotism, between 1969 and 1973. The trend towards self-development dates back to at least the eighteenth century. Lantz *et al.*, 1975, found an increasing emphasis on individual happiness as the main motive for marrying in American magazines between 1741 and 1850. For more evidence of the trend towards self-development in the sixties and seventies, see Spindler, 1977; and Duncan *et al.*, 1973. Inglehart, 1977, reports a similar trend in Europe.

61 The data on the increase in therapists is from the Encyclopedia of Associations, Vol. 20, Detroit, Gail Research Co.

62 The question on making plans is from Mason *et al.*, 1976. Thornton, *et al.*, 1983, review the changes in sex-role attitudes. On motherhood, see Gallup, 1980; Duncan *et al.*, 1973; and Blake, 1979.

63 Inkeles, 1979, comments on change since the eighteenth century. On the reversal in the fifties, Hoge (1974) shows that in 1954, 81% of a national sample said that communists should not be allowed to speak on the radio, compared to 40% in 1943. The recent revival of fundamentalist Christianity may be part of another brief reversal.

64 De Charms and Moeller, 1962.

65 See Bain, 1936; Buck, 1936; and Hoge, 1974, pp. 94–100.

66 Duncan *et al.*, 1973, p. 40; Bush *et al.*, 1977.

67 Caplow and Bahr, 1979. Bahr, 1980, found a larger drop in the percentage of female high-school students in Muncie who thought that "being a good cook and housekeeper" was a most desirable quality in a mother. For girls the percentage dropped from 52% to 24% between 1924 and 1977; the drop for boys was only from 57% to 41%. In addition, several surveys of college students found a larger shift towards equalitarian sex-role attitudes for women than for men between the fifties and the late seventies; for example, Hudson and Henze, 1969; Scanzoni, 1976; Parelius, 1975.

68 Cherlin, 1981, Chapter 1.

69 Glick and Spanier, 1980.

70 Gordon, 1978. In the forties, women and men were expected to be very interested in sex, but women were portrayed as sexually passive, while men were expected to master the complex skills required to awaken a woman and be a good lover. Lewis and Brissett's analysis of marriage manuals (1967) concludes that, by the sixties, sex had become work.

4 *The history of love*

1 As Lasch has observed, 1978, family sociologists typically stress the persistence of the family. For an example, see Bane, 1976.

2 Exchange theories that do not emphasize mutual dependence, culture, and power relations are usually politically conservative and do not challenge current gender roles. Economists use exchange models, but they tend to treat people as isolated individuals with pre-set needs that are not culturally determined. They assume that people are free to exchange or not, depending on their preferences: they ignore the way the structure of society provides different resources to different people and the fact that coercion is often part of exchange. Criticisms of exchange theory by radicals and feminists focus on this tendency to view relationships in terms of marketplace exchange. See, for example, Ehrenreich and English, 1978. Some versions of exchange theory, like Homans, 1961, take their model from classical economics and are more deserving of this criticism. In contrast, Richard Emerson's version, on which I rely most heavily, suggests a view of interaction that is much closer to Marx's than to that of free-market economists. See Emerson, 1976. Turner, 1982, presents an extremely useful and detailed discussion of exchange theory. Wallace and Wolf, 1980, point out the similarities between Marx and exchange theorists.

3 The particular resources that people value and need are shaped by their culture and social position, and their psychological makeup.

4 Blumstein and Schwartz, 1983, p. 167.

5 Lukes, 1972, pp. 26–7.

6 Durkheim, 1951. Also see Peter Marris's provocative discussion, 1974, of how meaning depends on close relationships and is threatened when these relationships are lost.

7 On the positive psychological effect of economic security, see Catalano *et al.*, 1985. The effects of security in relationships is discussed in Chapter 8.

8 In *What are Norms?*, 1975, I argue that norms and constraining rules need not be internalized into the unconscious, but can be more conscious criteria of rank and of membership in groups.

9 See Fischer's critique of these theorists, 1977. I have taken the term "decline-of-community" from him.

10 Tönnies presented the concepts of *Gemeinschaft* and *Gesellschaft* in a book published in 1887, but, as Sorokin comments in the foreword of a new edition of Tönnies, this distinction, "like many fundamental categories of social thought, . . . is in a sense eternal" and appears in the theories of Confucious and Plato (Tönnies, 1963, p. viii). These quotes are from pp. 35 and 65.

11 Bane, 1976, documents the stability of rate of marital disruption in her excellent review of evidence on the continued strength of the family. See also Uhlenberg, 1980.

12 Laslett, 1972.

13 Fischer, 1977; Crowe, 1978.

14 I am drawing mostly on "early" Marx and the *1844 Manuscripts*. See Thom, 1983, for an interesting analysis of the way Marx ignores the positive aspects of society.

15 These assumptions are supported by research on alienation at work. See, for example, Kohn and Schooler, 1983. On the relation between work roles and gender, see Kahn-Hutt *et al.*, 1982.

16 See the evidence presented in Chapter 6.

17 The review of Parsons's theory is based primarily on the following works of Parsons and his associates: *Family, Socialization and Interaction Process*, 1955; *The Social System*, 1951; and *Societies: Evolutionary and Comparative Perspectives*, 1966; and his essay on the family and kinship, 1954. Parsons made several useful contributions to understanding the trend from role to self, pointing out how family relationships became more intimate and more attuned to self-development – or personality maintenance – as a result of the split between the family and the workplace.

18 See Gilligan, 1982, for an analysis of such theories of psychological development. Weinstein and Platt, 1969, exemplify the same pattern in sociological theory.

19 See Engels, 1902, p. 79, and Marx's *1844 Manuscripts*. For a radical, feminist theory, see Firestone, 1970.

20 Psychological studies of androgyny are reviewed in Cook, 1985. On the negative consequences for children of sharp gender differentiation by parents see Slater, 1970; and Stockard and Johnson, 1980. Lewis and Spanier, 1979, present evidence on the causes of marital happiness and stability.

21 Rieff, 1966, p. 4.

22 *Ibid.*, pp. 30–31.

23 Bellah *et al.*, 1985, pp. 82–3 and 282–3.

24 *Ibid.*, pp. 72, 76 and 101.

25 Bellah *et al.*, 1985, p. viii.

26 See for example, Fisher, 1982. Bellah *et al.*, 1985, qualify their attack on 'lifestyle enclaves,' as they qualify almost all their assertions (pp. 72–5). But I ignore this in my brief analysis of their position because their qualifications take back almost all their assertions.

27 Bellah *et al.*, 1985, pp. 102–7.

28 See Clecak, 1983.

29 Lasch, 1977 and 1978.

30 See, for example, Jacoby, 1975. Their argument is based on Herbert Marcuse's concept of "repressive desublimation," 1964. The clearest statement of this position is in Jacoby, 1975. It is also used by Lasch, 1977 and 1978; Sayre, 1978; and Sohn, 1980.

31 Lasch, 1977, pp. xiii and xiv.
32 Lasch, 1977 and 1978. Social critics also explain the crisis in the family in terms of the split between the public and the private sphere. They argue that people are increasingly disengaged, powerless, and isolated in the face of a bureaucratic government, alienating jobs, and disintegrating communities and kin networks. As a result, they lose interest in the public realm and withdraw to private, egoistic concerns that permit them to experience human contact and power. Relationships also become more fragile because such a great burden is placed on them, in the absence of ties to other groups. Sennett, 1977, has an idiosyncratic interpretation of the retreat to intimacy that is based almost entirely on the public–private distinction. His main argument is that the expressive orientation of the private sphere has invaded and destroyed the instrumental, rule-bound public sphere. See Brittan, 1977, for a more orthodox discussion of the public–private split.
33 The conservative bias of Lasch and others has been criticized by Poster, 1978; Wolin, 1977; and Wrong, 1979. See Zaretsky, 1977, for an apt critique of the elitist and apolitical nature of much social criticism. Clecak, 1983, Chapter 12, gives a perceptive analysis of why critics labeled the seventies as narcissistic or selfish. Studies on contemporary Americans are described in the last half of Chapter 3, and include Veroff *et al.*, 1981. It is interesting that the magazine articles on marriage analyzed in Chapter 3 began to de-emphasize self-development as opposed to self-sacrifice after the middle of the seventies. The attack on "narcissism" by Lasch and others may have been part of this decline and may also have helped bring it about.
34 Zaretsky, 1976, p. 30.
35 *Ibid.*, pp. 30 and 69. Zaretsky underemphasizes the importance of gender roles and the identification of personal life with the feminine role. He also neglects the effects of education and affluence on the concern for self-fulfillment. However, our positions are very similar in assuming a human need for love or attachment, in valuing self-development and autonomy for women and men, and in emphasizing the social and historical foundations of personal life.
36 See Lasch, 1984, for a review and criticism of these writers.
37 Clecak, 1983, p. 115.
38 See studies reviewed in the beginning of Chapter 8.
39 Morgan, 1973, pp. 82–3.
40 *Ibid.*, pp. 96–7, 20 and 244–5.
41 "Who Cares About Housewives," E.R.A. Orange County, Irvine, California, 1982.
42 Morgan, pp. 14–15.
43 This is why the backing for the radical right comes from the most conservative political and financial organizations in our society. See Boles, 1979, pp. 200–202.
44 Betty Friedan's book, 1981 is flawed – Friedan blithely asserts that men will share childrearing equally with women, despite all the evidence to the contrary. Left feminists have been intensely critical of the attempt to develop a socialist, feminist, profamily line. See Ehrenreich, 1982. On the other hand, Morgan, 1978, praises heterosexual love combined with radical politics, according to each woman's personal bent, and family commitments are emphasized by Elshtain, 1981. For reviews of different feminist perspectives, see Flax, 1982; and MacKinnon, 1982.
45 Ehrenreich and English, 1978, p. 304.
46 Ehrenreich, 1983. Her argument that men are rejecting the breadwinner role is contradicted by men's high rates of marriage and remarriage and by the fact that in marriage and cohabiting relationships, men more than women oppose the woman's going to work (see Blumstein and Schwartz, 1983, p. 125).
47 Ehrenreich and English, 1978, pp. 311 and 319.
48 For American radicals, as Peter Clecak has commented, "it is always the worst of times

in the larger society"; in all periods, "the 'hegemonic' system is relentlessly evil." See Clecak, 1983, Chapter 4 for a perceptive analysis.

49 Ehrenreich, 1983, p. 170.

5 Feminine and masculine love

1 The quotations are from a study by Ann Swidler. For useful reviews of the history of love see Hunt, 1959; and Murstein, 1974.

2 See Bowlby, 1969, on mother–infant attachment. The quotation is from Walster and Walster, 1978, p. 9. Conceptions of love and adjustment used by family sociologists are reviewed in Lewis and Spanier, 1979, pp. 268–94.

3 Alternative definitions of love are reviewed in Walster and Walster, 1978; Hendrick and Hendrick, 1983; Reiss, 1980, pp. 113–41; Reedy, 1977.

4 Maslow, 1970, pp. 182–3.

5 Stinnett *et al.*, 1970.

6 Lillian Rubin's book on marriage is *Intimate Strangers*, 1983. Intimacy is defined on page 90.

7 The emphasis on mutual aid and instrumental love among poor people is described in Rubin, 1976; Rapp, 1982, pp. 168–87; and Miller and Riessman, 1964, pp. 24–36.

8 See the evidence in Chapter 3.

9 Webster's New Collegiate Dictionary, 1977.

10 Rosencrantz *et al.*, 1968, pp. 287–95, and Rosencrantz, 1982. See also Ruble, 1983.

11 Chodorow, 1978, p. 169. Dinnerstein, 1976, presents a similar theory. Freudian and biological dispositional theories about women's capacity to nurture are surveyed in Stockard and Johnson, 1980.

12 Gilligan, 1982, pp. 159–61.

13 Radical feminist theories also support the feminized conception of love but they have been less influential in social science, e.g., Daly, 1979.

14 Ryan, 1979 and 1981.

15 Miller, 1976. There are, of course, many exceptions to Miller's generalization, e.g., women who need to be independent or who need an attachment with a woman.

16 Chodorow refers to the effects of the division of labor and power differences between men and women, and most historians, including Ryan, acknowledge the special effects of women being the primary parents.

17 The data on Yale men is from Komarovsky, 1976 and the quote is from Veroff *et al.*, 1981, p. 240. Campbell, 1981, reports that children are closer to their mothers than fathers, and daughters feel closer to their parents than sons, on the basis of large national surveys. However, people also tend to criticize their mothers more than their fathers; for example see Payne and Mussen, 1956.

18 Studies of differences in friendship by gender are reviewed in Dickens and Perlman, 1981; and Hess, 1981. While almost all studies show that women have more close friends, Tiger, 1969, argues that there is a unique bond between male friends.

19 Komarovsky, 1962.

20 Levinson, 1978, p. 335.

21 The argument about the middle age switch was presented in the popular book *Passages*, by Gail Sheehy, 1976, and various more scholarly works, such as Levinson, 1978. These studies are reviewed in Rossi, 1980. However, a careful survey by Fischer and Oliker, 1980, reports an increasing tendency for women to have more close friends than men beginning in middle age.

22 Studies on gender differences in self-disclosure are reviewed in Peplau and Gordon, 1985. Also see Rubin *et al.*, 1980.

23 Working-class patterns are described in Komarovsky, 1962. Middle-class patterns are

reported by Davidson and Duberman, 1982. Similar findings are reported in Lewis, 1978.

24 Rubin *et al.*, 1980.

25 These studies are based on the self reports of men and women college students, and may reflect norms more than behavior. The findings are that women say they feel and express more affect and bodily reactions than men, except for hostile feelings. See Allen and Haccoun, 1976; and Balswick and Avertt, 1977. Gender differences in interaction styles are analyzed in Henley, 1977. Also see Fishman, 1978.

26 Gender differences in leisure are described in Rubin, 1976, Chapter 10. Also see Davis, unpublished manuscript.

27 Adams, 1968, p. 169.

28 Lowenthal and Haven, 1968.

29 Pleck, 1981, argues that family ties are the primary concern for many men. On life goals see Campbell and Converse, 1976.

30 Reedy, 1977. Her subjects were from southern California, of a wide age range, and were selected because they seemed to be very much in love. Unlike most studies, Reedy did not find that women emphasized communication more than men.

31 Parelman, 1980.

32 Both spouses thought their interaction was unpleasant if their spouse engaged in negative or displeasurable instrumental or affectional actions. Wills *et al.*, 1974.

33 Rubin, 1976, p. 147.

34 See Rubin, 1976; also Sennett and Cobb, 1973.

35 More stable relationships for lesbians than for gays are reported by Bell and Weinberg, 1978. However, Blumstein and Schwartz, 1983, did not find this pattern. On sex differences in friendship, see Caldwell and Peplau, 1982. Part of the reason for these differences in friendship may be men's fear of homosexuality and of losing status with other men. An exploratory study found that men were most likely to express feelings of closeness if they were engaged in some activity like sports that validated their masculinity; see Swain, 1984. For discussions of men's homophobia and fear of losing power, see Brannon, 1976, pp. 1–48.

36 The quote is from an intensive interview by Cynthia Garlich. For evidence on men separating sex and love, see Hunt, 1974, p. 231; and Clark and Wallin, 1965.

37 For example, see Mackinnon, 1982. For a thoughtful discussion of this issue from a historical perspective, see Gordon and Dubois, 1983.

38 Kephart, 1967. See Peplau and Gordon, 1985, for an analysis of research on gender and romanticism.

39 Yankelovich, 1974, p. 98.

40 The link between love and power is explored further in Cancian, 1985.

41 See Flax, 1982.

42 See Chodorow, 1971 on being and doing in gender role socialization.

43 Inkeles, 1979 confirms this description of American values.

44 See Bose and Rossi, 1983.

45 Broverman *et al.*, 1970.

46 Levinson, 1978, p. 206.

6 Illness and split gender roles

1 Maccoby and Masters, 1970, review the empirical findings; see especially pp. 136–7. For a readable and clear review of the need for attachment in children, see Lynch, 1977. Some of the key works in this area are by Bowlby, 1969; and Ainsworth, 1972; see also Harlow and Harlow, 1962.

2 Gore, 1978. Other major studies of social support, stress, and illness include Nuckolls

et al., 1972; Myers *et al.*, 1975; and Eaton, 1978. For useful reviews, see Heller, 1979; and Gottlieb, 1983.

3 The evidence on the coronary care patients is reported by Lynch, 1977. The psychological experiments on the presence of strangers and reduced anxiety are reviewed in Heller, 1979.

4 These findings are reported in Parkes *et al.*, 1969. On the effects of widowhood and bereavement on health, see the review article by Jacobs and Ostfeld, 1977. On the effects of loss and the importance of grieving, see Marris, 1974. The link between losing a close relationship and cancer and other illness is documented in Schmale, 1958; and LeShan, 1959.

5 Lynch, 1977, p. 56. The case, quoted by Lynch, was taken from Engel, 1971.

6 For discussions of this scale and the methodology of measuring stress, see Holmes and Rahe, 1967; Dohrenwend and Dohrenwend, 1978; and Thoits, 1981. Studies of social stress and health were very fashionable in the seventies. For example, see Gunderson and Rahe, 1972; Liao, 1977; and Gersten *et al.*, 1977.

7 Yankelovich, 1974, and Campbell *et al.*, 1976. In most studies of quality of life, relationships outside of marriage are not carefully examined. A relation between happiness and a variety of social ties is reported by Bradburn, 1969; and Campbell *et al.*, 1976. Attachments to children have a complex relationship to happiness. If asked directly, people say that their children make them happy (see, for example, Gurin *et al.*, 1960), but people without young children are somewhat happier with their lives in general and much happier with their marriages. The negative relation between children and marital satisfaction is reviewed in Schram, 1979; also see Renne, 1971; and Glenn, 1975.

8 The estimates of murders are from Curtis, 1974, while the figures on spousal violence are from a national survey by Straus *et al.*, 1980. Heller, 1979, reviews some studies on the costs of attachment.

9 Several studies of social support and health have investigated the different dimensions of social support, among them instrumental help, emotional support, sociability, and shared beliefs or shared meanings. See Caplan and Killilea, 1976. Lofland, 1982, proposes a thoughtful list of the qualities that comprise close relationships. See also Fischer, 1982.

10 See Seligman, 1975 for the psychological theory of overdependency, and Phillips, 1980, for confirming evidence. The relation between locus of control and depression is challenged by Aiken and Baucom, 1982. The findings on alienation cannot be explained by differences in education, race, social class background, or various other characteristics, because the researchers controlled for the effects of these variables. The results of these studies are described in Kohn and Schooler, 1983. Blauner, 1964, also shows how alienation at work produces low self-esteem and a stunting of creativity and intellectual growth. However, according to Blauner, alienated workers may feel contented, especially if they are closely attached to family and friends and are socially integrated into their communities. For evidence on alienation at work and poor mental and physical health, see Frankenhauser, 1977, and Gardell, 1976.

11 For excellent reviews and analyses of the complex findings on sex and mental and physical illness, see Nathanson, 1980; Verbrugge, 1976; Kessler and McRae, 1980. Gove and Hughes, 1979, and Tudor *et al.*, 1977, argue that men go to doctors less frequently than women because they actually are healthier since their lives are less stressful.

12 Kalmuss and Straus, 1982.

13 See Blood and Wolfe, 1960.

14 Studies that have found superior mental helath among employed wives include Rosenfield, 1980; Gove and Geerken, 1977; Kessler and McRae, 1980. On the other hand, many studies have found no differences in health between the two groups, e.g., Anenshensel *et al.*, 1981. Studies of happiness usually find no difference or a slight

tendency for working women to be happier (Wright, 1978). Among highly educated women, the wives who work are much happier than housewives (Campbell *et al.*, 1976). Nathanson, 1980; and Vanfossen, 1981, document the burdens of working wives.
15 The quote is from Heller's review, 1979.
16 This study is reported in Keefe *et al.*, 1978.
17 These figures are based on national helath statistics for 1959–61, see Gove, 1973.
18 Shurtleff, 1956. He analyzed national death certificates from 1949 to 1951.
19 More physical and mental illness for the unmarried is convincingly demonstrated in Carter and Glick, 1976; Redlick and Johnson, 1974; Pearlin and Johnson, 1977; and Verbrugge, 1980. However, one national survey found no relation between symptoms of mental illness and marital status (Gurin *et al.*, 1960) and Bernard, 1972, cites several studies to support her conclusion that married women are in worse mental and physical health than unmarried women.
20 The key studies are by Cantril and Roll, 1971; Campbell *et al.*, 1976; Gurin *et al.*, 1960, and Bradburn, 1969.
21 For example, this interpretation is used by Shurtleff, 1956, and is discussed by Gove, 1973.
22 Renne, 1971, found more chronic disability and illness among the unhappily married than the happily married. Also see Gore, 1978. Mortality rates had no relation to the quality of the mariage in the study by Berkman and Syme, 1979.
23 On reasons for marrying, see the survey data described in Duncan *et al.*, 1973, p. 7. Several studies show that married people have more friends, for example, Martin, 1976; Pearlin and Johnson, 1977. Obviously, marriage usually creates ties with kin and children.
24 The Chicago study is by Pearlin and Johnson, 1977. The strong relation between low income and premature death and illness is documented in Kitagawa and Hauser, 1973; Hollingshead and Redlick, 1958; and Berkman and Syme, 1979. Also see Kessler, 1982, for an attempt to analyze why there is a relation between low social status and mental illness. Berkman and Syme also show the importance of health care practices.
25 The effects of friendships are reported in Berkman's dissertation (1977). Other studies showing that people with friends are healthier include Lowenthal and Haven, 1968, and Phillips, 1967. See the reviews of this research by Heller, 1979; and David Mechanic, 1975. A study by Brown *et al.*, 1975, found that superficial friends provided no protection against depression and other psychological symptoms for women who experience a stressful life event, but an intimate, confiding realtionship with their husband or boyfriend gave the women almost complete protection from mental illness. Also see Miller and Ingham, 1976.
26 Carter and Glick, 1976. Also see Shurtleff, 1956. Another consistent finding in studies of mortality and marital status is that the "protective" effect of marriage declines as people get older. It remains a mystery why marital status makes less difference to people's health as they age.
27 Marcuse, 1964. His concept is similar to Marx's concept of false consciousness.
28 Waldron, 1976.
29 Verbrugge, 1980. Men's reluctance to define themselves as sick and to ask for help is probably part of the reason for their higher mortality. It also helps explain why women are more likely to say they are sick and go to the doctor, but more men die prematurely.
30 This discussion of male mortality is based largely on Waldron, 1976. Males have a higher rate of fetal death and infant mortality than females, but biological factors cannot easily explain why the difference in mortality continues to widen, even after death in childbirth became very rare, and why a pattern of high mortality for men occurs in some societies but not others. Men more than women engage in risky, dangerous behavior. They smoke more; they are four times as likely as women to be heavy drinkers, and they drive

much less safely. One of the reasons that men's health benefits from marriage may be that men who live with women become more "feminine" and less likely to live dangerously and neglect their health.

31 Gove and Hughes, 1979. A study in Scotland found that women who had trusted friends were much less anxious and depressed than women who lacked such friends, but men's mental health did not depend on their close friendships. These results are reported in Miller and Ingham, 1976. Men also may need wives to help them relate to other people. Thus Berkman and Syme, 1979, found that married men have more contact with friends and relatives than unmarried men, but marital status has no effect on women's contacts.

32 Jessie Bernard's influential book, *The Future of Marriage*, 1972, is an insightful analysis of the many ways that a wife's experience of marriage is different from her husband's.

33 A repeat of a 1950 survey of mental health in New York City in 1974 found an improvement in women's mental health but not men's when some of the same people were interviewed (Srole and Fischer, 1980); and a 1976 repeat of a large national survey originally done in 1957 also found an improvement in women's mental health (Kessler and McRae, 1980).

7 *Marital conflict over intimacy*

1 Mornell, 1979, pp. 2–3.

2 Rubin, 1976, pp. 120–21. On working-class marriage, see also Komarovsky, 1962.

3 This quote and all others in this chapter not attributed to published studies are from intensive interviews about marriage and close friendship conducted by myself, Eileen Pinkerton, and Cynthia Garlich (see Appendix I).

4 The laboratory study is described in Raush *et al.*, 1974. The couple survey is reported in Ronald Burke *et al.*, 1976.

5 The 39 respondents younger than twenty-five were much more concerned with closeness. Most of them (29) were unmarried.

6 Another parallel, at least in middle-class couples, is that husbands typically seem to control the amount of talking, by vetoing or going along with their wives' efforts to talk, while wives control the frequency of sex, by vetoing or going along with their husbands' initiative. For an analysis of husbands' and wives' preferences for sex, see Laws, 1971.

7 Rubin, 1976, pp. 136 and 146.

8 Collier, 1966.

9 Rosenblatt and Phillips, Jr, 1975.

10 Similarly, if the couple believes that love is shown by an activity which is usually defined as men's "turf," such as sex, the wife is likely to feel controlled when he wants to "be intimate" and respond with withdrawal and passivity.

11 Collier, 1966.

12 Gould, 1974, p. 26.

13 Being in love seems to make it acceptable for men to be emotionally dependent and powerless in relation to a woman.

14 The cartoon was published in Calendar, the *Los Angeles Times*, 23 January 1983.

15 This pattern was reported by the national surveys described in Gurin *et al.*, 1960; and Veroff *et al.*, 1981.

16 Men may have more difficulty than women in experiencing work as intrinsically gratifying because being successful at work is required of them.

17 The power difference between the sexes has been the major focus of feminist research. For a sampling of this work, see Thorne, 1982; and Millman and Kanter (eds.), 1975.

18 Bernard, 1972.

19 Blumstein and Schwartz, 1983, p. 176 report that it is mostly young wives who want more closeness.

20 On variations in marital satisfaction over the life cycle, see Blood and Wolfe, 1960; and Glenn and McLanchan, 1982.
21 For excellent descriptions of the negative effects of their economic position on working-class couples, see Rubin, 1976; and Komarovsky, 1962. Kohn, 1969, shows the negative effects on family life of alienating jobs that allow workers little self-direction.
22 Joan Aldous makes this interpretation on the basis of several studies of marriage in different social classes. See Aldous *et al.*, 1979.
23 For example, see the description of British managers and their wives by Pahl and Pahl, 1971.
24 Hochschild, 1975, describes how a young woman professor with a young child and successful husband experiences this situation.
25 She goes on to mention the non-physical things she also needs: "I guess I never knew I needed emotional support and connections. I always tried to find that with other friends, other women, when in fact I would like some from him ..."
26 This is a nice example of how couples establish a shared definition of reality, or congruent images of each other, as discussed in Hess and Handel, 1959.
27 This is from an interview done six months after those quoted previously.

8 Self-development

1 Most psychological theories of self-development focus on becoming independent, as Gilligan, 1982, has pointed out.
2 For example, see Bellah *et al.*, 1985. However, Lasch, 1978, presents a clear psychoanalytic theory of self-development that differs from the one in this chapter. In a recent book, Lasch argues that Americans are now oriented to a more minimal, restricted self (1984).
3 Blumstein and Schwartz, 1983, p. 11, and the cases described on pp. 333–94.
4 The study is described in Chapter 3.
5 Bellah *et al.*, 1985, pp. 90 and 110.
6 The divorce figures are from Glick and Lin, 1985, and the survey data is from Veroff *et al.*, 1981.
7 The causal arguments in *Habits of the Heart* are not clearly stated. They are suggested in elegant prose and are heavily qualified, but a negative assessment of the therapeutic ethic and a positive regard for tradition permeates the book.
8 Bellah *et al.*, 1985, pp. 93–8, 130 and 135. The chapter on love in this book, based on Ann Swidler's research, is more sympathetic to the therapeutic ethic than the rest of the book. Some paragraphs imply that a paradoxical but workable concept of commitment through choice is part of the therapeutic ethic, such as the discussion of the Rowan couple on p. 101. But the chapter as a whole rejects this view.
9 Rothman, 1978, p. 253.
10 Lasch, 1978, pp. 139 and 141.
11 Berne, 1967, pp. 178–80. One reason that human potential theories of the self undervalue commitment, discipline, and obligation may be that the psychologists who produced them had grown up in the forties and fifties and had an excess of these qualities in themselves. They may have taken their own overdeveloped superegos for granted and created theories that dealt with their own failings.
12 Bellah *et al.*, 1985, p. 79.
13 *Ibid.*, p. 99.
14 *Ibid.*, pp. 121 and 130.
15 Rogers, 1961, pp. 184–96.
16 Peck, 1978, pp. 175–8.
17 Bettleheim, 1983. Other psychoanalysts who stress the importance of expressing affec-

tion towards patients include Kohut, 1968; and Winnicott, 1975. Also see Becker, 1973, for a rich, thoughtful analysis of love and transference in psychotherapy.

18 "Self" here means personality – enduring ways of thinking, feeling, and behaving. It implies some degree of awareness, actually or potentially. Though the term is not precise, it is widely used and alternatives such as "personality" are no clearer. For definitions of "self" and related concepts, see Rosenberg, 1979; and Turner, 1976. Psychoanalytic views of the self are reviewed in Hedges, 1985.

19 See Freud, 1957.

20 Leary, 1957. I have simplified his scheme.

21 The technique used to identify underlying dimensions is factor analysis. The dimensions that usually emerge in these studies have been labeled "potency" and "evaluation," "control" and "affection," or similar terms. A third factor, focusing on activity, sociability, or interaction rate, is also found in some studies. For a review of this research, see Foa, 1961; and Cancian, 1963.

22 These two dimensions also seem to emerge in non-industrialized societies, suggesting that universal differences in power and nurturance by gender, not the modern separation of the home from the workplace, may be the basis of these dimensions.

23 I am relying especially on object relations theory as presented by Guntrip, 1961. Recent psychoanalytic work on self–object psychology, narcissism, and borderline conditions continues to emphasize relationships with others; see the useful overview by Hedges, 1985.

24 See Mahler et al., 1975. Children raised by several caretakers tend to be less intensely dependent; see Maccoby and Masters, 1970.

25 Guntrip, 1961, pp. 291–2.

26 Ibid., p. 293.

27 When an adult repeats infantile dependence, according to Guntrip, there is an added voraciousness and anxiety resulting from traumatic experience; an infant's dependency is less angry. Psychoanalytic theories of borderline conditions examine the effects of the failure to develop a satisfactory dependence or symbiosis in infancy; see Hedges, 1985.

28 Nancy Chodorow argues that girls are much less likely to repress childhood dependency because they have more gratifying relations with their mothers and are less likely to be punished or pushed away. If this is so, many more women than men will be able to attain mature interdependence. I believe, however, that most women show signs of such repression, although their repression may be less intense than men's. Many women avoid intimacy or repeat the dependency of childhood; many are estranged from their bodies, their sexuality, and their capacity for spontaneous joy and anger. Such women may devote their lives to their families and caring for others, following the feminine gender role, but they will not have interdependent relationships that promote the development of themselves and the ones they love. See Evan Connell's brilliant novel, Mrs. Bridge, for a description of such a woman.

29 Another basis for resisting change indirectly suggested by Guntrip, 1961, is that internalized images of bad parents constitute an important bond to parents. Giving up the bad internal image or childhood pattern thus means losing an aspect of this attachment.

30 The psychoanalytic theorist, Heinz Kohut, emphasizes the importance of the analyst's empathically mirroring the patient's self and believing in the patient's worth and ideals. He argues that narcissistic patients need analysts who will empathically listen, perceive, and mirror the patient's fragile self and strengthen his sense of worth "through the expression of a warm glow of pleasure and participation" that the patient has lived up to his own values (Kohut, 1968, p. 902). Winnicott maintains that for patients who have lost the core of their "real self," "the analyst and the setting he arranges for the treatment must function symbolically as the mother who adapts 'perfectly' to the needs of the infant" (quoted in Guntrip, 1961, p. 410).

31 Winnicott, 1975, discusses the reemergence of a person's real, physical self. See Guntrip, 1971, for a discussion of Winnicott.

32 The quantitative evidence on whether therapy helps people develop and have better relationships is mixed. See the review in Kelley *et al.*, 1983, Chapter 10.

33 Rogers, 1961, p. 38. Different personality types require different kinds of therapy, and this simplified exposition emphasizes kinds of therapy that would be effective with people who used repression as a major defense. "Borderline" personalities are sometimes seen as lacking a strong enough ego and super-ego to use repression. Hedges, 1985 reviews different therapies that are useful for different personalities.

34 Hawkins *et al.*, 1977. In my survey of forty-six couples and fourteen individuals in 1982, the activities respondents said that they most enjoyed with their partners were "being alone together and talking about our feelings and experiences" (the first or second choice of 61% of the respondents), "being alone quietly," (ranked first or second by 53%), and "physical lovemaking" (ranked first or second by 40%). The other two activities they could choose from were "being with children, friends or relatives at home" (28%) and "being with friends at a party" (16%). Other studies reporting the importance of self-disclosure and communication, warmth, and acceptance include Levinger, 1964.

35 For example, psychological studies show that when they are being evaluated in a test, many people become very anxious and perform poorly; they also think less of themselves and anticipate rejection from others; see Sarason, 1980. Other studies suggest that empathy from teachers produces higher self-esteem and improved learning by students; see, for example, Chang *et al.*, 1981.

36 Some marriage counselors who use Rogerian principles train couples to use a clear set of rules in taking turns at genuinely expressing their own feelings and empathically listening to their partner. This method is described in Kelley, 1983, Chapter 10.

37 Thus Abraham Maslow assumes that self-fulfillment naturally leads to an altruistic concern for others. As self-actualizing people gratify their needs for belonging, affection, and respect, Maslow argues, the idea of the self becomes enlarged "to include aspects of the world." They become interested in "seeing justice done, doing a more perfect job, advancing the truth," and their goals become "transpersonal, beyond-the-selfish, altruistic satisfactions" (1970, Chapter 11).

9 Androgynous love in marriage

1 Gould, 1974, p. 14.
2 *Ibid.*, pp. 24–5.
3 *Ibid.*, p. 25.
4 *Ibid.*, p. 80.
5 *Ibid.*, p. 193.
6 The Gerrards were interviewed by Eileen Pinkerton.
7 Blumstein and Schwartz, 1983, p. 412.
8 This case is from Blumstein and Schwartz, 1983, pp. 436–47.
9 Greg and Lisa were interviewed by Kim Thompson.
10 See Winnicott's description of ego-relatedness between mother and child in Guntrip, 1961, pp. 116–17.

10 Friends and relatives

1 Rossi, 1984.
2 The social science literature on friendship is small, and some of the best work is by anthropologists; see Leyton, 1974; and Brain, 1976. For a review of data on friends and

acquaintances, see Duck and Gilmour, 1981 as well as the studies cited in Chapter 5. Fischer, 1982 points out the advantages of associating with friends, who can be freely chosen to fit individual interests. This argument is a useful corrective to the romanticizing of the close kin and community ties of the past.

3 Scholars, especially men, often exaggerate the uniqueness of friendship, portraying it as extremely free, pure, moral, and generally beyond compromise and conflict.

4 Chris and Jenny were interviewed by Nancy Broomfield.

5 These data are presented in Fischer, 1982, p. 40. For a discussion of friendship and self-development, see Rubin, 1985.

6 The national survey data are reported in Campbell, 1981. Fischer, 1982, documents the importance of the parent–child tie, and the tendency of people to turn to kin for long-term help is reported by Litwak and Szelenyi, 1969.

7 Komarovsky, 1962, p. 239.

8 Adams, 1968.

9 Rapp, 1982.

10 Novak, 1983.

11 For an insightful description of the cooperative orientation of working-class men, see Little, 1980, and his description of the "attachment-need" type of political orientation. Class differences in husbands dominating their wives are documented by Blood and Wolfe, 1960. However, some sociologists, like Rainwater *et al.*, 1959, have argued that women are more powerless and dependent in the working class than in the middle class.

12 Komarovsky, 1962, p. 292. Sennett and Cobb, 1973, also describe how working-class men blame themselves for their class position and avoid talking about parts of their experience to protect their dignity. Also see Rubin's sensitive account of working-class marriage, 1976.

13 The Blaines were interviewed by Kitty Rowley.

14 See Rubin's discussion of these two working-class life-styles, 1976, Chapter 3.

15 This pattern of the wife doing the giving yet being dependent and powerless is fascinating. Apparently, because he does not overtly admit his need for what she is giving, his dependency does not reduce his power.

11   Current trends and future possibilities

1 Quoted in Cherlin, 1981, Introduction.

2 See Bane, 1976, for an excellent review of the evidence on the persistence of the family. The commitment to getting married and having children has been strong throughout the twentieth century. In fact, with rising affluence and economic security more people were able to live the "preferred life cycle," to use Peter Uhlenberg's term, and the proportion of people who never married and who remained childless steadily dropped. Of white women who were born between 1890 and 1894 and who survived to age fifty, 22% were childless; this percentage declined steadily to 5% for women born between 1930 and 1934; see Uhlenberg, 1969 and 1974.

3 The figures on marriage and living together are from U.S. Bureau of the Census, Current Population Reports, No. 399, March 1984. The survey data on monogamy are from Blumstein and Schwartz, 1983, p. 585, n. 27. On cohabitation, see Spanier, 1983.

4 Strober and Weinberg, 1980. Several studies report that working wives spend from three to four hours per day less on housework than full-time housewives and have an hour or two less leisure time per day. Studies of time use are reported by Robinson and Converse, 1972. On women's occupational segregation and low wages, see Kahn-Hutt *et al.*, 1982.

5 Dowling, 1981, p. 215.

6 Mason *et al.*, 1976; see also Gerstel, 1978.

7 Zuckerman, 1982, pp. 17–18.
8 I do not have any hard evidence on this cultural trend. Unger, 1975, makes a similar interpretation.
9 The data on poverty are from 1981 (U.S. Commission on Civil Rights, 1983); 7% of the husband–wife families were below the poverty level. The data on single parents is from the U.S. Census Current Population Reports, No. 398, 1984. 89% of single-parent households were headed by the mother in 1984. In 1970, 1% of single-parent households were headed by the father compared to 3% in 1984 – a small change in spite of all the media attention to fatherhood. Cherlin, 1981, discusses trends in divorce. Furstenberg, 1983, documents the lack of involvement of fathers after divorce, and Rossi, 1984, summarizes the evidence on men's declining involvement in childrearing.

Appendix IV: Biology and gender

1 See Rossi, 1984, for a somewhat different set of criteria for establishing biological sex differences and an eloquent and well-documented plea for considering the biological dimension of gender roles, especially as it relates to parenthood.
2 See Whiting and Edwards, 1973.
3 Zelditch, 1955.
4 The only other consistent sex differences reported in the classic review by Maccoby and Jacklin, 1974, is that males are better in spatial perception. For more recent reviews, see Stockard and Johnson, 1980.
5 But Rossi, 1984, argues that there is evidence for a biological basis for nurturance.
6 See Money and Ehrhardt, 1972.
7 Whiting and Edwards, 1973; Munroe and Munroe, 1975.
8 Whiting and Edwards, 1973.
9 See Maccoby and Masters, 1970.
10 Only elites such as men of wealth and education in ancient Greece or the knights of medieval Europe developed a concept of love that emphasized the expression of feelings; see Hunt, 1959; and Murstein, 1974.

References

Adams, Bert (1968). *Kinship in an Urban Setting*. Chicago: Markham Publishing Co.

Aiken, Pamela and Donald Baucom (1982). "Locus of Control and Depression." *Journal of Personality Assessment* 46:391–5.

Ainsworth, Mary (1972). "Attachment and Dependency." In Jacob Gewirtz (ed.) *Attachment and Dependency*. Washington, D.C.: Winston, pp. 97–137.

Aldous, Joan, Marie Osmond and M. Hicks (1979). "Men's Work and Men's Families." In Wesley Burr, R. Hill, F. Nye and I. Reiss (eds.) *Contemporary Theories about the Family*, Vol. 1. New York: Free Press, pp. 227–58.

Allen, Jon and Dorothy Haccoun (1976). "Sex Differences in Emotionality." *Human Relations* 29:71–722.

Almond, Richard (1977). "Character, Role and Self: Evolution in Personality Styles." Unpublished manuscript. Palo Alto, California.

Anenshensel, Carol, R. Fredricks and V. Clark (1981). "Family Roles and Sex Differences in Depression." *Journal of Health and Social Behavior* 22:379–93.

Bahr, Howard (1980). "Changes in Family Life in Middletown, 1924–1977." *Public Opinion Quarterly* 44:35–52.

Bain, Read (1936). "Changed Beliefs of College Students." *Journal of Abnormal and Social Psychology* 31:1–11.

Bakan, David (1966). *The Duality of Human Existence*. Boston: Beacon Press.

Balswick, Jack and Christine Avert (1977). "Gender, Interpersonal Orientation and Perceived Parental Expressiveness." *Journal of Marriage and the Family* 39:121–8.

Bane, Mary Jo (1976). *Here to Stay: American Families in the Twentieth Century*. New York: Basic Books.

Barker-Benfield, G. J. (1976). *The Horrors of the Half-known Life: Male Attitudes Toward Women and Sexuality in 19th Century America*. New York: Harper and Row.

  (1978). "The Spermatic Economy: A 19th Century View of Sexuality in The American Family in Social-Historical Perspective." In Michael Gordon (ed.) *The American Family in Social-Historical Perspective*. Second Edition. New York: St Martin's Press.

Becker, Ernest (1973). *The Denial of Death*. New York: Free Press.

Bell, Alan and Martin Weinberg (1978). *Homosexualities*. New York: Simon and Schuster.

Bellah, Robert, Richard Madsen, William Sullivan, Ann Swidler and Steven Tipton (1985). *Habits of the Heart*. Berkeley: University of California Press.

Bem, Sandra (1977). "Beyond Androgyny." In Arlene Skolnick and Jerome Skolnick (eds.) *The Family in Transition*. Second Edition. Boston: Little Brown, pp. 204–221.

(1983). "Gender Schema Theory and Its Implications for Child Development." *Signs* 8:598–616.

Berkman, Lisa (1977). "Social Networks, Host Resistance and Mortality." Unpublished Ph.D. Dissertation. School of Public Health, Berkeley, California.

Berkman, Lisa F. and S. L. Syme (1979). "Social Networks, Host Resistance and Mortality: A 9-year Follow-up Study of Alameda County Residents." *American Journal of Epidemiology* 109:186–204.

Bernard, Jessie (1972). *The Future of Marriage*. New York: World Publishing.

Berne, Eric (1967). *Games People Play*. New York: Grove Press.

Bettleheim, Bruno (1983). *Freud and Man's Soul*. New York: Alfred Knopf.

Blake, Judith (1979). "Is Zero Preferred? American Attitudes Towards Childlessness in the 1970s." *Journal of Marriage and the Family* 41:245–58.

Blau, Peter (1964). *Exchange and Power in Social Life*. New York: Wiley:

Blauner, Robert (1964). *Alienation and Freedom*. Chicago: University of Chicago Press.

Blood, Robert and Donald Wolfe (1960). *Husbands and Wives*. New York: Free Press.

Blumstein, Philip and Pepper Schwartz (1983). *American Couples*. New York: William Morrow.

Boles, Janet K. (1979). *The Politics of The Equal Rights Amendment*. New York: Longman.

Booth, Alan (1972). "Sex and Social Participation." *American Sociological Review* 37:183–92.

Bose, Christine and Peter Rossi (1983). "Prestige Standings of Occupations as Affected by Gender." *American Sociological Review* 48:316–30.

Bowlby, John (1969). *Attachment and Loss*. New York: Basic Books.

Bradburn, Norman M. (1969). *The Structure of Psychological Well-Being*. Chicago: Aldine.

Brain, Robert (1976). *Friends and Lovers*. New York: Basic Books.

Brannon, Robert (1976). "The Male Sex Role." In Deborah David and Robert Brannon (eds.) *The Forty-Nine Percent Majority*. Reading, Massachusetts: Addison-Wesley.

Braverman, Harry (1975). *Labor and Monopoly Capital; The Degradation of Work in the 20th Century*. New York: Monthly Review Press.

Brittan, Arthur (1977). *The Privatised World*. London: Routledge and Kegan Paul.

Broverman, Inge, Donald Broverman, Frank Clarkson, Paul Rosenkrantz and Susan Vogel (1970). "Sex-Role Stereotypes and Clinical Judgments of Mental Health." *Journal of Consulting Psychology* 34:1–7.

Brown, G. W., Marie Bhrolchain and Terril Harris (1975). "Social Class and Psychiatric Disturbance Among Women in Urban Population." *Sociology* 9:225–54.
Buck, Walter (1936). "A Measurement of Changes in Attitudes and Interests of University Students Over a Ten Year Period." *Journal of Abnormal and Social Psychology* 31:12–19.
Burgess, Ernest W. and Harvey J. Locke (1960). *The Family: From Institution to Companionship*. New York: American Book Co.
Burke, Ronald, Tamara Weir and Denise Harrison (1976). "Disclosure of Problems and Tensions Experienced by Marital Partners." *Psychological Reports* 38:531–42.
Bush, Diane, Roberta Simmons, Bruce Hutchinson and Dale Blyth (1977). "Adolescent Perception of Sex Roles in 1968 and 1975." *Public Opinion Quarterly* 41:459–74.
Caldwell, Mayta A. and Letitia Peplau (1982). "Sex Differences in Same-Sex Friendship." *Sex Roles* 8:721–32.
Calhoun, Arthur W. (1917). *A Social History of the American Family*. Cleveland: Arthur Clark.
Campbell Angus (1981). *The Sense of Well-Being in America*. New York: McGraw Hill.
  (1976). "Subjective Measures of Well-Being." *American Psychologist* 31:117–24.
Campbell, Angus, Philip Converse and Willard L. Rodgers (1976). *The Quality of American Life*. New York: Russell Sage.
Cancian, Francesca (1975). *What Are Norms?* New York: Cambridge University Press.
  (1963). "Interaction Patterns in Zinacanteco Families." *American Sociological Review* 29:540–50.
  (1985). "Gender Politics: Love and Power in the Private and Public Sphere." In Alice Rossi (ed.), *Gender and the Life Course*. New York: Aldine, pp. 253–64.
Cancian, Francesca and Bonnie Ross (1981). "Mass Media and the Women's Movement." *Journal of Applied Behavioral Science* 17:9–26.
Cantril, A. H. and Charles W. Roll (1971). *Hopes and Fears of the American People*. New York: Universe Books.
Caplan, Gerald, and Marie Killilea (1976). *Support Systems and Mutual Help*. New York: Grune and Stratton.
Caplow, Theodore and Howard Bahr (1979). "Half a Century of Change in Adolescent Attitudes: Replication of a Middletown Survey by the Lynds." *Public Opinion Quarterly* 43:1–17.
Carden, Maren L. (1974). *The New Feminist Movement*. New York: Russell Sage Foundation.
Carter, Hugh and Paul C. Glick (1976). *Marriage and Divorce: A Social and Economic Study*. Cambridge, Massachusetts: Harvard University Press.
Catalano, Ralph, D. Dooley, R. L. Jackson (1985). "Economic antecedents of help-seeking." *Journal of Health and Social Behavior* 26:141–52.

Chafe, William H. (1972). *The American Woman*. New York: Oxford University Press.

Chang, Alice, Stephen Berger and Betty Chang (1981). "The Relationship of Student Self-Esteem and Teacher Empathy to Classroom Learning." *Psychology* 18:21–5.

Cherlin, Andrew (1981). *Marriage, Divorce, Remarriage*. Cambridge, Massachusetts: Harvard University Press.

Chodorow, Nancy (1978). *The Reproduction of Mothering*. Berkeley: University of California Press.

(1971). "Being and Doing: a Cross-Cultural Examination of the Socialization of Males and Females." In V. Gornick and B. Moran (eds.) *Women in Sexist Society*. New York: Mentor Books, pp. 259–91.

Clark, Alexander and Paul Wallin (1965). "Women's Sexual Responsiveness and the Duration and Quality of their Marriage." *American Journal of Sociology* 21:187–96.

Clecak, Peter (1983). *America's Quest for the Ideal Self*. New York: Oxford University Press.

Collier, James (1966). "When a Man Marries." *Reader's Digest*, October.

Cook, Ellen Piel (1985). *Psychological Androgyny*. New York: Pergamon Press.

Cott, Nancy F. (1977). *The Bonds of Womanhood*. New Haven: Yale University Press.

Crowe, Paricia W. (1978). "Good Fences Make Good Neighbors: Social Networks at Three Levels of Urbanization in Tirol, Austria." Unpublished Ph.D. Dissertation, Department of Anthropology, Stanford University.

Curtis, L. (1974). *Criminal Violence: National Patterns and Behavior*. Lexington, Massachusetts: Lexington Books.

Daly, Mary (1979). *Gyn/Ecology: The Metaethics of Radical Feminism*. Boston: Beacon Press.

David, Deborah and Robert Brannon (eds.) (1976). *The Forty Nine Percent Majority: The Male Sex Role*. Reading, Massachusetts: Addison-Wesley.

Davidson, Lynne and Lucille Duberman (1982). "Friendship: Communication and Interactional Patterns in Same Sex Dyads." *Sex Roles* 8:809–22.

Davis, Margaret (n.d.). "Sex-Role Ideology as Portrayed in Men's and Women's Magazine Short Stories, 1935–1975." Unpublished manuscript, Stanford University.

De Beauvoir, Simone (1953). *The Second Sex* (H. M. Parsley, trans.). New York: Knopf.

De Charms, Richard and Gerald Moeller (1962). "Values Expressed in American Children's Readers: 1800–1950." *Journal Abnormal and Social Psychology* 64:136–42.

Degler, Carl N. (1974). "What Ought to Be and What Was, Women's Sexuality in the 19th Century." *American Historical Review* 79:1467–90.

(1980). *At Odds: Women and the Family in America from the Revolution to the Present*. New York: Oxford University Press.

Demos, John (1974). "The American Family in Past Time." *American Scholar* 43:422–46.

(1979). "Images of the American Family, Then and Now." In V. Tufte and

B. Myerhoff (eds.), *Changing Images of the Family.* New Haven: Yale University Press, pp. 43–60.

Derlega, Valerian and Alan Chaikin (1976). "Norms Affecting Self-Disclosure in Men and Women." *Journal of Consulting and Clinical Psychology* 44:376–80.

De Rougemont, Denis (1956). *Love in the Western World.* New York: Pantheon.

Dickens, Wenda and Daniel Perlman (1981). "Friendship over the Life Cycle." In Steve Duck and Robin Gilmour, *Personal Relationships,* Vol. 2, London: Academic Press.

Dinnerstein, Dorothy (1976). *The Mermaid and the Minotaur: Sexual Arrangements and Human Malaise.* New York: Harper and Row.

Dohrenwend, Barbara and Bruce Dohrenwend (1978). "Some Issues in Research in Stressful Life Events." *Journal of Nervous and Mental Diseases* 166:7–15.

Douglas, Ann (1977). *The Feminization of American Culture.* New York: Knopf.

Dowling, Colette (1981). *The Cinderella Complex.* New York: Pocket Books.

Duck, Steve and Robin Gilmour (eds.) (1981). *Personal Relationships,* Vol. 2. London: Academic Press.

Duncan, Beverly and Otis Duncan (1978). "Social Stratification and Mobility." In Eleanor Sheldon and Wilbert Moore (eds.) *Indicators of Social Change.* New York: Russell Sage, pp. 675–720.

Duncan, Otis Dudley, Howard Schuman and Beverly Duncan (1973). *Social Change in a Metropolitan Community.* New York: Russell Sage.

Durkheim, Emile (1951). *Suicide.* Glencoe, Illinois: Free Press.

Easterlin, Richard A. (1980). *Birth and Fortune.* New York: Basic Books.

Eaton, William W. (1978). "Life Events, Social Supports, and Psychiatric Symptoms." *Journal of Health and Social Behavior* 19:230–34.

Ehrenreich, Barbara (1983). *The Hearts of Men.* New York: Doubleday.
(1982). "Family Feud on the Left." *The Nation,* March 13.

Ehrenreich, Barbara and Deirdre English (1978). *For Her Own Good: 150 Years of the Experts' Advice to Women.* New York: Anchor Books.

Elder, Glen (1974). *Children of the Great Depression.* Chicago: University of Chicago Press.

Elshtain, Jena Bethke (1981). *Public Man, Private Woman.* Princeton, New Jersey: Princeton University Press.
(1979). "Feminists Against the Family." *The Nation,* Nov. 17.

Emerson, Richard (1976), "Social Exchange Theory." In A. Inkeles and N. Smelser (eds.) *Annual Review of Sociology,* Vol. 2, pp. 335–62.

Engel, George (1971). "Sudden and Rapid Death." *Annals of Internal Medicine,* 74:771–82.

Engels, Frederick (1902). *The Origin of the Family.* Chicago: Charles Kerr.

E.R.A. (1982). "Who Cares about Housewives." Irvine, California.

Erikson, Erik H. (1950). *Childhood and Society.* New York: W. W. Norton and Co.

Faderman, Lillian (1981). *Surpassing the Love of Men.* New York: William Morrow.

Fass, Paula S. (1977). *The Damned and the Beautiful.* New York: Oxford University Press.

Fiedler, Leslie A. (1966). *Love and Death in the American Novel.* Revised Edition. New York: Stein and Day.

Filene, Peter (1974). *Him/Her/Self: Sex Roles in Modern America.* New York: Harcourt Brace Jovanovich.

Firestone, Shulamith (1970). *The Dialectic of Sex.* New York: William Morrow.

Fischer, Claude S. (1977). *Networks and Places.* New York: Free Press.

——— (1982). *To Dwell among Friends.* Chicago: University of Chicago Press.

Fischer, Claude and S. Oliker (1980). "Friendship, Gender and the Life Cycle." Institute of Urban and Regional Development, Berkeley, Working Paper No. 318.

Fishman, Pamela (1978). "Interaction: the Work Women do." *Social Problems,* 25:397–406.

Flax, Jane (1982). "The Family in Contemporary Feminist Thought." In Jean Elstian (ed.) *The Family in Political Thought.* Amherst, Massachusetts: University of Massachusets.

Flexner, Eleanor (1974). *Century of Struggle.* New York: Antheneum.

Foa, Uriel G. (1961). "Convergences in the Analysis of the Structure of Interpersonal Behavior." *Psychological Review* 68:341–53.

Frankenhauser, Marianne (1977). "Quality of Life: Criteria for Behavioral Adjustment." *International Journal of Psychology* 12:99–110.

Freeman, Jo (1975). *The Politics of Women's Liberation.* New York: David McKay.

Freud, Sigmund (1957). *The Ego and the Id* (Joan Riviere trans.). London: The Hogarth Press.

Friedan, Betty (1963). *The Feminine Mystique.* New York: Norton.

——— (1981). *The Second Stage.* New York: Simon Schuster.

Fromm, Erich (1956). *The Art of Loving.* New York: Harper.

Furstenberg, Frank, Christine Nord, James Peterson and Nicholas Zill (1983). "The Life Course of Children of Divorce: Marital Disruption and Parental Contact." *American Sociological Review* 48:656–68.

Gadlin, Howard (1977). "Private Lives and Public Order: A Critical View of Intimate Relations in the U.S." In G. Levinger and H. Raush (eds.), *Close Relationships.* Amherst, Massachusetts: University of Massachusetts Press, pp. 33–72.

Gallup, George (1980). *Gallup Opinion Index.*

Gardell, Bertil (1977). "Psychological and Social Problems of Industrial Work in Affluent Societies." *International Journal of Psychology* 12:125–34.

Gecas, V. (1979). "The Influence of Social Class on Socialization." In W. Burr et al. (eds.) *Contemporary Theories about the Family,* Vol. 1. New York: Free Press.

Gerbner, George (1958). "The Social Role of the Confession Magazine." *Social Problems* 6:29–40.

Gerstel, Naomi (1978). "Commuter Marriage." Paper read at annual meetings of American Sociological Association, San Francisco.

Gersten, Joanne, Thomas Langer, Jeanne Eisenberg and Ora Sincha-Fagan (1977). "An Evaluation of the Etiological Role of Stressful Life Chance events in Psychological Disorders." *Journal of Health and Social Behavior* 18:228–44.

Gilligan, Carol (1982). *In a Different Voice*. Cambridge, Massachusetts: Harvard University Press.

Glenn, Norval (1975). "Psychological Well-Being in the Post-Parental Stage." *Journal of Marriage and Family* 37:105–24.

Glenn, Norval and Sara McLanchan (1982). "Children and Marital Happiness." *Journal of Marriage and Family* 44:63–72.

Glick, Paul C. and G. Spanier (1980). "Married and Unmarried Cohabitation in the U.S." *Journal of Marriage and the Family* 42:19–30.

Glick, Paul C. and Sung-Ling Lin (1985). "Recent Changes in Divorce and Remarriage." Paper read at Annual Meetings of the American Sociological Association, August 28, Washington D.C.

Goldman, Emma (1931). *Living My Life*. New York: A. A. Knopf.

Goode, William (1963). *World Revolution and Family Patterns*. New York: Free Press.

Gordon, Linda and Ellen Dubois (1983). "Seeking Ecstacy on the Battlefield: Danger and Pleasure in Nineteenth Century Feminist Thought." *Feminist Review*, 13:42–54.

Gordon, Michael (1978). "From Unfortunate Necessity to a Cult of Mutual Orgasm: Sex in American Marital Education Literature, 1830–1940." In J. Henslin and E. Sagarin (eds.) *The Sociology of Sex*. Revised Edition. New York: Schocken, pp. 59–84.

Gordon, Michael and M. Charles Bernstein (1970). "Mate Choice and Domestic Life in the Nineteenth-Century Marriage Manual." *Journal of Marriage and the Family* 32:665–74.

Gore, Susan (1978). "The Effect of Social Support in Moderating the Consequences of Unemployment." *Journal of Health and Social Behavior* 19:157–65.

Gottlieb, B. H. (1983). "Social Support as a Focus for Integrative Research in Psychology." *American Psychologist* 38:278–87.

Gould, Lois (1974). *Final Analysis*. New York: Random House.

Gove, Walter R. (1973). "Sex, Marital Status and Mortality." *American Journal of Sociology* 79:45–67.

Gove, Walter R., and Michael Geerken (1977). "The Effect of Children and Employment on the Mental Health of Married Men and Women." *Social Forces* 56:66–76.

Gove, Walter R. and Michael Hughes (1979). "Possible causes of the apparent sex differences in physical health." *American Sociological Review* 44:126–46.

Gratton, Lynda C. (1980). "Analysis of Maslow's Need Hierarchy with Three Social Class Groups." *Social Indicators Research* 7:463–76.

Gunderson, Eric and Richard Rahe (eds.) (1972). *Life Stress and Illness*. Springfield, Illinois; C. C. Thomas.

Guntrip, Harry (1961). *Personality Structure and Human Interaction*. New York: International Universities Press.

(1971). *Psychoanalytic Theory, Therapy and the Self.* New York: Basic Books.
Gurin, Gerald, J. Veroff and S. Feld (1960). *Americans View Their Mental Health.* New York: Basic Books.
Hantover, Jeffrey P. (1980). "The Boy Scouts and the Validation of Masculinity." In Elizabeth Pleck and Joseph Pleck, *The American Man.* Englewood, New Jersey: Prentice Hall.
Harlow, Harry and Margaret Harlow (1962). "Social Deprivation in Monkeys." *Scientific American* 206:1–10.
Harris, Louis and Associates (1979). *The Playboy Report on American Men.* Playboy Inc.
Harris, William H. and Judith Levy (eds.) (1975). *The New Columbia Encyclopedia.* New York: Columbia University Press.
Hawkins, James, Carol Weisberg and Dixie L. Ray (1977). "Marital Communication Style and Social Class." *Journal of Marriage and Family* 39:479–92.
Hedges, Lawrence (1985). *Listening Perspectives: Modes of Psychoanalytic Inquiry.* New York: Jason Aronson.
Heer, David M. and Amyra Grossbard-Shechtman (1981). "The Impact of the Female Marriage Squeeze and the Contraceptive Revolution on Sex Roles and the Women's Liberation Movement in the U.S. 1960–1975." *Journal of Marriage and the Family* February, 43:49–65.
Heinz, Kohut (1977). *The Restoration of the Self.* New York: International Universities Press.
Heller, Kenneth (1979). "The Effects of Social Support." In Arnold Goldstein and Frederick Kanfer (eds.) *Maximizing Treatment Gains.* New York: Academic Press.
Hendrick, Clyde and Susan Hendrick (1983). *Liking, Loving and Relating.* Belmont, California: Wadsworth.
Henley, Nancy (1977). *Body Politics.* Englewood Cliffs, New Jersey: Prentice Hall.
Hess, Beth (1981). "Friendship and Gender Roles over the Life Course." In Peter Stein (ed.) *Single Life.* New York: St Martin's Press.
Hess, Robert and Gerald Handel (1959). *Family Worlds: A Psychosocial Approach to Family Life.* Chicago: University of Chicago Press.
Hicks, Mary W. and Marilyn Platt (1970). "Marital Happiness and Stability: A Review of Research in the Sixties." *Journal of Marriage and the Family* 32:553–74.
Hilliard, Marion (1957). "The Act of Love – Woman's Greatest Challenge." *Reader's Digest*, June.
Hochschild, Arlie (1975). "Inside the Clockwork of a Male Career." In Florence Howe (ed.) *Women and the Power to Change.* New York: McGraw-Hill.
Hoge, Dean R. (1974). *Commitment on Campus: Changes in Religion and Values Over Five Decades.* Philadelphia: Westminster Press.
Hole, J. and E. Levine (1971). *The Rebirth of Feminism.* New York: Quadrangle.
Hollingshead, August and Frederick Redlich (1958). *Social Class and Mental Illness.* New York: John Wiley.

Holmes, T. H. and R. H. Rahe (1967). "The Social Readjustment Rating Scale." *Journal of Psychosomatic Research* Vol. 11, 213–18.

Homans, George C. (1961). *Social Behavior: Its Elementary Forms.* New York: Harcourt, Brace Jovanovich.

Hudson, John and L. Henze (1969). "Campus Values in Mate Selection: A Replication." *Journal of Marriage and the Family* 31:772–5.

Hunt, Morton (1959). *The Natural History of Love.* New York: Knopf.

_____ (1974). *Sexual Behavior in the 1970s.* Chicago: Playboy Press.

Inglehart, Ronald (1977). *The Silent Revolution.* Princeton, New Jersey: Princeton University Press.

Inkeles, Alex (1979). "Continuity and Change in the American National Character." In Seymour Lipset (ed.) *The Third Century: America as a Post-Industrial Society.* Stanford, California: Hoover Institution Press, pp. 390–416.

Inkeles, Alex and David H. Smith (1974). *Becoming Modern.* Cambridge, Massachusetts: Harvard University Press.

Jacobs, Selby and Adrian Ostfeld (1977). "An Epidemiological Review of the Mortality of Bereavement." *Psychosomatic Medicine* 39:344–57.

Jacoby, Russell (1975). *Social Amnesia.* Boston: Beacon Press.

Johns-Heine, Patrick and Hans Gerth (1949). "Values in Mass Periodical Fiction, 1921–1940." *Public Opinion Quarterly* 13:105–113.

Johnson, Paul E. (1978). *A Shopkeeper's Millennium.* New York: Hill and Wang.

Johnstone, Margaret (1954). "How to Live with a Woman." *Reader's Digest,* July.

Jouraud, Sidney M. (1971). *The Transparent Self.* Revised Edition. New York: Van Nostrand.

Kahn-Hutt, Rachel, Arlene Daniels and Richard Colvard (eds.) (1982). *Women and Work.* New York: Oxford University Press.

Kalmuss, Debra and Murray Straus (1982). "Wife's Marital Dependency and Wife Abuse." *Journal of Marriage and the Family* 44:277.

Keefe, Susan E., Amado M. Padilla and Manuel L. Carlos (1978). *Emotional Support Systems in Two Cultures: A Comparison of Mexican Americans and Anglo Americans.* Spanish Speaking Mental Health Research Center, Occasional Paper No. 7, U.C.L.A., Los Angeles, California.

Kelley, Harold, E. Berscheid, A. Christensen *et al.* (1983). *Close Relationships.* New York: W. H. Freeman.

Kephart, William (1967). "Some Correlates of Romantic Love." *Journal of Marriage and the Family* 29:470–74.

Kessler, Ronald (1982). "A Disaggregation of the Relationship between Socioeconomic Status and Psychological Distress." *American Sociological Review* 47:752–64.

Kessler, Ronald and James McRae (1980). "Trends in the Relationship between Sex and Mental Illness: 1957–1976." Unpublished manuscript. University of Michigan.

Kett, Joseph (1977). *Rites of Passage.* New York: Basic Books.

Kidd, Virginia (1974), "Happy Ever After and Other Relationship Styles." Ph.D Dissertation. Department of Speech, University of Minnesota.

(1975). "Happily Ever After and Other Relationship Styles: Advice on Interpersonal Relations in Popular Magazines, 1951–1973." *Quarterly Journal of Speech* 61:31–9.

Kingsdale, Jon M. (1980). "The Poor Man's Club." In E. Pleck and J. Pleck (eds.) *The American Man.* Englewood Cliffs, New Jersey: Prentice Hall, pp. 255–83.

Kitagawa, Evelyn and Philip Hauser (1973). *Differential Mortality in the United States.* Cambridge, Massachusetts: Harvard University Press.

Kohn, Melvin (1969). *Class and Conformity: A Study in Values.* Homewood, Illinois: Dorsey Press.

Kohn, Melvin and Carmi Schooler (1983). *Work and Personality.* Norwood, New Jersey: Ablex Publication Co.

Kohut, Heinz (1968). "The Psychoanalytic Treatment of Narcissistic Personality Disorders." *The Psychoanalytic Study of the Child* 23:86–113.

Komarovsky, Mirra (1962). *Blue-Collar Marriage.* New York: Random House.

(1976). *Dilemmas of Masculinity.* New York: W.. W. Norton.

Lantz, Herman R., Jane Keyes and Martin Schults (1975). "The American Family in the Preindustrial Period: From Base Lines in History to Change." *American Sociological Review* 40:21–36.

Lasch, Christopher (1977). *Haven in a Heartless World.* New York: Basic Books.

(1978). *The Culture of Narcissism: American Life in an Age of Diminishing Expectations.* Norton: New York.

(1984). *The Minimal Self.* New York: Norton.

Laslett, Peter (ed.) (1972). *Household and Family in Past Time.* Cambridge, England: Cambridge University Press.

Laws, Judith Long (1971). "A Feminist Review of the Marital Adjustment Literature." *Journal of Marriage and the Family* 33:483–517.

Leary, Timothy (1957). *Interpersonal Diagnosis of Personality.* New York: Ronald Press.

Lebergott, Stanley (1976). *The American Economy.* Princeton, New Jersey: Princeton University Press.

Lederer, William and Don Jackson (1974). "Do People Really Marry for Love?" *Reader's Digest,* January.

LeShan, Lawrence (1959). "Psychological Status as Factors in the Development of Malignant Disease." *Journal of National Cancer Institute,* Vol. 22, 1–18.

Levinger, George (1964). "Task and Social Behavior in Marriage." *Sociometry* 27:433–48.

Levinger, George and Harold Raush (eds.) (1977). *Close Relationships.* Amherst, Massachusetts: University of Massachusetts Press.

Levinson, Daniel L. (1978). *The Seasons of a Man's Life.* New York: Knopf.

Lewis, Lionel S. and Dennis Brissett (1967). "Sex as Work: A Study of Avocational Counseling." *Social Problems* 15:8–18.

Lewis, Robert (1978). "Emotional Intimacy among Men." *Journal of Social Issues,* 34:108–121.

Lewis, Robert and Graham Spanier (1979). "Theorizing about the Quality and Stability of Marriage." In *Contemporary Theories about the Family,* W. Burr *et al.* (eds.). New York: Free Press, pp. 268–94.

Leyton, Elliott (ed.) (1974). *The Compact: Selected Dimensions of Friendship.* Newfoundland, Canada: Newfoundland University Press.

Liao, Winston (1977). "Psychological Stress, Health Status and Health Behavior: Application of the Life Changes Concept." *Psychological Reports* 41:246.

Little, Graham (1980). "Leaders and Followers: a Psychosocial Prospectus." *Melbourne Journal of Politics* 12:3–29.

Litwak, Eugene and Ivan Szelenyi (1969). "Primary Group Structures and Their Functions." *American Sociological Review* 34:465–81.

Lofland, Lyn (1982). "A Loss and Human Connection: An Exploration into the Nature of the Social Bond." In William Ickes and Eric Knowles (eds.) *Personality, Roles and Social Behavior.* New York: Springer-Verlag, pp. 221–42.

Lowenthal, Marjorie F., M. Thurnher and D. Chriboga (1975). *Four Stages of Life.* San Francisco: Jossey-Bass.

Lowenthal, Marjoria and Clayton Haven (1968). "Interaction and Adaptation: Intimacy as a Critical Variable." *American Sociological Review* 33:20–30.

Luker, Kristin (1984). *Abortion and the Politics of Motherhood.* Berkeley: University of California Press.

Lukes, Steven (1973). *Individualism.* Oxford, Basil Blackwell.

    (1972). "Alienation and Anomie." In A. Finifter (ed.) *Alienation and the Social System.* New York: Wiley, pp. 24–32.

Lynch, James J. (1977). *The Broken Heart: The Medical Consequences of Loneliness.* New York: Basic Books.

Lynd, Robert S. and Helen Lynd (1929). *Middletown.* New York: Harcourt, Brace and Co.

    (1937). *Middletown in Transition.* New York: Harcourt, Brace and Co.

Lyons, John O. (1978). *The Invention of the Self.* Carbondale, Illinois: Southern Illinois University Press.

Maccoby, Eleanor and Carol Jacklin (1974). *The Psychology of Sex Differences.* Stanford, California: Stanford University Press.

Maccoby, Eleanor, and John Masters (1970). "Attachment and Dependency." In P. Mussen (ed.) *Carmichael's Manual of Child Psychology*, Vol. 2. New York: Wiley, pp. 73–157.

MacKinnon, Catharin (1982). "Feminism, Marxism, Method and the State." *Signs* 7:515–44.

Mahler, Margaret, Fred Pine and Anni Bergman (1975). *The Psychological Birth of the Human Infant: Symbiosis and Individuation.* New York: Basic Books.

Marcuse, Herbert (1964). *One-Dimensional Man.* Boston: Beacon Press.

Marin, Peter (1975). "The New Narcissism: Follies of the Human Potential Movement." *Harper's*, October.

Marris, Peter (1974). *Loss and Change.* New York: Pantheon.

Martin, Walter (1976). "Status Integration, Social Stress, and Mental Illness: Accounting for Marital Status Variations in Mental Hospitalization Rates." *Journal of Health and Social Behavior*, 17:280–94.

Marx, Karl (1964). *Economic and Philosophical Manuscripts of 1844.* D. Struik (ed.). New York: International Publishers.

Maslow, Abraham (1970). *Motivation and Personality*, Second Edition. New York: Harper and Row.

Mason, Karen, John Czajka and Sara Arber (1976). "Change in U.S. Women's Sex-Role Attitudes, 1969–1974." *American Sociological Review* 41:573–96.

Maurois, Andre (1940). "The Art of Marriage." *Ladies' Home Journal*, April.

McDonald, Gerald (1980). "Family Power: the Assessment of a Decade of Theory and Research, 1970–79." *Journal of Marriage and the Family* 42:841–54.

Mechanic, David (1975). "Sociocultural and Social-Psychological Factors affecting Personal Responses to Psychological Disorder." *Journal of Health and Social Behavior*, 16:393–404.

Miller, Jean Baker (1976). *Toward a New Psychology of Women*. Boston: Beacon Press.

Miller, P. and J. C. Ingham (1976). "Friends, Confidents and Symptoms." *Social Psychiatry*, 11:51–8.

Miller, Ruth Scott (1925). "Masterless Wives and Divorce." *Ladies' Home Journal*, January.

Miller, S. M. and F. Riessman (1964). "The Working-Class Subculture." In A. Shostak and W. Greenberg (eds.) *Blue-Collar World*. Englewood Cliffs, New Jersey: Prentice-Hall, pp. 24–36.

Millman, Marcia and Rosabeth Kanter (eds.) (1975). *Another Voice*. Garden City, New York: Doubleday.

Money, John and Anke Ehrhardt (1972). *Man and Woman: Boy and Girl*. Baltimore: Johns Hopkins Press.

Morgan, Marabel (1973). *The Total Woman*. New York: Pocket Books.

Morgan, Robin (1978). *Going Too Far*. New York: Vintage.

Mornell, Pierre (1979). *Passive Men, Wild Women*. New York: Ballantine Books.

Mukhopadhyay, Carol Chapnick (1980). "The Sexual Division of Labor in the Family: A Decision Making Approach." Ph.D. Dissertation, Department of Anthropoology: University of California, Riverside.

Munroe, Robert and Ruth Munroe (1975). *Cross-Cultural Human Developemnt*. Monterey, California: Brooks/Cole Publication Co.

Murstein, Bernard (1974). *Love, Sex and Marriage through the Ages*. New York: Springer.

Myers, J., J. Lindenthal, and Max Pepper (1975). "Life Events, Social Integration and Psychiatric Symptomology." *Journal of Health and Social Behavior*, 16:421–7.

Nathanson, Constance A. (1980). "Social Roles and Health Status among Women: the Significance of Employment." *Social Science and Medicine* 14A: 463–72.

Newcomb, Theodore (1937). "Recent Changes in Attitudes Toward Sex and Marriage." *American Sociological Review* 1:659–67.

Novak, William (1983). "What do Women Really Want." *McCall's*, February.

Nuckolls, K. B., J. Cassell and B. H. Kaplan (1972). "Psychosocial Assets, Life Crisis and the Prognosis of Pregnancy." *American Journal of Epidemiology*, 95:431–41.

O'Neil, William (1978). "Divorce in the Progressive Era." In M. Gordon (ed.) *The American Family in Social-Historical Perspective*. New York: St Martin's Press, pp. 140–51.
Oppenheimer, Valerie Kincade (1973). "Demographic Influence on Female Employment and the Status of Women." *American Journal of Sociology* 78: 946–61.
Osmond, Marie W. and Patricia Y. Martin (1975). "Sex and Sexism." *Journal of Marriage and the Family* 37:744–59.
Pahl, J. M. and R. E. Pahl (1971). *Managers and their Wives*. London: Allen Love and Penguin Press.
Parelius, Ann P. (1975). "Emerging Sex-Role Attitudes, Expectations and Strains among College Women." *Journal of Marriage and the Family* 37:146–54.
Parelman, Sara Allison (1980). "Dimensions of Emotional Intimacy in Marriage." Ph.D. Dissertation, University of California, Los Angeles.
Parkes, C. Murray, B. Benjamin and R. Fitzgerald (1969). "Broken Heart: A Statistical Study of Increased Mortality among Widowers." *British Medical Journal* I:740–43.
Parsons, Talcott (1951). *The Social System*. Glencoe, Illinois: The Free Press.
 (1966). *Societies: Evolutionary and Comparative Perspectives*. Englewood Cliffs, New Jersey: Prentice-Hall.
 (1954). "The Kinship System of the Contemporary United States." In *Essays in Sociological Theory*. Revised Edition. Glencoe, Illinois: Free Press, pp. 177–97.
Parsons, Talcott and Robert F. Bales (1955). *Family, Socialization and Interaction Process*. Glencoe, Illinois: The Free Press.
Payne, Donald and Paul Mussen (1956). "Parent-Child Relations and Father Identification among Adolescent Boys." *Journal of Abnormal and Social Psychology* 52:358–62.
Pearlin, Leonard and Joyce Johnson (1977). "Marital Status, Life Strains and Depression." *American Sociological Review* 42:704–15.
Peck, M. Scott (1978). *The Road Less Traveled*. New York: Simon and Schuster.
Peplau, Letitia and Steven Gordon (1985). "Women and Men in Love: Sex Differences in Close Relationships." In Virginia O'Leary, R. Unger and B. Wallston (eds.) *Women, Gender and Social Psychology*. Hillsdale, New Jersey: Erlbaum, pp. 257–91.
Phillips, D. L. (1967). "Mental Health Status, Social Participation and Happiness." *Journal of Health and Social Behavior*, Vol. 8, 285–91.
Phillips, Walter (1980). "Purpose in Life, Depression and Locus of Control." *Journal of Clinical Psychology* 36:661–7.
Pleck, Elizabeth H. and Joseph H. Pleck (1980). *The American Man*. Englewood Cliffs, New Jersey: Prentice-Hall.
Pleck, Joseph (1981). *The Myth of Masculinity*. Cambridge, Massachusetts: M.I.T. Press.
 (1985). *Working Wives, Working Husbands*. New York: Sage Publications.
Poster, Mark (1978). *Critical Theory of the Family*. New York: Seabury Press.

Quinn, Naomi (1982). " 'Commitment' in American Marriage: a Cultural Analysis." *American Ethnologist* 9:775–98.

Rainwater, Lee, Richard Coleman and Geranl Handel (1959). *Workingman's Wife*. New York: Oceana Publications.

Rapp, Rayna (1982). "Family and Class in Contemporary America." In Barrie Thorne (ed.) *Rethinking the Family*. New York: Longman.

Raush, Harold, William Barry, Richard Hertel and Mary Ann Swain (1974). *Communication, Conflict and Marriage*. San Francisco: Jossey-Bass.

Redlick, R. W. and C. Johnson (1974). "Marital Status, Living Arrangements and Family Characteristics of Admissions to State and County Mental Clinics, U.S. 1970." Statistical Note 100: N.I.M.H. Washington, D.C.: G.P.O.

Reedy, Margaret N. (1977). "Age and Sex Differences in Personal Needs and the Nature of Love." Ph.D. Dissertation, Department of Psychology, University of Southern California.

Reiss, Ira L. (1980). *Family Systems in America*. Third Edition. New York: Holt, Rinehart and Winston.

Renne, Karen (1971). "Health and Marital Experience in an Urban Population." *Journal of Marriage and the Family* 33:338–50.

Rieff, Philip (1966). *The Triumph of the Therapeutic*. New York: Harper and Row.

Robinson, John P. and Philip E. Converse (1972). "Social Change Reflected in the Use of Time." In Angus Campbell and Philip Converse (eds.) *The Human Meaning of Social Change*. New York: Russell Sage, pp. 17–86.

Rogers, Carl R. (1961). *On Becoming a Person*. Boston: Houghton Mifflin.

Roper, Brent S. and Emily Labeff (1977). "Sex Roles and Feminism Revisited: An Intergenerational Attitude Comparison." *Journal of Marriage and the Family* 39:113–20.

Rosaldo, Michelle (1973). "Woman, Culture and Society: A Theoretical Overview." In Michelle Rosaldo and Louise Lamphere (eds.) *Woman, Culture and Society*. Stanford, California: Stanford University Press.

Rose, Willie Lee (1982). "Reforming Women." *New York Review of Books*, Oct. 7.

Rosenberg, Charles E. (1980). "Sexuality, Class and Role in 19th Century America." In Elizabeth H. Pleck and Joseph H. Pleck (eds.) *The American Man*. Englewood Cliffs, New Jersey: Prentice-Hall.

(ed.) (1975). *The Family in History*. University of Pennsylvania Press.

Rosenberg, Morris (1979). *Conceiving the Self*. New York: Basic Books.

Rosenblatt, Paul C. and Robert A. Phillips, Jr (1975). "Family Articles in Popular Magazines." *Family Coordinator* 24:267–71.

Rosencrantz, Paul (1982). "Rosencrantz Discusses Changes in Stereotypes about Men and Women." *Second Century Radcliffe News*. Cambridge, Massachusetts.

Rosencrantz, Paul *et al.* (1968). "Sex Role Stereotypes and Self-Concepts in College Students." *Journal of Consulting and Clinical Psychology* 32:287–95.

Rosenfeld, Sarah (1980). "Sex Difference in Depression." *Journal of Health and Social Behavior* 21:33–42.

Rossi, Alice (1980). "Life-Span Theories and Women's Lives." *Signs* 6:4–32.
(1984). "Gender and Parenthood." *American Sociological Review* 49:1–18.
Rothman, Sheila M. (1978). *Women's Proper Place: A History of Changing Ideals and Practices 1870 to the Present.* New York: Basic Books.
Rubin, Lillian (1976). *Worlds of Pain.* New York: Basic Books.
(1983). *Intimate Strangers.* New York: Harper and Row.
(1985). *Just Friends.* New York: Harper and Row.
Rubin, Zick (1970). "Measurement of Romantic Love." *Journal of Personality and Social Psychology* 16:265–73.
Rubin, Zick, Charles T. Hill, Letitia Peplau and Christine Dunkel-Schetter (1980). "Self-Disclosure in Couples." *Journal of Marriage and Family* 42:305–318.
Ruble, Thomas (1983). "Sex Stereotypes: Issues of Change in the 1970s." *Sex Roles* 9:397–402.
Ryan, Mary (1979). *Womanhood in America (From Colonial Times to the Present).* Second Edition. New York: New Viewpoints.
(1981). *The Cradle of the Middle Class: the Family in Oneida County, N.Y., 1790–1865.* New York: Cambridge University Press.
Sarason, Irwin (ed.) (1980). *Test Anxiety.* Hillsdale, New Jersey: L. Erlbaum.
Sayre, Robert (1978). *Solitude in Society.* Cambridge, Massachusetts: Harvard University Press.
Scanzoni, John (1976). "Sex Role Change and Influences on Birth Intentions." *Journal of Marriage and the Family* 38:43–60.
Schmale, Arthur (1958). "Relationship of Separation and Depression to Disease." *Psychosomatic Medicine,* 20:259–77.
Schneider, David M. and Raymond Smith (1973). *Class Difference and Sex Roles in American Kinship and Family Structure.* Englewood Cliffs, New Jersey: Prentice Hall.
Schram, Rosalyn W. (1979). "Marital Satisfaction over the Family Life Cycle." *Journal of Marriage and the Family* 41:7–14.
Secor, Cynthia (ed.) (1974). *Women's Studies,* 2, no. 2, Special issue on androgyny.
Seligman, Martin (1975). *Helplessness: on Depression, Development and Death.* San Francisco: W. H. Freeman.
Sennett, Richard (1977). *The Fall of Public Man.* New York: Alfred Knopf.
Sennett, Richard and Jonathan Cobb (1973). *Hidden Injuries of Class.* New York: Vintage.
Sheehy, Gail (1976). *Passages.* New York: Dutton.
Shorter, Edward (1975). *The Making of a Modern Family.* New York: Basic Books.
Shostak, A. and W. Greenberg (eds.) (1964). *In Blue-Collar World.* Englewood Cliffs, New Jersey: Prentice-Hall.
Shurtleff, Dewey (1956). "Mortality among the Married." *Journal of the American Geriatrics Society* 4:654–66.
Skolnick, Arlene (1978). *The Intimate Environment.* Boston: Little, Brown and Company.
Slater, Philip (1970). *The Pursuit of Loneliness.* Boston: Beacon Press.

Smith, Daniel Scott (1978). "The Dating of the American Sexual Revolution." In M. Gordon (ed.) *The American Family in Social-Historical Perspective.* New York: St Martin's Press, pp. 426–38.

Smith-Rosenberg, Carroll (1975). "The Female World of Love and Ritual." *Signs* 1:1–29.

Sohn, Ira (1980). "The Rise and Decline of the Nuclear Family." Ph.D. Dissertation. Department of Economics, University of California, Riverside.

Spanier, Graham (1983). "Married and Unmarried Cohabitation." *Journal of Marriage and the Family* 45:277–88.

Spindler, George (1977). "Change and Continuity in American Core Cultural Values." In Gordon Di Renzo (ed.) *We the People: American Character and Social Change.* Westport, Connecticut: Greenwood Press, pp. 20–39.

Srole, Leo and Anita Fischer (1980). "The Midtown Manhattan Longitudinal Study vs. the Mental 'Paradise Lost' Doctrine." *Archives of General Psychiatry* 37:209–21.

Stinnett, Nick, Janet Collins and James Montgomery (1970). "Marital Need Satisfaction of Older Husbands and Wives." *Journal of Marriage and the Family* 32:428–34.

Stockard, Jean and Miriam Johnson (1980). *Sex Roles.* Englewood Cliffs, New Jersey: Prentice-Hall.

Stone, Lawrence (1979). *The Family, Sex and Marriage in England 1500–1800.* New York: Harper Colophon Books.

Straus, Murray, R. Gelles and S. Steinmetz (1980). *Behind Closed Doors: Violence in the American Family.* New York: Anchor Books.

Strober, Myra and Charles Weinberg (1980). "Strategies Used by Working and Non-Working Wives to Reduce Time Pressures." *Journal of Consumer Research* 6:338–48.

Swain, Scott (1984). "Male Intimacy in Same-Sex Friendships: The Impact of Gender-Validating Activities." Paper read at annual meetings of the American Sociological Association.

Swidler, Ann (1980). "Love and Adulthood in American Culture." In N. Smelser and E. Erikson (eds.) *Themes of Work and Love in Adulthood.* Cambridge, Massachusetts: Harvard University Press, pp. 120–47.

(1982). "Ideologies of Love in Middle Class America." Paper read at Annual Meeting of Pacific Sociological Association, San Diego.

Thernstrom, Stephan (1964). *Poverty and Progress: Social Mobility in a Nineteenth Century City.* Cambridge, Massachusetts: Harvard University Press.

Thoits, Peggy (1981). "Undesirable Life Events and Psychophysiological Distress: A Problem of Operational Confounding." *American Sociological Review* 46:97–109.

Thom, Gary (1983). *The Human Nature of Discontent.* Totowa, New Jersey: Rowman and Allanheld.

Thorne, Barrie (ed.) (1982). *Rethinking the Family.* New York: Longman.

Thornton, Arland, Duane Alwin, and Donald Camburn (1983). "Causes and Consequences of Sex-Role Attitudes and Attitude Change." *American Sociological Review* 48:211–27.

204 *References*

Tiger, Lionel (1969). *Men in Groups.* London: Thomas Nelson.
Tönnies, Ferdinand (1963). *Community and Society* (Charles Loomis, trans. and ed.). New York: Harper Torchbooks.
Tudor, William, Jeannette Tudor and Walter Gove (1977). "The Effect of Sex Role Differences on the Social Control of Mental Illness." *Journal of Health and Social Behavior* 18:98–112.
Tufte, Virginia and Barbara Myerhoff (1979). *Changing Images of the Family.* New Haven: Yale University Press.
Turner, Jonathan H. (1982). *The Structure of Sociological Theory.* Third Edition. Homewood, Illinois: Dorsey Press.
Turner, Ralph (1976). "The Real Self: From Institution to Impulse." *American Journal of Sociology* 81:789–1,016.
U.S. Bureau of the Census (1976). *The Statistical History of the United States.* New York: Basic Boosk.
  (1982). *Current Population Reports,* Series P-20, No. 367 and No. 371.
  (1984). *Current Population Reports,* Series P-20, No. 398 and No. 399.
U.S. Commission on Civil Rights (1983). *Disadvantaged Women and their Children.* Washington, D. C.: Clearinghouse Publication 78.
Uhlenberg, Peter (1969). "A Study of Cohort Life Cycles: Cohorts of Native Born Mass. Women, 1830–1920." *Population Studies* 23:407–420.
  (1974). "Cohort Variations in Family Life Cycle Experiences of U.S. Females." *Journal of Marriage and the Family* 36:284–92.
  (1980). "Death in the Family." *Journal of Family History* 5:313–29.
Unger, Roberto Mangabeira (1975). *Knowledge and Politics.* New York: Free Press.
Vahanian, Tilla and Sally Olds (1978). "How Good is Your Marriage." *Ladies' Home Journal,* January.
Vanfossen, Beth (1981). "Sex Differences in Mental Health Effects of Spouse Support and Equity." *Journal of Health and Social Behavior* 22:130–43.
Verbrugge, Lois (1976). "Females and Illness: Recent Trends in Sex Differences in the U.S." *Journal of Health and Social Behavior* 17:387–403.
  (1980). "Sex Differences in Complaints and Diagnoses." *Journal of Behavioral Medicine* 3:327–55.
Veroff, Joseph, Elizabeth Douran and Richard Kulka (1981). *The Inner American: A Self-Portrait from 1957 to 1976.* New York: Basic Books.
Wahlstrom, Billie Joyce (1979). "Images of the Family in the Mass Media." In Virginia Tufte and Barbara Myerhoff (eds.) *Changing Images of the Family.* New Haven: Yale University Press, pp. 193–229.
Waldron, Ingrid (1976). "Why Do Women Live Longer Than Men?" *Social Science and Medicine* 10:349–62.
Wallace, Ruth A. and Alison Wolf (1980). *Contemporary Sociological Theory.* Englewood Cliffs, New Jersey: Prentice-Hall.
Walster, Elaine and G. William Walster (1978). *A New Look at Love.* Reading, Massachusetts: Addison-Wesley.
Webster's New Collegiate Dictionary (1977). Springfield, Massachusetts: G. C. Merriam Co.

Weinstein, Fred and Gerald Platt (1969). *The Wish to be Free*. Berkeley: University of California Press.

Welter, Barbara (1966). "The Cult of True Womanhood: 1820–1860." *American Quarterly* Summer, 151–74.

Whiting, Beatrice and Carolyn Edwards (1973). "A Cross-cultural Analysis of Sex Differences in the Behavior of Children Aged Three Through Eleven." *Journal of Social Psychology* 91:171–88.

Wills, Thomas, Robert Weiss and Gerald Patterson (1974). "A Behavioral Analysis of the Determinants of Marital Satisfaction." *Journal of Consulting and Clinical Psychology* 42:802–11.

Winnicott, D. W. (1975). *Through Pediatrics to Psycho-Analysis*. New York: Basic Books.

Wolfenstein, Martha (1955). "Fun Morality: An Analysis of Recent American Child-Training Literature." In M. Mead and M. Wolfenstein (eds.) *Childhood in Contemporary Cultures*. Chicago: University of Chicago Press, pp. 168–78.

Wolin, Sheldon (1977). Review of *Fall of Public Man* by Richard Sennett. *New York Review*, April 14.

Wright, James D. (1978). "Are Working Women *Really* More Satisfied? Evidence from Several National Surveys." *Journal of Marriage and the Family* 40:301–14.

Wrong, Dennis (1979). "Bourgeois Values, No Bourgeoisie? The Cultural Criticism of Christopher Lasch." *Dissent*, Summer: 308–14.

Yankelovich, Daniel (1974). *The New Morality*. New York: McGraw-Hill. (1981). *New Rules*. New York: Random House.

Young, Michael and Peter Willmott (1957). *Family and Kinship in East London*. London: Routledge and Kegan Paul.

Zaretsky, Eli (1976). *Capitalism, the Family and Personal Life*. New York: Harper Colophon. (1977). Review of *Social Amnesia* by Russell Jacoby. *Insurgent Sociologist* 7:41–6.

Zelditch, Morris (1955). "Role Differentiation in the Nuclear Family." In T. Parsons and R. Bales, *Family, Socialization and Interaction Process*. Glencoe, Illinois: Free Press, pp. 307–52.

Zelnick, Melvin and John Kantner (1977). "Sexual and Contraceptive Experience of Young Unmarried Women in the United States, 1976 and 1971." *Family Planning Perspectives* 9:55–71.

Zelnik, Melvin and John Kantner (1980). "Sexual Activity, Contraceptive Use and Pregnancy." *Family Planning Perspectives*, 12:230–37.

Zube, Margaret (1972). "Changing Concepts of Morality: 1948–1969." *Social Forces* 50:385–96.

Zuckerman, Diana (1982). "Career and Life Goals of Freshmen and Seniors." *Radcliffe Quarterly*, September.

Zweig, Paul (1968). *The Heresy of Self-Love*. Princeton, New Jersey: Princeton University Press.

Index

abortion, and traditional values 39, 41
Adams, Bert, study of kinship 74–5
aggression: and health 86–90; within
    marriage 83, 93, 96; in men 7, 74
Alameda County, California, study of
    marriage and health 87–8
androgyny: benefits 11, 56–7, 90; and
    friendship 136, 138; and love 27–8;
    opposition to 8, 49, 78; trends towards
    7–9, 30, 38–9, 151–2; see also gender
    roles; independence, interdependence;
    self-development
arguments, marital 97–8, 99, 102, 125,
    126–7; see also conflicts
attachment; and development 72, 81–2,
    113; and health 82–3, 85–90; see also
    commitment; interdependence

Bakan, David, on gender roles 5–6
Bellah, Robert et al. 28–9; criticises new
    trends 8, 9–10, 49, 58; on independence
    40–1, 53; on interdependence 106–7; on
    therapy 108–9, 110
Berkman, Lisa and Leonard Syme, health
    survey 87
Bernard, Jessie, on women and
    marriage 90
Berne, Eric, Games People Play (1967) 108,
    109, 120
Blaine, Carol and John 141–5
Blumstein, Philip and Pepper Schwartz,
    study of couples 106, 127, 129
Burgess, Ernest, on the family 34

Calhoun, Arthur, on the family 32
Campbell, Angus, on quality of life 83
capitalism: Marxist analysis 55, 58–60; and
    personal life 60–1, 152–3; rise of 15,
    16–19, 25–9; see also elites; self-made
    man; work
Case, Luella, on friendship 25

Chafe, William, on social change 32, 35
Child, Lydia Maria, compares women
    with slaves 26
children: attitudes towards 5, 16–17,
    18–19, 60; family size 36, 47; and
    marriage 34, 83, 84, 96–7, 132; mother's
    responsibility 7, 16, 19, 151, 152; see also
    fatherhood; motherhood
Chodorow, Nancy, on feminine love
    71–3, 98
Cinderella Complex, The (1981), Colette
    Dowling 151
class 36, 59; and relationships 37, 48, 96–7,
    106, 139–41
Clecak, Peter, on self-development 10, 61
commitment: rejection of 127–9, 133, 149,
    152; to relationships 3, 8, 58, 105–8; see
    also attachment; constraints; individual-
    ism; interdependence
communication: and friendship 134–5, 136,
    142; importance of 40, 41, 42–8, 62; as
    love 7, 8, 70–1, 73–5, 78; in marriage
    91–2, 93, 99, 101–2; and self-
    development 79, 118–19, 150
Companionship marriage 34–7, 40, 93;
    costs 45, 63, 91–2, 150; decline 37–9,
    151–2; persistence 48, 50, 64, 150–1; and
    social theory 55–6, 62–3, 71
communities 9, 58; decline of community
    theorists 53–4, 60; modern involvement
    59; see also public life
competition: men drawn to 74, 89–90; and
    relationships 140, 152–3
conflicts: freedom v. commitment 21–2,
    38, 54–5, 57–61; love v. self-develop-
    ment 3–4, 63–5, 79–80, 91–102, 110,
    132–3, 150; in marriage 11, 39–40, 97–9,
    102, 125–7
conservative attitudes 35–6, 59, 150–1
constraints, and relationships 51–5, 57–60,
    119–20; 149–50; see also freedom

206

42